# RECIPROCITY

A Celebration
on the life of
Jean-Paul Delamotte

Edited by Marie Ramsland

**Editorial Team**
John Beach
Gerry Collins
John Ramsland
Marie-Laure Vuaille-Barcan

*'amour et labeur'*

ETT IMPRINT
Newcastle-Paris Link

This edition published by ETT Imprint, Exile Bay 2023

This book is copyright. Apart from any fair dealing for the purposes of private study, research, criticism or review, as permitted under the Copyright Act, no part may be reproduced by any process without written permission. Enquiries should be addressed to the publisher:

ETT Imprint
PO Box R1906
Royal Exchange NSW 1225
Australia

Copyright © this edition ETT Imprint
Copyright essays © individual authors

Design by Tom Thompson

Cover: Portrait of Jean-Paul Delamotte by Daniel Pata

ISBN   978-1-923024-26-7  (pbk)
ISBN   978-1-923024-27-4  (ebk)

# CONTENTS

Préface / Preface  6
*Mise-en-scène* : 'amour et labeur'  9
*Domaine australien*, Australia  15
CONTRIBUTIONS :
Jean-Paul Delamotte : Three Vignettes; Cinema – Ken Dutton  17
*Amour d'Elle* – Ross Steele  27
'with trepidation' – Colyn Whitehead  36
Early years in Newcastle – Denise Yim  37
'Born in a House of books' – Guibourg Delamotte  44
My First French Friend – Israel Horovitz  50
An amazing Frenchman – Tony Maniaty  53
Vale Jean-Paul – Xavier Pons  58
Unlocked doors and impossible reciprocity: a student's perspective on
    the Delamottes – John West-Sooby  61
Evening Lessons – Barbara Kelly  70
'The Paris end of Newcastle' : Perkins Street – Brian Suters  72
Frank Moorhouse and the Delamottes: A Reciprocity –
    Tom Thompson  81
Jean-Paul, Coonardoo and me – Hélène Jaccomard  87
Friendship and Remembrance – Dianne Reilly  91
Home  Paris 1988 – Allan Chawner  97
The Studio Ici-*Aussie* – John Emerson  103
Jean-Paul Delamotte and I : outline of a thirty-year collaboration –
    Maurice Blackman  111
The Thread of Friendship – Joanna Murray-Smith  113
Two Extracts from *Les Amours de rencontre (1)* – translations by
    Marie-Laure Vuaille-Barcan, Marie Ramsland & Ken Dutton  117
How One Man Sparked My French Revolution – John Beach  123
The Early Years : Jean-Paul *par lui-même* – Ken Dutton  126
An Unforgettable Moment – Gionni Di Gravio  148
Memories of Good Friends – Peter Weir  151
Reciprocity in the cinema of David Gulpilil: Fables of Friendship and
    cultural identity – John Ramsland  158

Mentor and Friend : Journeys through Australian Cinema –
	Virginie Bauer   169
Art Exhibitions and an opening at Brousse-le-Château, Aveyron –
	Daniel Pata   176
A Tale of Two Years – Linda Barcan   180
How a Chance Discovery led to a Treasure Trove of French Literature
	– Gerry Collins   188
'A very special man' – Alan Ventress   197
Diary of a New Chum or The Road to Boulogne-Billancourt –
	Will Noonan   199
The making of a thesis: Memories of Jean-Paul Delamotte –
	Helen Ledwidge   211
Travelling back in time ... *à la rencontre de* Paul Wenz –
	Solène Anglaret   215
The Forgotten Legacy of Hettie Wenz and her books  –
	Merrill Findlay   226
Denis Wenz, '*Le Thé*' – Marie Ramsland   238
Chaleureuses rencontres –  Kevin Tang   241
Kelver Hartley and Marguerite Yourcenar: A Tale of Absence and
	Presence – Sandi Warren   251
Postgraduate Reminiscences – Travis Watters   255
In French, in English – Marion Halligan   260
*A French Village* : TV Series 2009-2017 – Suzanne Evans   264
*Un village français* : a Personal Take – Gay Bookallil   267
*Réminiscences et souvenirs affectueux* – Emmannuelle Souillac   273
*Jean-Paul ou la « douce obstination »* – Jean-Pierre Langellier   278
*Hommage à Jean-Paul Delamotte : éditeur, traducteur, romancier,
	homme de lettres* – Hélène Savoie Colombani   282
Life Enhancer & the Art of Reciprocity – Margie Bryant   287
A Series of Magic Moments – Virginia Wallace-Crabbe   290
'A staunch promoter of cultural reciprocity' – Michael Costigan   296
Australian Cultural Attaché in Boulogne – Peter Collins   299
Franco-Australian cultural exchange in mirror image: the papers of JP
	Delamotte and the ACFA – Alex Byrne   305
*Pour rendre hommage ...*  – Ilona Kiss   310
'Do You Remember ... ?' – Monique Delamotte   313
Contributors   321

EXTRAS

*Table des matières* for *Amours de rencontre* (1) & (2)   328
Reference from Eugène Ionesco, *Paris, le 9 mars 1974*   330
Newcastle gets a Film Festival *NMH*, 1975   331
*Livres d'Or* – Ken Dutton   334
Letter from Margaret Whitlam & Keen on travelling   335
Fêter la presence à Paris de Gough et Margaret Whitlam   335
Poetry by Jean-Paul   336
'Jean-Paul Delamotte, le cosmopolite' in *Express*   339
Publications – JP Delamotte : author, translator, subtitler   341
*Association Culturelle Franco-Australienne*   345
*Livres d'Or* – Bon Voyage Lloyd Rees   346
Promotion of Australian Culture in France   347
Australian Honours: AM & Honorary Fellowship   349 *Livres d'Or* – Keryl & Paul Kavanagh   350
*Livres d'Or* – Tom, Elizabeth & Frank   351
Enduring friendships   352
"Ici Aussi" – Lynn Hard   353
Monique apprend ses ancêtres   355
In the 'Studiolo'   357

# Préface / Preface
## Jean-Claude Poimboeuf
### Ancien consul général de France à Sydney (1997-2000)

J'ai un souvenir vivace de ma première rencontre avec Jean-Paul Delamotte. C'était au printemps 1997 : je servais alors à la cellule diplomatique de la présidence de la République et Jean-Paul avait adressé à Jacques Chirac, qu'il avait côtoyé à Sciences-Po, un courrier dans lequel il indiquait vouloir lui présenter ses idées sur les échanges culturels entre la France et l'Australie. Nous étions à ce moment-là dans une phase de reconstruction des relations franco-australiennes après les tensions qui avaient suivi la décision de Jacques Chirac de reprendre nos essais nucléaires. Ayant déjà été désigné pour exercer les fonctions de consul général de France à Sydney à compter de l'été 1997, il m'a été demandé de recevoir Jean-Paul à l'Elysée.

J'ai fait alors la connaissance d'un homme à la fois doux dans son expression et passionné dans son propos. Homme de conviction, Jean-Paul m'a exposé ce qui a été le combat de sa vie : celui d'une meilleure réciprocité culturelle entre nos deux pays rendue nécessaire selon lui par une situation asymétrique qui le chagrinait, les Australiens ayant une bien meilleure connaissance de notre patrimoine et de notre création que les Français des leurs. C'est aussi dans sa bouche que j'ai entendu pour la première fois le terme de « cultural cringe », les Australiens ayant tendance, selon Jean-Paul, à sous-estimer leur culture par rapport à celle de la vieille Europe.

Nous avons poursuivi cet échange jusqu'à mon départ pour Sydney en juillet 1997 à l'occasion d'agréables déjeuners chez Jean-Paul à Boulogne. J'ai alors fait la connaissance de son épouse Monique, tout aussi active que Jean-Paul dans la promotion de la culture australienne en France, à travers notamment la « petite maison » qui, au fond de leur grand jardin, accueillait année après année nombre d'écrivains et d'artistes australiens en résidence.

C'est donc un couple engagé et généreux qu'il m'a été donné de rencontrer avant même mon départ pour l'Australie, pays qui m'était encore peu familier et sur lequel j'ai pu bénéficier de judicieux conseils de lecture pour me préparer au mieux. Je suis infiniment reconnaissant à Jean-Paul et Monique pour cette introduction accélérée à la culture australienne qui s'est avérée très utile pendant les trois merveilleuses années passées que j'ai eu la chance de passer à Sydney.

Au-delà de la relation amicale qui s'est nouée entre nous, ce qui importe, bien sûr, c'est leur contribution unique à une meilleure connaissance réciproque de nos cultures, à laquelle Jean-Paul a consacré une grande partie de sa vie. L'Australie a bénéficié avec lui d'un formidable ambassadeur de sa culture. Comme quoi, on peut être un bon ambassadeur sans être diplomate de carrière !

Alors que Jean-Paul a lui-même écrit ou publié de nombreux livres, je me réjouis qu'un ouvrage rende hommage à son travail à travers une cinquantaine de contributions de personnes l'ayant connu et compris la mission qu'il s'était lui-même assignée. Je souhaite que cette publication suscite de nouvelles vocations de « passeurs » entre nos deux cultures.

***

I have a vivid memory of my first meeting with Jean-Paul Delamotte. It was in the spring of 1997: I was then serving in the diplomatic team of the Presidency of the Republic and Jean-Paul had sent a letter to Jacques Chirac, whom he had met at Sciences-Po [Institute of Political Studies, Paris], in which he indicated that he wanted to present his ideas on cultural exchanges between France and Australia. At that time we were in a phase of rebuilding Franco-Australian relations after the tensions that had followed Jacques Chirac's decision to resume our nuclear tests. Having already been appointed Consul General of France in Sydney from the summer of 1997, I was asked to receive Jean-Paul at the Elysée.

I met a man who was both gentle in his expression and passionate in his words. A man of conviction, Jean-Paul explained to me what had been his life's struggle: that of a better cultural reciprocity between our two countries, made necessary according to him by an asymmetrical situation that grieved him, the Australians having a much better knowledge of our heritage and our creation than the French of theirs. It was also from his lips that I first heard the term 'cultural cringe', as Australians tend, according to Jean-Paul, to underestimate their culture compared to that of old Europe.

We continued this exchange until I left for Sydney in July 1997 over pleasant lunches at Jean-Paul's home in Boulogne. I met his wife Monique, who was just as active as Jean-Paul in promoting Australian culture in France, notably through the "little house" which, at the bottom of their large garden, welcomed many Australian writers and artists in residence year after year. It was a committed and generous couple that I met even before my departure for Australia, a country I was unfamiliar with and about which I was able to benefit by taking their judicious advice on reading material to prepare myself as much as possible. I am infinitely grateful to Jean-Paul and Monique for this accelerated introduction to Australian culture which proved very useful during the three wonderful years I was lucky enough to spend in Sydney.

More than the personal friendship that developed between us, what is important, surely, is their unique contribution to a better mutual knowledge of our cultures, to which Jean-Paul had devoted a large part of his life. Australia has benefitted from a formidable ambassador of its culture. Just goes to show you can be a good ambassador without being a career diplomat!

While Jean-Paul wrote or published many books, I am delighted a book paying tribute to his work through some fifty contributions from people who knew him and understood the mission he had assigned himself. I hope that this publication will inspire new vocations of "passers-by" between our two cultures.

# *Mise-en-scène : 'amour et labeur'*

*'Labeur' est un acte de dévotion qui tient du mécénat, d'un état d'esprit et d'une hauteur d'âme. Comme le sep de la charrue (ou l'âme) laboure la terre ainsi va le Labeur d'un homme.*

My first encounter with Jean-Paul Delamotte was in Newcastle at the University on one of his many visits to Australia since he left permanently in 1977. He spoke at the Newcastle launch of the *festschrift* I had edited in honour of Emeritus Professor Dutton in 1996. I then had the opportunity to visit the Delamottes in Boulogne during my first Outside Study Leave from the University. The leave was to pursue my research of a prominent Australian writer, Dymphna Cusack, and her involvement in France. I was also to interview Michel Tournier whose novels were the subject of my PhD.

**Diary entry — *Mardi, 12 août 1997***

*Passée une superbe soirée chez Jean-Paul et Monique Delamotte; pris le métro et j'étais là en avance (no 25). Travaillé le matin à BN, trouvé peu. Mangé une salade, poulet et taboulé, glace et framboises et, bien entendu, des fromages ; champagne et rosé – délicieux ! J'ai offert des chocolats. Rencontré John [Emerson] d'Adélaïde et Marie, Française qui habite le 4e, gentils, les deux. Rentrée en taxi avec elle (je lui dois 50f).*

In 2001, the University of Newcastle agreed to a 'reciprocal' academic exchange for one semester with the University of La Rochelle between Dr Sue Ryan-Fazilleau and myself. I taught English language and Aboriginal and Maori culture. And Sue took my classes in French language and literature. John joined me towards the end of my stay there. Jean-Paul and Monique invited us to their home on 17 June where we were warmly welcomed. We both signed the *Livre d'Or* – 'good food & interesting talk – never long enough!' and Monique recorded the meal we enjoyed:

*Crudités variées : tomates, avocat, œufs durs, asperges vertes et salade de choux blanc coupé fin ; Beau poulet jaune (volaille de Bresse) et petites pommes de terre vapeur ; fromages ; flan aux pommes maison ; cerises et abricots.*

In *La Route de Nanima* (256), Jean-Paul records an occasion I had forgotten :

*Mardi 7 janvier 03  Je suis content d'avoir sympathisé avec John et Marie Ramsland [...] qui nous ont reçus dans leur jolie maison Art Déco, pour déjeuner, dimanche.*

Jean-Paul began his 1997 Kelver Hartley Fellowship address – 'For John Rowland: In Memoriam' – by explaining "Reciprocity" as the 'keyword that will pay tribute, first to the contribution made to French culture by so many Australian scholars, writers and artists; and second to the emergence in France of a serious interest in Australian culture, often amounting to love and fascination'.

The second point was strongly established by the lifetime labours of Jean-Paul : *'un proxène ardent et dévoué à une belle cause par amour et en remerciement de son accueil en 1974.'*

He claimed : 'Love of one's country coupled with love of one's chosen and adopted culture is a seductive and rewarding course to follow' (Reciprocity, 20). No wonder, when introduced to Joséphine Baker's *J'ai deux amours,* did he immediately feel a close connection.

Reminiscences about Jean-Paul and Monique Delamotte by a wide range of people with varying interests, backgrounds and experiences, play a significant part in this anthology of fifty contributions. The reader is presented with a kaleidoscope of images that – together and sometimes overlapping – form a powerful portrait of a French couple dedicated to their cause of promoting cultural reciprocity between France and Australia for more than forty years. Each contribution adds something new to the portrait of Jean-Paul and his dedication to ensuring the French become as aware of Australian literature as Australians have been of French literature.

There are threads that can be seen in the contributions that are found in Jean-Paul's "Reciprocity" speech: literary passions; comprehensive variety of artistic forms: painting, drawing and writing, music, photography, dance, film; the teaching of French language and culture; places that are emotionally 'special'; adhesion and room for hope despite the odds against them. For him, literature ignited friendships that flourished in an 'atmosphere of family' and camaraderie. And images abound – manifested in various forms.

What I knew of Jean-Paul was added to and reinforced with each contribution. I also discovered something new and surprising each time. It was like gathering and placing individual pieces of a jigsaw puzzle, each piece tinged with subtle colour and form. These 'extras' are there for the reader to discover in amongst the qualities of Jean-Paul which are repeatedly expressed from one contribution to the next.

His qualities included: genuine warmth, boundless generosity of spirit, enthusiasm, 'patience extraordinaire', sincerity, an 'impressive and encompassing mind', loyalty, modesty. He was kind, a 'gentleman', a 'fun' person with a sense of humour; he had vision and expertise.

It all began in 1974 when Jean-Paul and Monique arrived, as newly-weds, to be tutors in French at the University of Newcastle, New South Wales. They were soon celebrated as an 'exotic' couple by the surrounding community. As teachers, they were known to be patient, encouraging and inspiring. Australia provided Jean-Paul with a stronger sense of purpose and a mission. He was a tireless advocate for Australian culture in France marked by his substantial and multifaceted contributions – a 'cross cultural phenomenon'.

Although they stayed in the country for only three years, they subsequently made twenty-two journeys back to visit people they had met in Newcastle, Sydney, Melbourne, Forbes – the heart of Paul Wenz country – and elsewhere, thus establishing and cementing close lifetime friendships with like-minded people.

Relationships were reciprocal with Australians visiting them in their ever-welcoming home in Boulogne-Billancourt, Paris – experiencing warmth, generosity, always good food and wine and stimulating conversation. Such experiences were never to be forgotten. Many had 'the privilege to sit at the cultured table' of the Delamottes. And people spent various periods of time in the special accommodation so generously prepared by Jean-Paul and Monique. This gave them a rare freedom to achieve their goals, albeit in their specific field of artistic endeavour or research. A few stayed years; many returned several times. For many Australians, Jean-Paul opened doors and provided unexpected golden opportunities which they were never able to adequately repay.

Where knowledge was lacking on detail in the contributions, or when I became curious and wanted to know more, Monique was ready and able to fill the gaps skilfully using both her notebooks/cahiers and entries from Jean-Paul's typed diary of nearly 8,000 pages that he began as a sixteen-year-old! Monique's records were practical 'housekeeping' ones. These are priceless records of the hundreds of people, Australians, French and others, who have had contact with them and been helped, beyond their expectations, in their individual endeavours.

\* *Cahiers I-4 : Sociabilité – visitors and events. Such as: déjeuner/dîner/ soirée en l'honneur de ... / à l'hommage de ; Bienvenue à ..., Welcome back, cocktails, afternoon teas, lunches ; launches ; Inauguration of LPM (28/4/1984); Journées Conférences Littéraire Australiennes ; Soirée amicale franco-australo-japanaise ; Réunions ; Les Belles Etrangères ; Visites des Lauréates de la Kelver Hartley Foundation.*

*Hôtes de l'ACFA (Association Culturelle Franco-Australienne) puis de l'ALFA (Atelier Littéraire Franco-Australienne):*
\* *Cahiers 1 – La petite maison ; Cahiers 2 – Studio Ici AussiE ; Studio Noël.*

Their contacts and visitors included academics, students, architects, lawyers, filmmakers, directors, actors, politicians, diplomats, librarians, artists, photographers, authors, playwrights, poets, musicians and singers, educators of all types, publishers – the majority are represented here, often bringing a new and different perspective as they recount their own experiences.

Jean-Paul's close contact with ambassadors reinforced his goal. They became very close friends – in particular with Gough and Margaret Whitlam.

He also found a parallel connection between ACFA and ISFAR – the Institute for the Study of French-Australian Relations founded in Melbourne (1985) – of which he was granted honorary life membership.

Special thanks to Emeritus Professor Ken Dutton for his contributions and continued help with this project, especially for his analysis of Jean-Paul's life as recorded in his diary and before he and Monique came to Australia. I am grateful to John Ramsland and John Beach who proofread the entries in English, Marie-Laure Vuaille-Barcan for checking the French contributions and Gerry Collins who summarised, in English, the 'essence' of those written in French.

Thanks to all contributors who have made this publication possible – even the few who never met Jean-Paul, but are enthusiastic Francophiles.

Special thanks to publisher Tom Thompson for his encouragement and extreme generosity. Last but not least, my sincere appreciation to Monique and Guibourg who have tirelessly answered questions along the way and sent me an abundance of material to work with and to select from – a challenging but rewarding task. I have acquired a deep understanding of Jean-Paul: his abilities, interests, passions, frustrations, motivations as well as his highly commendable personal traits and social skills which are repeated and reinforced by individual contributors. The personality of each contributor also adds colour to the portrait of Jean-Paul.

While working on this volume, I have been inspired by the artwork of Daniel Pata which appears on the front cover. For me, there is a helpful calmness, a serenity captured in the portrait – and I feel an affinity with Jean-Paul's love of reading a printed book.

In VIVRE ET REVIVRE (4,903), Jean-Paul wrote:

Dimanche 8 juillet 1990 - 19h30  *Pour préparer le compte rendu que je veux faire des 10 années ACFA, j'ai été chercher des carnets, ceux que j'utilise pour le travail pratique. Et je succombe à la nostalgie: tant d'énergie ... gâchée? En pure perte?*

Monique's reply (20 avril 2023) : *Non, mon amour, certainement pas en pure perte ... grâce aux témoignages [...]*

... and I agree.

Marie Ramsland (editor)

# *Domaine australien – Australia**

This collection of articles is first and foremost my response to a very simple preoccupation: the creation of a convenient document to provide to those sensitive souls and curious minds who have sometimes been kind enough to ask me questions about Australian culture and the reasons for the deep interest that has inspired me for such a long time.

It is also a kind of 'invoice requiring payment' from those who tacitly or explicitly confided in me. Here is where I let them be the judge of my endeavours – hence a certain amount of repetition that would be omitted in a more standard work and for which I humbly apologise.

It is, like every written work, a kind of gamble as to the future, a game of chance.

I have put together, mainly from the *Monde des Livres* and the *Magazine littéraire,* scattered fragments of work inspired by the overweening ambition (as is only proper) to contribute towards making known in France the cultural richness of a country which should be remote from us only by its geography. Why, I ask you, would I be content with various anachronistic mechanisms, combined with the lack of common sense and widespread slow-mindedness, that still keep us so wide apart?

And so these pages are the signs of an effort that is often (though not always) isolated, and is largely (but, again, not always) unfruitful, to overcome that unfortunate delay.

Without wanting to prove to anyone that I know better than they do, I have a rather upbeat, even if obscure, idea of the writer's role. I like the fact that he tries to capture the occasion rather in the

Voltairean style, as opposed to those cheerful characters of whom Voltaire quite rightly said: 'Each of them covets both a position as valet and a reputation as a Great Man.' Having had the good fortune to fall under the spell of a foreign literature that is unknown on the banks of the Seine, I have simply tried to talk about it. A number of masters – Roger Caillois, Maurice Coindreau or Valery Larbaud – have done this for South America, the United States or Europe. I can only claim to come up almost to their shoulders – as a modest workman.

Thinking of Valery Larbaud, the one of whom I am fondest, and of the Domain (without an e), the park in Sydney where one evening I saw the audience rise to its feet to welcome Gough and Margaret Whitlam, I therefore offer to the adventurous reader this modest *Domaine australien* – in its present state, although by definition it is certainly destined to become more extensive.

I have come up against, and still come up against, various obstacles; but to be honest I want to keep going. Even if it's only a pipe dream.

**Jean-Paul D**

---

\* Jean-Paul Delamotte, *Amours de rencontre (Papiers australiens)(I)*, La Petite Maison, Boulogne, 1993, 9-10 (translated by Ken Dutton). See page 328 for *Table des matières of Amours de rencontre (1) & (2)*.

# *Jean-Paul Delamotte*
# THREE VIGNETTES
## Ken Dutton

**1. The Appointment**
When I took up the Chair of French at the University of Newcastle in 1969, the minimum staffing establishment for each academic department was five, except in the case of Modern Language departments in which case it was six – five plus a native-speaker. This had been decreed by the then Vice-Chancellor, Professor James Auchmuty – a graduate of Trinity College Dublin and a man favourably disposed to the teaching of languages both ancient and modern, who always attended the annual French Department play and the annual Alliance Française Dinner (the past is another country…).

In early 1974, the French Department's native-speaker took early retirement on the grounds of ill health. It was about that time that I received a letter from a certain Jean-Paul Delamotte, enquiring whether there might be a vacancy in the Department for which he would be suitable.

The letter provided a list of his qualifications. A doctorate in political science from Paris, a Master of Public Administration from Harvard, a number of novels, short stories, poems and articles in highly reputable publications, involvement in film production (including working on the multi-award-winning Algerian-French political thriller Z directed by Costa-Gavras) … The list went on and on.

Could this person be for real? Why wasn't he already in a Chair somewhere?

I replied, indicating that the only position that I had

available was that of native-speaker, but that this was at the lowly level of Tutor, a level well below that for which his academic credentials and experience qualified him. Nonetheless, I added, should he be interested in the position despite its lowly status, he should send me the names of three referees.

Back came a reply within only a few days. Yes, it stated, he was indeed interested and, as for referees, he provided three names: one of France's leading critical theorists, Serge Doubrovsky; the influential sociologist and philosopher Georges Friedmann of the École pratique des hautes études; and – last but not least – Eugène Ionesco, one of the most significant practitioners of the Theatre of the Absurd. A veritable Who's Who of referees!

I asked the University Personnel Department to write to the persons named – thinking (I'm somewhat ashamed to admit) that, even if the references were less than favourable, it would be something of a coup to be in possession of a letter actually signed by Eugène Ionesco. And back the letters came – all full of the highest praise for this man to whom Ionesco referred as 'un espoir de la nouvelle littérature française'.

(As an aside, I was particularly interested in Ionesco, as I had both lectured on his works and produced some of his plays – *La Cantatrice chauve* ('The Bald Prima Donna') in English for St Paul's College Mummers at the University of Sydney; *Les Chaises* – again in English – at Macquarie University; and *La Cantatrice chauve* again – in French, this time – at the University of Newcastle, with John West-Sooby in the role of Le Capitaine des Pompiers.)

In any case, on receipt of such favourable appraisals, I arranged for Jean-Paul to be offered the position. I have no recollection of the position being advertised or of a Selection Committee being established (again, another country…). I was at the time Dean of the Faculty of Arts, which gave me a certain discretion in the making of appointments and I think I simply wrote to the Vice-Chancellor recommending that he approve my action – knowing that

James Auchmuty would never pass up the opportunity to have on his staff someone to whom he could refer as 'my distinguished colleague'.

And so Jean-Paul was appointed. Although the traditional role of the native-speaker was to conduct conversation classes in French, it was obvious that it would have been a waste of Jean-Paul's expertise – not to mention a somewhat frustrating exercise for Jean-Paul himself – to restrict him to this activity. Accordingly, he and I worked together on a number of courses on literature and cinema that he was uniquely qualified to teach.

Equally, I recognised that in Monique we had a native-speaker of intelligence and charm who would bring to students in conversation classes a level of delightful engagement with the language that was an opportunity not to be missed. Fortunately, a small allocation of part-time teaching funds enabled us to welcome Monique to the staff of the French Department, an arrangement that continued until the birth of Guibourg the following year.
Those were halcyon days.

## 2. The Arrival
The excitement felt by the staff of the French Department at the imminent arrival of a new colleague was tempered by a certain apprehension at the possibility that this distinguished French scholar might be of less than congenial character. For my own part, I had vivid memories of a visit some years earlier by Professor Henry Bornecq of the University of Caen, who showed himself to be a model of incivility in every Australian university that he visited. Or perhaps our new colleague's wife would turn out to be a termagant, or to be otherwise insufferable.

Being tied up with administrative duties, I was unable to meet the Delamottes on their arrival by train from Sydney, so I entrusted this risky task to one of the most obliging lecturers in the Department, Colyn Whitehead. Having deposited them at the somewhat downmarket motel at which the University's Personnel Department had booked them for three nights' accommodation, Colyn phoned me in a state of mingled surprise and excitement. 'They're actually very nice!'

A reception had been arranged for that evening at the home of another member of the French Department staff, Janice Rubenach. Jan lived in a charming terrace house in Perkins Street in the Newcastle CBD, a steep street on what was known to Novocastrians as The Hill. When Colyn Whitehead picked up the Delamottes at their motel and brought them to Jan's house to meet the assembled staff, the atmosphere changed immediately from one of nervous anticipation to one of easy détente, as we marvelled at the command of English displayed by both Jean-Paul and Monique and found the conversation flowing seamlessly as the evening progressed. I think it was probably a case of relief on both sides.

The following day, the new arrivals decided that their first task was to find somewhere to live. The normal thing would have been to consult an estate agent, but the Delamottes had other ideas. Impressed by the charm of the 19th-century terrace houses in Perkins Street, they made what might be considered a bold decision for a couple who had just arrived in a foreign country: they would go back to Perkins Street and knock on a few doors.

Selecting a terrace house at random, that is just what they did. Their knock was answered by an attractive woman in her early 30s. 'Good morning,' said Jean-Paul. 'We've just arrived from Paris and we were wondering whether there might be any houses for rent in this area.'

'How lovely to meet you,' said the woman. 'Actually, I've just come back from Paris. Do come in and have a coffee. And yes, the house next door is for rent.'

As it happened, the attractive young woman was an up-and-coming artist by the name of Aldona O'Brien, who painted and exhibited under her maiden name of Aldona Zakarauskas. She had recently returned from a trip to Europe and would shortly be appointed to the teaching staff of the Newcastle College of Advanced Education.

This extraordinary meeting marked the beginning of what might almost be considered a love affair between the Delamottes and Perkins Street, Newcastle. It seemed that, whenever they returned to Newcastle, there was always a terrace house for rent somewhere in Perkins Street and it is surely no accident that one of the characters appearing most frequently in Jean-Paul's fictional writing is named Arabella Perkins.

**3. A Book Launch in Paris**
From 1982 to 1987, I occupied the position of Vice-Principal and Deputy Vice-Chancellor. In 1984, Auchmuty's successor as Vice-Chancellor, Professor Don George was in his last year in that role and decided that I should be rewarded for my years of assistance to him through some difficult times (I had also worked closely with him as Deputy Chairman of the University Senate in the late 1970s) by being sent to a conference on university education to be held in London under the auspices of the Association of Commonwealth Universities.

Earlier in 1984, I had been invited by the poet, playwright and essayist Dr Grace Perry, the founder of South Head Press and editor of the magazine *Poetry Australia*, to edit a special edition of the magazine under the title 'French Poetry Now'. Being conscious that *Poetry Australia* had an excellent reputation – having published poetry by such major poets as Ezra Pound, Ted Hughes and Seamus Heaney among many others – I considered that I was not up to the task and was on the point of declining when Jean-Paul (who had undoubtedly been the person who had suggested my name to Grace Perry) urged me to go ahead.

Jean-Paul offered, in fact, to contact a number of contemporary French poets and invite them to contribute one or more works to the volume. My role would be to translate the works into English and to write an Introduction. Despite some lingering hesitation as to whether I would be able to present what the poet Pierre Seghers had called a "forest of lone trees" in any coherent way, I accepted – as much out of respect for Jean-Paul and of not wanting to let him down, as anything else.

Some sixteen poets had responded to Jean-Paul's invitation – most of them contributing more than one work and some sending half-a-dozen, including a number of prose-poems (or, to use the term coined by Francis Ponge to refer to his works, *Proêmes*) or works referred to by their authors as *écrits* or *tranches d'écriture*. To be frank, some were impenetrable and a literal translation (the only option in such cases) made them appear even more so in English. On the other hand, some were quite beautiful, including two prose-poems sent by Michel Butor. I persevered.

The resulting publication had an appropriate cover photo – the Australian Embassy in Paris. It was one of a number of photographs of Paris taken by the great Australian photographer Max Dupain, who had accompanied his long-time colleague and friend Harry Seidler to Paris in 1978 with the specific intention of photographing the Embassy building which Seidler had designed and completed the year before.

By an interesting coincidence (or, more probably, contrivance on Jean-Paul's part), the book was launched in that very building and I was fortunate enough to be present, having come from London at the conclusion of the Commonwealth Universities Conference. The launching itself was conducted by none other than former Australian Prime Minister Gough Whitlam, who was at the time Australia's Ambassador to UNESCO. Referring to the building as the 'Palais Seidler' (a reference to the Paris Opéra, the *Palais Garnier*, which was not lost on those attending), Whitlam made an elegant speech interspersed with Gallicisms ('My consort and I, *Marguerite et moi*') and seemed very much at ease mingling with the half-dozen or so French poets who were present along with a select group of literati hand-picked by Jean-Paul.

An unexpected highlight of the evening took place when a small number of us were invited to stay on for dinner after the book launch. The event in question was Monique's presentation to Whitlam of his own well-thumbed copy of Liddell and Scott's Greek-English Lexicon (the authoritative dictionary first published in 1843 of which

Whitlam's copy was the revised edition of 1940); it had been beautifully re-bound by Monique herself and Jean-Paul typically had his camera at the ready to record the event.

Back at my accommodation in the famous Petite Maison in Boulogne-Billancourt, I was invited to sign the *Livre d'Or* which already bore the names and comments of so many outstanding figures in the world of literature and cinema. For some reason or other, I felt that a verse tribute would be appropriate. I take the liberty of reproducing it here.

### POETRY AUSTRALIA(N)

*Lorsque le voyageur, quittant les Antipodes,*
*Viendra refaire, un jour, le plus grand des exodes,*
*Il retiendra l'espoir (et donnons-lui raison)*
*D'occuper de nouveau la «Petite Maison».*
*Car, ayant éprouvé ce privilège unique*
*De partager la vie de Jean-Paul et Monique,*
*De se sentir «chez soi» dans un joli faubourg*
*Et d'entendre la voix de la belle Guibourg,*
*Il gardera toujours le souvenir précieux*

> *De livres, de rencontres, de repas merveilleux,*
> *En repensant souvent (ayant repris son vol)*
> *Aux jours heureux passés chez Monique et Jean-Paul.*
> **Envoi**
> *Amis, je vous salue! Vous vous en doutez bien – S'il est*
> *un coin de France où puisse l'Australien*
> *Se sentir vivre en roi, et non en étranger,*
> *C'est au Numéro 9 de la rue Béranger.*
> **Boulogne-Billancourt, le 28 septembre 1984**

The next day, my last before the trip back to Australia, we shared lunch at Jean-Paul and Monique's local restaurant in the rue Béranger. It no doubt had a name – if so, I've forgotten – but for Jean-Paul and Monique it was chez Mme Martin. Apart from the excellent food, two things stand out in my memory. One was the list of celebrities – largely film stars – who had eaten there. The other was the menu displayed on the wall, the meticulous chalked calligraphy being provided on a daily visit by Monique.

What times they were.

**NOTE from Monique:** 'rue Béranger was Madame Martin's petit resto, simply called 'Chez Martin' which had become part of our life. The food was 'simple et délicieuse'. [...] Her restaurant was famous when the Studios of Boulogne (where I met JP) were a hot spot for American shootings. C'était fréquenté par les techniciens du cinéma parce que 'c'était bon et très raisonnable'. Montand, Signoret, Costa Gravas y venaient régulièrement. Elle avait un Livre d'Or qu'elle nous avons montré qui portait de grandes signatures. Elle était merveilleuse, Madame Martin !

# Jean-Paul discovers Australian Cinema

## Ken Dutton

Towards the end of 1974, I had occasion to visit the French Embassy in Canberra and invited Jean-Paul to accompany me. At this distance, I can't recall exactly the purpose of the visit: I suspect that it was in connection with the Federation of Alliances Françaises in Australia, of which I spent some years as Vice-President; though it may also have been – perhaps as a semi-conscious adjunct – the opportunity to publicise the Newcastle French Department by showing off our newly-acquired Distinguished Colleague.

What I do clearly recall from that visit is that our host was the *Conseiller Culturel* at the Embassy, the unforgettable Albert Salon. Fortunately, others have paid tribute to this remarkable man, Ivan Barko for instance writing: 'Albert Salon was arguably the most unusual and possibly the most memorable of all the French Cultural Counsellors who have served in Australia.' My most vivid memory of our visit was Salon's demonstration of that impressive skill known as *l'action de sabrer le champagne* – not in the colloquial sense, in which it means simply to 'crack open a bottle of champagne', but rather in the literal sense in which it is said to have originated in a custom of the Cossacks during their occupation of the Champagne region in 1814, namely the removal of the neck of the bottle by a sharp blow from the blunt edge of a sabre.

In any case, after our visit to the Embassy we faced a wait of some three or four hours until our return flight to Newcastle. Noticing that there was a recently-released Australian film showing in a local Canberra cinema and remembering Jean-Paul's background in film production, I suggested that we might take it in while we waited. He enthusiastically agreed. At the time, our expectation was simply that it would be an opportunity to while away a few hours in an entertaining way. How wrong we were.

The film in question was *Petersen,* the film that shot Jack Thompson to stardom. In fact, he won the Hoyts Prize for the Best Performance at the 1975 AFI (Australian Film Institute) Awards for his performance in this movie. Not only that, but the cast-list contained some of the most talented actors of the time: Jackie Weaver, Wendy Hughes, Belinda Giblin, Arthur Dignam, Helen Morse and Charles "Bud" Tingwell among others. Directed by Tim Burstall to a script by David Williamson, it is considered one of the better social dramas of the early years of that movement variously known as the Australian Film Revival, Australian Film Renaissance or even (in David Stratton's words) the Australian 'New Wave'.

If my memory is correct (and it may be unreliable after almost 50 years), one of the sexual encounters in which the eponymous Tony Petersen engages is conducted to the strains of the Second Movement (*Andante* in F major) of Mozart's Piano Concerto No. 21, K. 467. This nod to the 1967 Bo Widerberg classic *Elvira Madigan* was, I thought, a sign of the increasing sophistication of the new Australian cinema.

What I do remember with certainty is Jean-Paul's almost ecstatic reaction to the experience we had just shared – and how I could almost read the mind of this passionate cinéphile as he decided that Australian cinema was an area that he would now pursue with characteristic enthusiasm. And the rest, as they say, is history.

# *Amour d'Elle*

# Ross Steele

Monique played an essential role in the success of the cultural mission that Jean-Paul orchestrated to promote Australian literature in France.

They were an extremely devoted couple. Their constant love for each other and their confidence in each other were obvious. It drew its strength from admiration and respect for each other. They shared the same values and worked together as a team, each bringing their special skills to enrich what they were undertaking. Love and working together, a combination of the heart and the mind formed the basis of their successful lifelong partnership. '*Amour et Labeur*' became their motto.

Jean-Paul in his diary (page 4,790) describes what united him with Monique:

- *Je suis plein d'amour et de tendresses pour ma femme. J'éprouve en ce moment pour toi, ma chérie, un désir qui me projette vers toi.*
- *Je me tourne de tout mon corps vers l'accueil délicieux de ton corps.*
- *Je ne pense qu'à te couvrir de caresses et à décrire pour toi la forme nouvelle de mon/notre amour conjugué. Les plaisirs dont je te parlais si souvent et que si souvent, si chaleureusement, tu m'as octroyés.*
- *J'ai de la chance. Ma femme est belle, ma femme a beaucoup de tenue. Ma femme a un sens aigu des valeurs que je trouve essentielles.*
- *Au début et parfois longtemps, il y a le corps, objet de plaisir. Puis il y a l'esprit, sujet de réflexion, coïncidence entre deux subjectivités.*
- *Puis il y a communion, union véritable.*

Monique was born in 1946 in Le Mans, Maine. She left home at seventeen to study English in London where she worked as an au pair in three socially different families. After passing the Oxford English Examination for Foreign Students in 1964, she returned home to spend

Christmas with her family. In January 1965, after answering a newspaper advertisement, she became a bilingual Secretary for an English Insurance Company on the Champs-Elysées. In that Company, there was a Cinema Insurance Section. A colleague there suggested she phone the Director of the Film Studios in Boulogne where she was interviewed by Julien Derode, the Director of Warner Seven Arts. In June 1965 aged nineteen, she became his bilingual Secretary.

Jean-Paul was working with him in the Franco-American Department as Production Director. He was born in 1931 in Boulogne-Billancourt where he lived until 1960. He spent a lot of time with his commercially successful grandfather and his family who lived there and frequently entertained artists.

### Boulevard d'Auteuil

*La demeure enchantée où vivait mon grand-père*
*Etait pour nous alors le boulevard d'Auteuil.*
*Elle seule comptait comme point de repère*
*Et c'est d'elle aujourd'hui que je porte le deuil.*
*La grille était discrète et l'allée accueillante*
*Avec un fin gravier semé au long des buis.*
*La cime du grand pin dominait, ondoyante,*
*Un flot de lilas blancs dont je rêve aujourd'hui.*

**J-P Delamotte**

After studying political science in Paris (1954-1956) in the same class as future President Chirac, who died three days after Jean-Paul, he continued his studies with a Fulbright Scholarship in the USA at Harvard. Back in France, he completed (1958-60) a Doctorate on *'Les Relations de l'Industrie cinématographique et de l'Etat.'*

Jean-Paul's ambition was to be a writer:
*Je me suis consacré à ce que j'aime: ECRIRE!*
(*Vivre et Revivre*, 146)

He had begun writing a diary in 1948 when he was seventeen and did not stop writing it until his death in 2019, leaving behind more than 7,600 pages. His novel *La Communauté* published by the prestigious publisher Gallimard in 1962 was the first of a series of novels.

In parallel with his writing, he began a second profession, the production of Franco-American feature films in the film studios in Boulogne where Monique obtained a position with MGM in the European Publicity Department. Cinema became their joint world. Jean-Paul used to say: 'At least one M in MGM stands for Monique!'

1969-1971 they lived together in Montmartre, before moving into the Delamotte family apartment building, 5 rue Vital in the wealthy sixteenth arrondissement. Jean-Paul's father and mother disapproved of Monique who didn't belong to their social class. This "*petite Provinciale*" was not an acceptable partner for their son. When Jean-Paul and Monique married on 15 January 1974, his parents didn't attend the wedding. In fact, there were only four people at their civil wedding.

Later that year their lives took a major change. They left the Boulogne Film Studios and came to Newcastle in Australia where they would stay until 1977. Their only child, a daughter Guibourg, was born there in 1975. In Newcastle Jean-Paul continued his career as a writer and discovered a new society whose literature was barely known in France. He began lecturing at the University in June 1974. He made it his mission to get Australian literature better known in France through his contacts with publishers. In Newcastle, Monique's role changed. She became a mother and her role was primarily social.

They made friends in Newcastle, Sydney and in Melbourne where Jean-Paul lectured on French Cinema at La Trobe University. They made contacts with writers and cultural leaders and discovered Paul Wenz (1869-1939), who arrived in Australia 1897, built a home "Nanima" in 1898 near Forbes and lived an Australian life as a grazier while writing novels. Jean-Paul republished them through ALFA – La Petite Maison and promoted Wenz as '*un conteur français d'une authentique Australie*'.

Their return to France was motivated by the illness of Jean-Paul's father. In fact both his parents died in 1978.

Jean-Paul worked again (1979-1981) as Director General of Les Productions United Artists and Paramount.

In 1980 the Association Culturelle Franco-Australienne (ACFA) was established by Jean-Paul and Monique with Margaret Whitlam as Honorary President. Jean-Paul continued to translate Australian writers including Marcus Clarke, Katharine Susannah Prichard, Frank Moorhouse and Tom Thompson and draw the attention of French publishers and journalists to Australian writers. ACFA created a network of French and Australian cultural and political contacts.

In 1981 Jean-Paul returned to live in Boulogne-Billancourt when he, Monique and Guibourg moved to 11, avenue du Maréchal de Lattre de Tassigny which would become their permanent home. It was Guibourg's first year in primary school. There was a garden with a small house called '*la petite maison*' where they would invite many Australian visitors and students to stay. Under the auspices of ACFA, Jean-Paul and Monique generously financed a hospitality programme where 11 Avenue de Tassigny became a meeting-place bringing together French and Australian writers, creatives, journalists, filmmakers, University researchers and students. Often these meetings were accompanied by meals elegantly prepared by Monique.

In 1986 'La Petite Maison' became a small publisher of limited editions of works by Australian and French authors. In 1985 ALFA (*Atelier littéraire franco-australien*) was established. It was thirty years since Monique and Jean-Paul met at the Boulogne Film Studios. Monique's joyful, generous and positive nature combined with the hard work and time preparing so many delicious meals contributed to the expansion of ACFA and ALFA.

In his diary, Jean-Paul observed that in France, a 'country where food is a national pastime', the actual food is less important than the taste with which it is presented and its role in sociability. Monique was an expert in both. From 1979 -2001, Monique was the cook and hostess for 3,361 guests at ACFA and ALFA lunches, dinners and social events and for 831 guests from 2001-2012.

From 1984-2008, she organised 475 short stays in their home and *la petite maison*. An amazing contribution to Franco-Australian friendship complementing Jean-Paul's continuous promotion of Australian literature and culture. The family returned frequently to Australia. In 2012, Jean-Paul and Monique had made 22 trips to Australia which always included a return to Newcastle.

Jean-Paul's poem "Bangkok" is a testament to his love for Monique and the central place she occupied in his life.

### BANGKOK

*Allez-y voir, c'est pas facile*
*Quand on veut écrire un poème*
*Et que l'on n'est pas fort agile*
*A chanter, en vers, que l'on aime…*
*Je l'aime, mon M qui sème*
*En ma vie un lot de bonheurs:*
*Celle qui a gardé mon cœur*
*Depuis Montmartre et la bohème!*
*Celle qui a une âme droite*
*Et qui m'aura fait tant d'honneur*
*A Paris, Sydney et ailleurs*
*Au long de notre longue route!*
*Savez-vous que je l'ai connue,*
*Elle était encore ingénue.*
*Je l'étais aussi, je crois bien,*
*Malgré mes quatorze ans d'avance,*
*Car je n'ai d'abord compris rien*
*A mon incroyable chance…*
*Nous devenons ce que nous sommes*
*Et c'est le Temps qui fait la somme*
*De ce qui a son prix en nous.*
*Tout a commencé un mois d'août*
*Dans mon atelier de la rue*

*Du Bac où tu étais venue*
*Un après-midi de congé.*
*Tu m'as choisi, tu m'as choyé,*
*Moi qui manquais de savoir-vivre,*
*Disant, grand sot que j'ai été:*
*'Ça ne durera qu'un été,*
*J'écris et je veux être libre!'*
*Libre, je le suis grâce à toi.*
*Je voudrais tant que tu le sois*
*Que tu te sentes épanouie…*
*Avant toi, j'étais écrivain,*
*Avec toi, je le suis encor.*
*Veillons à ce que notre sort*
*Nous garde à la littérature*
*Où notre place est aussi sûre*
*Au fil des ans que nous tissons*
*(Si tu le veux) qu'à la maison.*
*Notre maison, tu l'as bâtie*
*Et tu as bâti notre vie*
*Faite de dignité, d'ardeur,*
*De discrétion, de sympathie et de bonheur*
*Notre avenir, tu l'as bâti*
*Et c'est moi qui te dis merci,*
*A jamais, du fond de mon cœur.*
Lunch time, 6 mai 1994
Lord Jim, Oriental Hotel, Bangkok

**English translations:**

•[page 27]   I am full of love and tenderness for my wife. I experience at this moment for you, my darling, a desire that projects me towards you.
•        I turn myself with my whole body towards the delicious welcome of your body.
•        I think only of covering you with caresses and describing for you the new form of my/our combined love. The pleasures I have spoken to you about so often and that so often, so warmly, you have granted me.
•        I am lucky. My wife is beautiful. My wife has a lot of class. My wife has a keen sense of the values that are essential for me.
•        In the beginning and sometimes for a long time, there is the body, object of pleasure. Then there is the spirit, subject of reflection, coincidence of two subjectivities.
•        Then there is communion, veritable union.

[page 28]   **Boulevard d'Auteuil**

The enchanted dwelling where my grandfather lived
Was for us then the boulevard d'Auteuil.
It alone counted as our reference point
And it is for it today that I grieve.
The entrance gate was modest and the path welcoming
With fine gravel along the hedges.
The top of the large pine dominated, wavering,
A wave of white lilacs that I dream of today.

[page 31] **Bangkok**
Go and see, it isn't easy
When one wants to write a poem
And one isn't very agile
For singing, in verse, that one is in love…
I love you, my M who sows
In my life a bundle of happiness:
She who has kept my heart
Since Montmartre and the bohemian life!
She who has an upright soul
And who will have given me so much honour
In Paris, Sydney and elsewhere
All along our long route!
Do you know that I met her,
She was still naïve.
I was similar, I think,
In spite of my 14 year advance,
For at first I understood nothing
About my unbelievable luck…
We became what we are
And it's time which makes the totality
Of what is valuable within us.
Everything began one month of August
In my studio in the rue
Du Bac where you had come
One afternoon we had off.
You chose me, you spoilt me,
I lacked savoir-vivre,
Saying, fool that I was:
'It will only last a Summer,
I am a writer and I want to be free!'
Free, I am thanks to you,
I so much want you to be free,
To feel radiant…

Before you, I was a writer,
With you, I am still one.
Let us take care that our destiny
Associates us with literature
Where our place is as sure
During the years that we weave
(If you wish) as in our home.
Our home, you have built it
And you have built our life
Made of dignity, fervour,
Discretion, Congeniality and Happiness
Our future, you have built it
And it is me who thanks you,
Forever, from the bottom of my heart.

# 'with trepidation …'

## Colyn Whitehead

In 1974, I was a lecturer in the French Section of the Department of Modern Languages at the University of Newcastle, NSW. I was asked by the Head of Department Professor Ken Dutton to meet Jean-Paul Delamotte at the railway station and then drive him to his hotel. He had been invited to join the Department as tutor for the benefit of undergraduate students.

This task probably fell to me as the junior member of the teaching staff with access to a car and I remember viewing the task with some trepidation – how would I fare with my version of the French language with this French intellectual and *'homme de lettres'* of international standing? I need not have been worried. Jean-Paul spoke perfect English and if ever there was a perfect gentleman, it was Jean-Paul Delamotte: polite, quiet and unassuming, eminently *'abordable'* and *'délicat'* in this and every other interaction with him – academic or social.

I don't remember much about his work with the undergraduates, only that he lectured to them. It would be more accurate to say he discussed with them – at Professor Dutton's request – one or more of his own works (maybe *Signe de Vie*). He also gave tutorials on Henri Alain-Fournier's *Le Grand Meaulnes* (1913). I wish I had been in his class! He also did for me masterly French renditions of two passages from Henry D Thoreau's *Walden* (1854) for use in the weekly prose translation, or *'thème'* that I continued in the Kelver Hartley tradition.

I have none but fond and pleasant memories of the Delamottes – Jean-Paul, Monique and Guibourg.

# Early years in Newcastle

## Denise Yim

I first met Jean-Paul in 1975. Professor Ken Dutton had invited me to apply for a lectureship in French at Newcastle University and I was looking for accommodation, having relocated from Sydney. I rather fancied the area known by Novocastrians as 'The Hill' and went door knocking in Perkins Street. One of the doors was opened by a heavily pregnant French woman, who herself was a new arrival, so could not help me with lodgings. I eventually found an apartment in Bar Beach and arrived at work, to be told that I would be sharing an office with the other new recruit to the Newcastle University French Department, Jean-Paul Delamotte, who had arrived six months earlier. The lady in Perkins Street was Monique his wife, who shortly after gave birth to a baby girl. Thus began a close friendship over many years.

The Delamotte couple was quite a novelty in the Newcastle community. They were extremely exotic, firstly for being French and secondly for having worked in the film industry, notably at MGM. Jean-Paul had worked on some big-name films, including *The Sleeping Car Murders (Compartiment tueurs,* 1965). Newcastle soon fell in love with them and they with Newcastle.

Jean-Paul himself, I soon discovered, was rather vague and whimsical, a sort of absent-minded philosophiser. His baby daughter, he explained to me, would be called Guibourg after the eponymous French medieval queen. Sharing an office with him, I found him to be an out-of-the-ordinary colleague. He loved nothing better than to indulge in that quintessential French café pastime of discussing in abstractions, roaming freely in his ruminations. He used the same free-roaming approach to his teaching as he did to our conversations. It baffled some of the students, but it had its advantages. This floating ethereally from one topic to the next might have appeared to a bystander as having no purpose, but it soon became apparent that Jean-Paul was a man on a mission. And the mission was forging close ties between French and Australian culture, especially in film and literature. His persistence in this endeavour ultimately led in 1980 to the formation of the Association Culturelle Franco-Australienne, which Jean-Paul, I think, viewed as the highlight of his Australian career. It was a prime example of his enormous contribution to the Australian arts. For such a softly-spoken, retiring and modest man Jean-Paul was remarkably determined in his quest to achieve his objectives. I admired his sheer tenacity.

In the 1970s Australian film was going through a renaissance and Jean-Paul was quick to recognise this. He sought out directors such as Bruce Beresford and Peter Weir long before they were household names. He confided in me one day that, unannounced, he was going to phone Bruce Beresford and introduce himself. Phoning strangers unannounced became his *modus operandi* and in this way he acquainted himself intimately with the Australian literary intelligentsia. He made contact with Australian film directors, poets (AD Hope), novelists (Frank Moorhouse) and publishers (Tom Thompson) one after the other. If these Australians were surprised and bemused by the attentions of an unknown Frenchman, they were certainly gratified to be offered the opportunity to promote their work in France. Over the years Jean-Paul and Monique generously welcomed many, many Australian literary figures into their Paris home, which became a French hub for Australians with connections to the arts.

Of Frank Moorhouse's *The Americans, Baby* (1972), Jean-Paul wrote presciently in 1975, '*Frank Moorhouse a trente-six ans et mériterait d'être [connu], avec un talent aussi original, mais c'est loin d'être le cas !*' [1] Jean-Paul believed that Moorhouse was under-appreciated in Australia and promised to make his and other Australian authors' work known in France. He honoured this commitment. He translated several works by Moorhouse, one being a collection of three short stories (*Un Australien garanti d'époque*, 1987), including *Letters to Twiggy* of which the only other known iteration is in *The Australian of 27 November 1971*. There was also *The Coca Cola Kid* (*Coca-Cola kid; et autres récits*, 1985), *Forty-Seventeen* (*Quarante/dix-sept*, 1992) and *Grand Days* (*Tout un monde d'espoir*, 1996).

Jean-Paul first met Moorhouse on 3 October 1975 in the restaurant of the Art Gallery of New South Wales. It must have been a significant moment for him, as he writes of the occasion in two different publications: in the preface of *Un Australien garanti d'époque* and in his *Signe de Vie 2*: 'Rencontre de Frank Moorhouse. Avec son accord, je m'apprête à traduire et publier, pour la première fois en français, des textes de lui, auxquels je souhaite consacrer le prochain Signe de Vie.' The third issue of *Signe de Vie* did not eventuate, but the first two contain important information on Jean-Paul's aims.

The slim paperback *Signe de Vie 2* was a pot pourri of pieces by Jean-Paul and others, but mostly by Jean-Paul. Jean-Paul describes his *Signe de Vie* in words which, especially the last sentence, typify his whimsical style:

> **Signe de Vie** *n'est pas une revue. Son ambition, démesurée comme il convient, est d'être à l'origine d'une collection publiant des textes, courts probablement, d'auteurs australiens et français. Le premier* **Signe de Vie**, *paru en janvier 1975, a été cordialement salué par le Magazine Littéraire et le Monde en a publié un large extrait dans son numéro du 22 février [1975].*
> *On trouve* **Signe de Vie,** *en cherchant bien, à la librairie La Hune, Saint-Germain-des-Près, Paris.*

The publication details at the front of the book tell us that this, the second issue of *Signe de Vie*, was printed in Newcastle on 21 October 1975, the first issue having appeared in January 1975. It had a print run of 500 and each copy was numbered and signed. I was gifted No 9 by Jean-Paul.[3] The volume is divided into three parts. Part 1 is entitled *Six Fines de Claires, nouvelles* and accordingly, Jean-Paul addresses his readers as '*écaillers*', or oyster openers. This part consists of short pieces, all written in the first person, the first three being 'situations' in the form of rather flirtatious dialogues and the second three, about four pages long, also 'situations' written as personal musings. All are somewhat Kafkaesque. Part 2, entitled *La part belle,* contains poetry by Raymond Queneau, translated by KR Dutton, by AD Hope, translated by Didier Coste, and by Didier Coste, translated by himself.

On discovering this slim paperback on my bookshelves, I was chuffed to find an inscription at the front in Jean-Paul's handwriting, in fountain pen of course:

> *pour Denise et aussi pour Tom en attendant de*
> *prendre quelques huîtres à Paris un jour ensemble*
>
> *avec la vive amitié de Jean Paul, 5 nov 75, Newcastle*

Again Jean-Paul kept his word. Tom and I and even our three children enjoyed the hospitality of Jean-Paul and Monique over many years in their Paris home in the leafy suburb of Boulogne-Billancourt.

Jean-Paul's other pet project was making known and appreciated the writings of Paul Wenz, the French novelist, who in the late nineteenth century settled in Forbes in rural New South Wales, and, except for his *Diary of a New Chum*, wrote exclusively in French. For Jean-Paul, Wenz epitomised the Franco-Australian cultural connection. He campaigned to have him studied at Australian universities and vowed to publish and reprint his little-known books, which he proceeded to do, setting up his own modest publishing house called 'La Petite Maison', a description of the cottage in his Paris garden where Australian writers and others stayed. He campaigned equally hard to have Paul Wenz recognised in France and was instrumental in having a street in Reims (Paul Wenz's hometown) named after him. The street would be inaugurated on 4

February 2008, Jean-Paul told me in his email of 31 December 2007, and was the reason that his and Monique's forthcoming visit to Australia was delayed. But since Paul Wenz is the subject of other contributions to this book, enough said here.

While Jean-Paul's attention was focused mainly on Paul Wenz, he did also like to 'resurrect' other forgotten French writers. I have just come across some old correspondence with Jean-Paul, sent from the email address of Monique, who was Jean-Paul's gentle guide and advisor in all practical matters. In one message, dated 4 December 2006, Jean-Paul could not remember if he had sent me his latest book, a republication of two one-act plays of a little-known eighteenth-century playwright, Louis de Boissy. In another three-way correspondence with Ken Dutton regarding an obscure character in an even more obscure Madame de Genlis novel, Jean-Paul displays a remarkably deep knowledge of this eighteenth-century education author. It is in this email (6 February 2007) that Jean-Paul mentions a lost manuscript of Genlis's entitled 'Les Dangers de la célébrité'. It reminded him of an experience from his student days in France, when he attended a lecture given by the French writer and humourist Pierre Daninos at Reed Hall, Columbia University's campus in Paris. During question time he asked the speaker, who was then enjoying considerable fame for his *Carnets du major Thompson*: 'Quels sont les inconvénients de la célébrité?' to which Daninos answered: 'I tend to disagree, but of course I have good reason for that.'

This was the sort of exchange that caught Jean-Paul's fancy.

Once, on a visit to our home on Lake Macquarie in Toronto, just out of Newcastle, Jean-Paul had, after the fashion of houseguests in eighteenth-century France or England, come equipped with reading matter. While I was in the kitchen at the back of the house he had ensconced himself in an armchair on the front verandah overlooking the lake with a book. Quite unexpectedly, I came upon him immersed in Rousseau's *Rêveries d'un promeneur solitaire*. The book was a peculiarly apt metaphor for Jean-Paul himself, not because he felt isolated, as did Rousseau, from society, but because it deals, in Rousseau's own words, with *'la douceur de converser avec mon âme'*.[4] Jean-Paul liked nothing better than to sit quietly with his own thoughts, to reflect, to ruminate, to reminisce and to recollect. Nothing illustrates this better than his *Signe de Vie 2* that contains a selection of whimsical random jottings about various episodes, events and even objects that struck him as quaintly noteworthy. The title of the present book, Reciprocity, is particularly well-chosen, not only for the obvious reason, which is the interaction between French and Australian culture, but also for the personal dialogues that Jean-Paul so enjoyed with his own soul.

There was, however, another unlikely love of Jean-Paul's and that was tennis. To my knowledge, it was the only sport that he indulged in and in 1975 we enjoyed many games on the University courts in our spare time. I was taken aback when, on a visit to Newcastle a few years later, he declined the offer of a game, pleading 'old age'. I certainly did not view him as 'old', but that is the way he saw himself and nothing I said could persuade him to change his mind.

I can still hear Jean-Paul's voice addressing me as *'chère Denise'* and the abiding image of his cardiganed figure will stay with me forever. Tom and I were in Japan when we received news of Jean-Paul's death in September 2019 and we straightaway went in search of a suitable card to send to Monique and Guibourg. The Japanese, in their inimitable way, create large decorative mourning cards for just such an occasion, but the salesgirl, fearing I was purchasing it to be sent as an ordinary greeting card, was visibly anxious lest I did not understand exactly what I was buying. Sadly, I did.

It is fitting, given the significant service that Jean-Paul has done untold numbers of Australian writers, film directors and other literati, that in 2015 his papers were acquired by the State Library of New South Wales and it was a pleasure to attend the celebration of that event at the Library last year, together with many of his Newcastle friends.

Sydney, 22 September 2022

**Notes:**

1. Jean-Paul Delamotte, *Signe de vie 2* (Newey & Beath, Newcastle, 1975), 49.
2. Delamotte, *Signe de Vie,* 50. In the end only two volumes of *Signe de vie* were published, January & October 1975.
3. Ken Dutton received No 1: *'pour Ken en souvenir des bonnes journées passées et en prévision des bonnes journées à venir, dans l'un ou l'autre hémisphère ... en attendant un dîner chez Drouant en place Clichy – spécialité d'huitres ... avec l'amitié de JP.D. 3 xi 75.*
4. *Les Confessions de JJ Rousseau,* vol 3, London [Neuchâtel], 1786, 11.

[**Ed's Note : 'French language lessons popular'** was the headline in the *Newcastle Morning Herald* (14 August 1975) to announce the arrival of 'a newly appointed lecturer in French at Newcastle University' from the University of NSW, **Miss Denise Maroney**. The article pointed out the important role language laboratories played in teaching a foreign language. Denise Maroney graduated with a BA with first class honours in French from Sydney University. 'From 1969 to 1972 she studied at the Sorbonne to gain her MA'.

# 'Born in the house of books'*

## Guibourg Delamotte

Before discovering Australian literature, Jean-Paul, my father, was a remarkable reader and a tireless writer himself. When he arrived in Australia, he met a rising generation of writers and film-makers and the connection was instantaneous.

Jean-Paul had devoured French literature in his maternal grandparents' library, 16 Boulevard d'Auteuil, in Boulogne – a house which he never ceased to adore and which his father soon sold. JP was made to decide which of his 'friends', which of the collector-item books would be sold with the house and which would be allowed to reach the country house. He never recovered from the trauma.

The country house in Andelu, now a 40-minute drive from Paris, is where he spent most of the Second World War with his mother Yvonne and beloved maternal grandparents, Paul and Marie Guibourg. I was named after them – Guibourg, their last name, is also a medieval girl's name, which my parents found out through Norman Million, a Medievalist from the French Department of the University of Newcastle.

JP's unmissed father was held in detention by the Germans until French officers could return, once 'collaboration' had been signed on. JP spent most of his childhood, from 8 to 14 years old (1939 to 1945), reading, climbing up trees, feeding a pig (Adolf) and a donkey (more conventionally named, although Adolf may have become a common name for pet pigs in occupied France) and helping out the gardener. The personnel grew thinner with the war and the former (relative) grandeur was lost forever – but my grandparents kept a cook, Marie, whom JP, my mother and I visited in Chartres for many years (and later on, her grave).

Food was scarce but in the countryside non-Jewish people lived well enough (JP's best friend in Boulogne was a Jewish boy, who was able to keep safe, a future Doctor, whom JP always kept in touch with). JP's big brother, Yves, whom he looked upon and loved, was 10 years older than him. Yves left the household to join the Résistance, crossing into Switzerland, to evade 'STO' – *Service du Travail Obligatoire*, the compulsory work service – labour force sent to Germany (of the Vichy government's own accord; Vichy is most ignominiously responsible for handing over Jewish children, rather than just the adults, to the Nazis).

This big brother, who never approved of JP's literary call and life choices, would prove bitterly disappointing. Yves took the father-approved path of Ecole nationale d'administration and became a high-ranking civil servant, in the tradition of the paternal side of the family. On the mother's side, the family sold coal in Boulogne. The Seine river allowed the transport of coal on barges and provided abundant water for laundering – a prosperous sector in that part of the town. On the coal yard were showers for the workers. My grandfather, Yvonne's husband, was at work from 5 am. The carpenter on the coal yard had made my father a treasured little desk.

Jean-Paul got little formal schooling during the War years and I believe they left him with a deeply engrained sense of freedom. Unless it was the experience of the War and Occupation itself? He did attend some private classes, but he acquired his culture through books. Jean-Paul was educated at a time and in a world where people read and were well-read. He read Ovide and Heraclitus in Latin and Greek, though later in life he resorted to the bilingual editions. So I, too, grew up with '*Alea jacta est*' and '*Tu quoque mi filii*'. In those days, even people with a primary school education knew verses of Racine and Corneille, so if you could quote them, you didn't sound pedantic; you were just letting slip a common reference. The verses simply came back, to punctuate the thought. He may well have been the last of that time, the last of a generation who could quote with simplicity, because classics were a part of their lives. So I benefited and heard the beauty people forget. '*Même, elle avait encor cet éclat emprunté/Dont elle eut soin de peindre et d'orner son visage,/Pour réparer des ans l'irréparable outrage.*' (*Athalie*, Racine).

    JP attended a very good public (state) high school in Paris and rode his bike there across the Bois de Boulogne. He was admitted to the *lycée* Henri IV's one-year literary class (HK), became a Fullbright scholar, attending Amherst in the US, aged 19, with an interest in nearby Mills College's girls, then Harvard. He did his military service in Freiburg, Germany, was always fond of speaking German and had a passion for Vienna and its pre-War feel. He was admitted at the Political Institute of Paris with former president Jacques Chirac, but his studies there were interrupted by the Algerian War. He benefited from his brother's influence then, himself a civil servant in Algiers. JP read Law and completed his doctoral degree in Political Science at the Sorbonne.

    But Jean-Paul's personality was much more than his education was meant to produce. He called himself : '*écrivain en liberté*' (freedom writer). He was free-spirited and was very fond of Voltaire. He loved Stendhal, too, for his literary style and life. To him they lived on through their books. Writing kept you alive. Indeed living on, was an obsession.

    He wrote every day of his life from the age of 14 at least, keeping a diary, publishing with Gallimard and Plon, prestigious French publishers – a worthy '*ouvrier des lettres*' (he liked Sainte-Beuve's expression). He worked on his manuscripts from 5 am before setting off to his paid job in the film industry. He met Monique at the Boulogne Film Studios. He moved to the subtitling of American and Australian films in the 1980s which provided more time for writing and translating. At one stage he had a work program: one poem, one short story, a dialogue ('*scénette*'), one book chapter, per week. He called his study 'studiolo'.

    It took me a few years to grasp and appreciate the breadth and depth of my father's personality. We never knew what book he would pick for reading over breakfast – when he had croissants with rather a lot of butter and jam and dipped it all in his tea distractedly, spilling quite a bit of it. All the while, he read The *Illiad* - for quite some time at least. I was 7 years old and lost in the story, yet enjoyed the liveliness and diversity of the characters. Other times he pulled a book at random, or so it seemed. Occasionally, I was embarrassed. His voice would break reading Victor Hugo. *Demain dès l'aube* – Hugo had lost his daughter. *'Mon père ce héros au sourire si doux'* still wrings in my ears and seems so fitting to JP. Funnily enough, I don't recall not understanding them – perhaps I got distracted by the croissants! They did leave an everlasting memory. I too read to my daughter over meals. I used to think he had a gift, that he could open any book and find *the* beautiful lines in it. It never seemed to work quite as well when I tried it. Then I realised: it wasn't the pages and the books he picked, it was his ability to see the words as the writer had meant them and bequeathed them to posterity.

When I was seven my parents would take me to the opera and, again how disturbed I was to see my father shedding tears over lines – '*He says* "I love you" and despite myself I feel/My heart beating and beating' (*The Queen of Spades*, Tchaikovsky). Those lines, those melodies of Jacques Offenbach (*Les Contes d'Hoffman*) or Franz Lehár (*Die Lustige Witwe*), remain the ones I find most beautiful now. It's interesting how much gets passed on even though you feel bored as a child.

I started understanding who he was as a young adult. Past the early teenage-hood, when I could enjoy a conversation. He had left paternity till late, 42. I feel great continuity between him and me, the blood carrying the soul.

His perception of Humanity was tinged with that long-gone world of beauty he could share with so few. He found his soulmates, men and women, in Australia. A month before my father died, Frank Moorhouse, August 12th, wrote to me:

> My dear Guibourg, how is JP? And how are you affected? If there is anything I could do please ask. I doubt I could

> afford to come to France but have been looking into it and if needed I will.
>
> Remember you and Eva always have a home here if or when you need a break. Or a long stay. Or to live.
>
> JP meant so much to me, as do you.
>
> My heart and mind are with you.
>
> A very dear American friend of mine died here in Sydney on Saturday – he had the room next to Jean-Paul at Amherst College for a year when students – David Gyger – they weren't close friends but remembered each other – weird they ended coming independently to know me here in Sydney and lived here for a time.
>
> Much love to JP

On 12th September, Frank wrote to JP:

> Subject: Get well
>
> My dear Jean-Paul, have received bulletins from Guibourg and hear you are recovering – great news. Hope we can get together in Sydney or Paris soon. Ageing isn't much fun is it? I spent most of yesterday with doctors about age related problems. I miss your company and your mind. Get well, we need you in our lives. You are often mentioned in conversation. With love and great respect, Frank.

Frank Moorhouse ("mon Frankie") was my father's soulmate. Brian Suters ("mon Brian") was his true brother. When I was 8 years old, we were about to land in Sydney and on the plane my mother told me Brian and Kay would be at the airport, waiting for us. She added: 'If anything happened to us, you'd go live with Brian and Kay.' (Not her sisters or brother.) My father went to the other side of the earth, far away from his father, with a woman who adhered to everything he offered, agreed to follow him, had the same ability to love passionately and would let him be who he needed to be, a writer.

Australia provided a purpose and a mission. French literature was taught in Australian universities, but this would not last unless the French reciprocated. French publishers, readers, academics, students, were to discover Australian literature; French museums and collections were to discover and open up to Australian art; French diplomats must understand the importance of Australia for French political influence to endure in the South Pacific: only superpowers can be influential alone, others must realise influence is a two-party process. My father was a pioneer, including a literary one, and pioneers have a hard time. But he had the inner conviction he would be proved right, as visionaries are. Indeed, he has been. He chose every bit of his life – my mother, Australia, writing – a free soul.

* As begins Geoffrey Dutton's *Out in the Open*, University of Queensland Press, 1994 – translated and published by Jean-Paul Delamotte : Et Voilà ! Souvenirs d'enfance, La Petite Maison, 1998, 9.

# My First French Friend

## Israel Horovitz

A film I had written was in competition at the 1970 Festival de Cannes. M-G-M's publicity person assigned to my film was a young woman named Monique Desgrouas, who introduced herself to me by saying: 'You must meet my boyfriend Jean-Paul. He's a writer and filmmaker and I know you will be friends.'

And so began a friendship that would last half a century.

Jean-Paul and Monique soon married and made their Rue Vital apartment's guest room my Paris home away from home. This generosity eventually took solid form when they moved to their final home in Boulogne-Billancourt and their garden house became free digs for literally hundreds of writers visiting Paris.

One of my earliest memories of Jean-Paul was his unusual skill at parking. He would choose a spot exactly where he wanted to park his car, crack open a book or manuscript and wait. I remember to this day Jean-Paul telling me: 'Eventually, someone will move a car. It will happen.' As a New Yorker given to driving in endless circles until a parked car was finally moved, usually somewhere quite far from my home, I was duly impressed by Jean-Paul's extraordinary patience. And, yes, somewhere in Paris, a parked car would soon enough be moved and Jean-Paul Delamotte would have the parking spot of his dreams.

Jean-Paul's patience was extraordinary.

Much has been written about Jean-Paul's romance with Australia. I would like to write about Jean-Paul's romance with writing and writers.

Samuel Beckett was among the writers Jean-Paul admired greatly. He saw Beckett on the street one say, but was embarrassed to talk with him. I knew Beckett well and was certain he would benefit from knowing Jean-Paul Delamotte and so I suggested to Jean-Paul that he write a note to Beckett. And he did. And Beckett replied, immediately, saying: 'When you next see me on the street, block my path.'

Jean-Paul Delamotte wrote virtually every day of his long life. His serious writing began when he was a student in America, with a novel ironically entitled *Le vain labeur*. And his serious writing never stopped. His published books include *La Communauté*, Gallimard, 1962; *Sans hâte, cette nuit*, Plon, 1967; *La Bourelle*, Plon, 1973; *Un Dimanche à Melbourne*, La Petite Maison, 1998; *La Place de la Concorde*, La Petite Maison, 1998; *L'Indien-Pacifique*, La Petite Maison, 2000 ... but this list is only the tip of a glorious mountain of work. Jean-Paul wrote more than one hundred short stories and scores of essays on writers and writing. He generously translated the work of many writers, mostly from Australia – his beloved second home. He kept a daily diary of events of his day, as well as events of the world around him. Only partly edited, this thousand-plus page diary is a masterful chronicle of nearly seventy years of life on the planet Earth. When I visited with Jean-Paul two months before his death, he talked at length about Samuel Pepys, the seventeenth-century diarist. Jean-Paul was re-reading Pepys and books written about Pepys. Clearly, Jean-Paul had found a soul-mate.

Jean-Paul's erudition was extraordinary. He was a consummate teacher with the gentlest of teaching skills, somehow managing to make his chamber-lectures seem like give-and-take conversation. During my fifty years of friendship with Jean-Paul Delamotte, I cannot remember a single conversation between us from which I did not learn something literary and large.

But Jean-Paul's extraordinary patience was most striking. When publishers were less than enthusiastic about taking on Jean-Paul's work, he never flinched. He never judged himself by other people's standards. He knew his work was unique and important. He knew that his work would be read one day. His identity as writer was precious and clear.

As an American, bred with the very-American notion that external success is the barometer by which talent is judged, Jean-Paul's absolute lack of panic was more than impressive. We had a conversation in the early 1980s that I shall never forget. I asked Jean-Paul if he were worried about his not being published by commercial French publishers. He smiled at me and said, simply: 'I love to write. Nothing can interfere with my writing. I know my work will be read, one day.'

Again, I learned something literary and large.

Like the parking spot that would somehow appear precisely where Jean-Paul wanted to place his automobile, Jean-Paul had faith his work would someday find its way to readers. And I, too, have faith that it will.

Jean-Paul Delamotte died on September 21, 2019 – a few weeks short of his 88th birthday. My wife and I were visiting with Jean-Paul and Monique on the day Jean-Paul died. Ever polite, Jean-Paul's final words were: 'Thank you for coming to visit.'

Thank you, Jean-Paul, for visiting my particular life. You are loved ... and already gone too long.

**Note from Guibourg Delamotte:**
I could not have Israel's [obituary for JP] published in France. He died of cancer one year after JP. He was at my parents' home with his wife Gillian, on the very day JP died.

This is the last message I received from him dated Nov. 1st, 2020: 'Unfortunately I'm doing very poorly. The cancer is winning the battle. Hard to know how much time I have left. I want you to know how much I love Jean-Paul and Monique. And you. Your family is my family.

# 'An amazing Frenchman'

## Tony Maniaty

My earliest encounter with Jean-Paul was in Sydney in the early 1980s, at a long and sunny lunch hosted by my then literary agent Rosemary Creswell. She wanted to introduce me to 'an amazing Frenchman' who was apparently passionate about Australian literature (as if the French didn't have enough grand literature of their own). Rose was keen to open up any publishing possibilities between Australia and France, which Jean-Paul was spearheading with considerable, even irrepressible, enthusiasm (which, I would quickly discover, was how he approached everything he did).

I dropped everything and headed to The Mixing Pot in Glebe and found the gathering in a garden courtyard – Italian-style like the food. I seem to remember the late Frank Moorhouse was there and Richard Hall as well – in such heavyweight company, the wine was flowing freely and I could see a hangover was more than likely the next day, but what stood out immediately was Jean-Paul's passion for everything Australian, which matched my long-held passion for anything French. We hit it off and talked for what seemed hours and promised to stay in touch.

A few years later, in 1989, I was on an Air France jet bound for Paris for a six-month residency at the Internationale Cité des Arts. Only then – when I reconnected with the unstoppable Delamotte operation – did I realise the depth and spread of Jean-Paul's influence over the Franco-Australian literary scene and Monique's input likewise. Perfectly-prepared lunches at their book-filled home with daughter Guibourg were attended by an extraordinary range of guests, be they literary, academic or political, and always Jean-Paul was saying: 'We must do more…'

I stayed on in France for three years, working as European Correspondent for SBS Television and revisited the Delamotte household many times. I'm sure it was Jean-Paul who arranged for my invitation to a Paris Town Hall reception as 'an important Australian author' (which certainly wasn't how I saw myself) so I could meet his old classmate, the then Mayor of Paris, Jacques Chirac. One of JP's great skills and pleasures was bringing people together, making the connections and generating enthusiasm. Hence his constant refrain: 'We must do more...'

In a world hungry for celebrity and success, Jean-Paul was charmingly old-school – engaging, intelligent, talented and with a mission he never stopped believing in.

\*\*\*

## 'The bush to Boulogne or bust'
(*Weekend Australian*, May 13-14, 1989)

PARIS LETTER

'That's where Ionesco lives,' says Jean-Paul Delamotte as we drove down the Boulevard Montparnasse.

Just as I'm thinking it's true, that so much mythology stalks these streets – de Beauvoir, Miller, Hemingway, Beckett, Sartre – he yells: 'Ah, there's Tom Keneally!' And standing at the corner is a definite lookalike with balding pate and goatee beard, except it's silky white. Perhaps he's aged suddenly.

But no! we assure ourselves it's just another imposter – climbing aboard the Australian literary bandwagon that's rolling across Paris, like a wave. Would I lie to you?

People here are living on their reputations. Delamotte adds, swerving to avoid a sluggish taxi. Since 1980, when he founded the French-Australian Cultural Association, Delamotte has been doing a lot of this – hosting visiting writers and conducting a love-hate affair with the French literary scene.

He rolls his eyes. 'And publishers – it would be terrible if we needed another war or a revolution to bring new blood to our literature.' He refers to several big names off the record. 'I talk too much, of course.'

But about Australian literature, he can't stop. For more than a decade, Delamotte has been driven by a singular passion: how to bring Boulogne and the Bush together without causing offence to anyone.

He can't be too crazy … so far he's attracted 300 members to the cause, and I'm the next candidate.

\*\*\*

At the Australian Embassy things are calmer. 'It's not as though we are being killed in the rush', says Trevor Baldock, gazing over his permanent display of Australian books in the foyer. Back in 1987, our Chief Trade Commissioner in Paris organised an exhibition of Australiana at the Printemps department store.

'Between a synthetic Ayers Rock and Lloyd Rees paintings,' Baldock says, 'we threw in a whole raft of Australian books, and they sold faster than anything.' That was the catalyst he adds with the voice of a man who doesn't confuse business with literature: 'In the subsequent year […] I included Australian books in my operational plans.'

He wrote to 113 Australian publishers and got positive replies from about 20 – another 50 French publishers showed interest in taking a closer look at Australian books and sent his newsletter to French literary critics and booksellers.

So far he's clinched one deal – Geoffrey Badger's *Explorers of the Pacific* (Kangaroo Press) has just been sold to Editions Raymond Chabaud for translation. There's strong interest in Australian children's books too which have a big reputation over here.

\*\*\*

On the Left Bank two days later, I discover the Librairie Attica (34, rue des Ecoles) where Tanguy Le Puloch and his offsider, Patrice Carrer, stock about 120 Australian titles on three shelves.

They're waiting for the paperback Oscar and Lucinda by Peter Carey (since hardbacks are virtually unknown in France and unsaleable) and report that Patrick White is still their biggest seller.

It's not exactly a roaring trade, admits Le Puloch: 'about 10 or 15 books a month, but interest is definitely picking up.' So who buys them? 'Tourists, French academics, Australians living in Paris, and especially students ...'

Right on cue, in walk Carina and Chrystele – with their Sorbonne reading list and scanning the shelves. They're third-year English students doing Australian and New Zealand history units and they ask my advice for something historical in novels.

Like clever students everywhere, they insist it shouldn't be 'too long' ... we settle on *The Chant of Jimmy Blacksmith*.

I scan the list of the most prestigious university in France and find – between B for Rolf Boldrewood and W for Judith Wright – the very esteemed Barry Oakley, author of the ever-popular Bedfellows.

\*\*\*

We're almost there, but still Delamotte seems worried. 'How to do this ...' he mumbles. Being naïve, I assume he's looking for a parking space – he's taking me to lunch at his favourite place near the Opera.

'A certain aura must be created ...'

'About what?'

He looks slightly incredulous. 'To promote this glorious friendship between France and Australia.' he says, 'You know, perhaps a publicist ...'

'Bonne idee.' I reply. 'What's that restaurant again?'

'Capucine,' says Delamotte vaguely. 'On the rue Scribe, just opposite Qantas. To be honest, I think a publicist would be too brutal for the French ...'

'But things seem to be going okay,' I urge, as hunger descends on me. 'Right now you're translating the latest Frank Moorhouse (*Forty-Seventeen*) and you've just done the sub-titles for *Evil Angels* (*A Cry in the Dark* over here) and every week you're organising a visit by some Australian writer or other ...'

'Yes, but did you know that at the turn of the century our French literary magazines published short stories by Henry Lawson, and a Frenchman wrote a major book on Australian socialism. There were a lot more contacts ...'

It's the impatience of a true convert, I realise. A genuine Australophile, Monsieur Delamotte, this piece of ironbark plonked down 'in our little place beside the Seine', as he calls the city ... a nice bloke.


**Note:** Quote from Albert Camus – 'We are all special cases.'

# Vale Jean Paul

# Xavier Pons

To talk to Jean-Paul Delamotte, even for a few minutes, was to sense his abiding passion for Australia. If his wife Monique and his daughter Guibourg were the great loves of his life, Australia had insinuated itself into the very substance of those loves.

Nothing in his first few decades suggested that Australia might come to play such an important part in his life. He studied at the elite Science-Po school of political studies, where he rubbed shoulders with a fellow student, Jacques Chirac, with whom he stayed in touch even when the latter became President of the Republic. He continued his studies in the USA at Amherst College and Harvard University and capped them with a doctoral dissertation at the Sorbonne on the relationship between the French State and the cinema industry. The cinema was indeed another of his passions. He came to play a significant part in this industry, where he had first-class connections. (Once when staying at his house, enjoying his usual generous hospitality, he asked me to look up a phone number in his address book, under the letter 'D' – and there the number was, among those of Gérard Depardieu and Catherine Deneuve …) The time he spent in the US had allowed him to become quite proficient in the English language, a proficiency he put to good use, becoming a translator and making his mark as a writer of French subtitles for English-language movies. His subtitles were always of the highest quality as Jean-Paul attached a great deal of importance to language issues. He was a very literary person and the author of various novels and essays.

With hindsight (and no doubt a little imagination), one can see his many interests converging towards Australia. His work for the cinema allowed him to meet his future wife Monique, who worked in the same industry. They married in 1974 and, strangely enough perhaps, they decided to spend their honeymoon in Australia. His academic qualifications and his experience as a writer and a translator allowed him to be appointed a tutor in French at the University of Newcastle. The appointment process made him a minor celebrity, as the two referees who supported his application were none other than Jacques Chirac – then Prime Minister of France – and world-famous dramatist Eugène Ionesco. It is fair to assume that the selection committee had never encountered such distinguished referees for the relatively humble position of tutor!

Jean-Paul and Monique felt very much at home in Australia and, even after they returned to France, the country continued to play a very significant part in their lives. It is Australia that brought us together. We met in 1979 at a lunch organised by then Australian Ambassador John Rowland at his residence. Like Jean-Paul I was there with my wife, as a young academic who had recently completed his PhD on Henry Lawson. We hit it off immediately, brought together by our common love for Australia – and so we stayed in touch.

Jean-Paul had always been keenly interested in literary matters. He was himself a published writer, having authored a number of novels. But, far from being obsessed by his own writing, he wanted to promote the writings of others, especially if they were Australian. He noted with regret that Australian writers had very little impact on the French literary scene and he was determined to make a difference. His endeavours took many different forms. In 1980 he founded the French-Australian Cultural Association in order to promote awareness of Australian culture in France and of French culture in Australia – reciprocity mattered very much to him. He generously gave much of his time to assist a succession of Australian ambassadors in organising various cultural events, including a prize for the best translation into French of a work by an Australian author. He himself translated works by such authors as Frank Moorhouse or Geoffrey Dutton and, most notably, Marcus Clarke's *For the Term of His Natural Life*. The confluence of French and Australian cultures that he embodied so passionately found its perfect expression in his taking up of Paul Wenz, a neglected French novelist who settled in Australia and wrote mainly in French. Jean-Paul rescued him from obscurity and restored him as a significant literary figure.

As well as writing about Australia and in order to promote Australian writing, Jean-Paul set up his own publishing house, La Petite Maison. The name was that of the actual 'little house' which stood at the bottom of the garden of his Boulogne mansion and where he generously accommodated visitors, Australian and otherwise. He thus published a variety of texts dealing with Australia, his own as well as those of other authors, including my wife's MA thesis, an introduction to Australian journalist John Stanley James, better known as "The Vagabond", and a translation of his work *The War in New Caledonia*, which dealt with the Kanak rebellion and its ferocious repression by the French army: *La Guerre en Nouvelle-Calédonie* (1878), (trans & presented by Géraldine Pons-Ribot, Petite Maison, 1989).

In addition to my natural affection for Jean-Paul and Monique, my own enduring interest in all things Australian kept us on the same wavelength – he reviewed my work and I reviewed his and this, at a time when Australia didn't loom large on France's cultural scene, was no mutual backscratching; rather, it was a persistent and honest effort to give greater visibility, in academia and beyond, to the achievements of Australian culture, especially where literature and cinema were concerned.

Jean-Paul's contribution to Australian studies was multi-faceted and very substantial. He wasn't a professional academic, but moved easily in all the circles that had a connection with Australia, whether literary or diplomatic. A tireless advocate for Australian culture, he was also a very charming man and exceedingly pleasant company – he was a fun person to be around, always upbeat, always looking forward to his next project.

I hardly need to emphasise how badly I miss him.

# *Unlocked doors and impossible reciprocity: a student's perspective on the Delamottes*
# John West-Sooby

The Delamottes, as we know, moved in exalted circles, rubbing shoulders and establishing firm friendships with renowned figures on the cultural and political scene, in both Australia and France (and beyond).[1] To the French students at the University of Newcastle, New South Wales in 1975, however, they were simply Jean-Paul and Monique, teachers whose sudden appearance in our midst offered a new dimension to our studies, along with a dose of exoticism. International travel was less commonplace in those days and for many of us the Delamottes were the first 'authentic' French people we had encountered. In so many ways, they embodied the language and culture we were studying, thereby providing us with a concrete manifestation of what we were learning in the abstract. And they did so to great effect, opening many doors and offering opportunities and experiences that we could never hope to reciprocate. Others, no doubt, will pay due homage to the role Jean-Paul and Monique played as intercultural mediators on the larger stage. The aim here, in contrast, is to offer some more personal, idiosyncratic recollections in the hope that these anecdotes, however trivial, will provide some insights into the profound and lasting impact that Jean-Paul and Monique had on the students they taught.

**From the Paris end of Newcastle …**
I was in my second year of French study at the University of Newcastle when Jean-Paul and Monique entered my orbit. Monique taught some of our second-year language classes, working from a textbook that bore the practical if underwhelming title: *Second French*. Its sub-title was a little more creative, though somewhat foreboding: *Le français non sans peine*.

I remember Monique being tickled by this. It was a hefty hardback tome of over 500 pages with an emerald green cover featuring a purple motif. Each of its 25 chapters, or '*Leçons*', had a themed vocabulary section (*La Maison, Les Repas,* etc) leading to particular grammar topics. It was fairly standard fare, though the grammar coverage was comprehensive – we had to confront the uses of the imperfect and pluperfect subjunctives as early as '*Leçon VIII*'. One of the book's more interesting features was its focus on directed composition. This provided the opportunity for some fun. My approach to these assignments was to use recurring characters whose paths crossed through loosely connected adventures. Apparently Balzac had already come up with that idea. In any event, Monique showed great tolerance in marking those pieces. I secretly hoped that she found them entertaining, a notion which her positive comments helped to nurture. Monique's classes were joyous affairs. With her trademark smile and unflappable cheerfulness, she guided us through the various chapters, offering her own personal observations and pointing out where idiomatic usage departed from grammatical rules. This was insider information, a door being opened. We were very grateful for this.

Meanwhile, Jean-Paul was opening doors of a different kind through his classes on French literature which covered an eclectic range of texts. We were unaware at the time that he was himself a writer, but that helps to explain in retrospect the personal perspectives he shared with us and the pensive approach he took to talking about texts. The first work we studied with him was *Athalie*. This was the final instalment in a block of three Racine tragedies on the program, each taught by a different lecturer. My guess is that *Athalie* is a work Jean-Paul might not have spontaneously chosen to teach. But if that was the case and he was simply fulfilling his duty and fitting in where needed, it must be said that he approached the task with great commitment and certainly with more enthusiasm than we students could muster: we had enjoyed the grandiose soap opera of *Phèdre* and had soldiered our way bravely through *Britannicus*, but by the time we reached *Athalie*, we were a little alexandrine-weary. Under his guidance, though, we managed to get something out of the play and emerged (largely) unscathed.

Other texts seemed a more natural fit for Jean-Paul. Julien Gracq's *Un balcon en forêt* was one. Gracq seemed to us to be very much a writer's writer, as seen through Jean-Paul's eyes. There was some irony in this, given the fact that Gracq had always distanced himself from the Parisian literary milieu – with which Jean-Paul seemed to have some mysterious connections – and famously rejected the Prix Goncourt in 1951 for *Le Rivage des Syrtes*. We were afforded a glimpse of that literary scene, in contrast, through our study with Jean-Paul of a very different kind of text: Jean Paulhan's *Les Incertitudes du langage*. I doubt whether this work has ever figured before or since on the curriculum of an Australian university French department, though I would be happy – if surprised – to be corrected on that score. Our class certainly had the impression that we were reading something out of the ordinary, but we were a little unsure how much of a privilege it was. For Jean-Paul's sake, I would like to say that I remember the text vividly, but what I mostly recall is the contextual discussion about Paulhan and the *Nouvelle Revue française*, of which Paulhan had twice been director. Jean-Paul was very discreet about his own connections to the *NRF* – he was never one to blow his own trumpet – but the detail in the many asides and the warmth in his voice when he offered such tangential information made it clear to us that we were (once again) being offered a rare insider's perspective. I regret not telling Jean-Paul in later life that I studiously kept that book, which cost me the princely sum of $1.60 at the Newcastle University Coop Bookshop. It sits on my shelf primarily as a memento of Jean-Paul's classes rather than as a text valued in its own right. I wonder whether it would have been a source of comfort or disappointment if he had known that …

Jean-Paul was equally discreet about his relationship with Eugène Ionesco when we came to study *La Cantatrice chauve* with him. We sensed that he had a particular affinity with both the text and the author, but we had no inkling that he had an actual personal connection to Ionesco. That would have been a cause for much excitement and many questions – a good reason, perhaps, for keeping such information to himself. In any event, that was one door we were destined not to step through. In our test on that term's literature program, Jean-Paul's essay question for Ionesco was: '*La Cantatrice chauve est-elle chauvine ?* An excellent question, in retrospect. If only I had known what "chauvine" meant! It being a test, there was no option but to plough on and make a guess at the question while trying to recall the main themes of Jean-Paul's lectures so as to concoct an essay that might contain some relevant points. It must have been obvious that I had not fully understood the question, but I was pleasantly surprised to find that Jean-Paul had given me a reasonable mark. Perhaps, by some fluke, I had managed to make a few pertinent comments, or else everyone else was in the same boat and some allowance was made for that. Jean-Paul was the soul of kindness.

One door which was always literally open – on Thursday evenings at least – was that of the Delamottes' home in Perkins Street, in the inner city precinct known as The Hill. Thanks to the Delamottes, this was now the Paris end of Newcastle. Jean-Paul and Monique showed great generosity in opening their home to students on Thursday evenings and we jumped on the chance to go and practise our French with them. I recall that, on one such occasion, Jean-Paul and Monique spent an extended session with me trying to perfect my pronunciation of words starting with an aspirate h – words such as '*le hasard*' or '*le héros*'. I thought I had this pronunciation challenge largely under control, but there was evidently still room for improvement. So Jean-Paul and Monique sat with me and modelled the pronunciation of such words which I did my best to imitate. It required a good deal of patience on their part, but it was all done in good humour and the session produced much mirth. Students were of course not the only visitors to Perkins Street. We were aware that a host of friends and notables also frequented their home and had a chance to mingle with some of them on those Thursday evenings. Jean-Paul and Monique were especially charmed by a visitor of a different kind: a small lizard that would come and sun itself on their kitchen window-sill. They called it "*César*", to rhyme with '*lézard*'. We liked that. As I recall, the Thursday *soirées* came to a halt, understandably enough, once Guibourg was born. Her birth was of sufficient import for Prof. Dutton to interrupt one of our French classes to give us the news. We registered the vital statistics – weight, length – with interest, but were mostly just happy to know that mother and baby were happy and healthy. The baby's name was the source of much speculation. It only added to the aura of the Delamottes.

No sooner had Jean-Paul, Monique and now Guibourg entered our lives, it seemed, than they disappeared from it. When they moved on to other pastures in 1976, they left a large gap that was the measure of the impact they had made on us. I was far from imagining then that our paths would once more cross, this time on the other side of the world …

### … to the Newcastle end of Paris

In September 1979 I arrived in Paris, where I planned to spend a week or so before heading down to Grenoble to begin my postgraduate studies which had been made possible thanks to a French Government scholarship. In those days, this was a very generous award, in terms of its length, at least (four years). The monthly stipend of 1,400 francs proved to be (just) adequate, if frugal. The Delamottes were the only people I knew in France at the time, so it seemed only natural to go and knock on their door. At the time Jean-Paul was working for *Les Artistes associés,* the French arm of United Artists, and I somehow found the means of contacting him and paying him a visit at his office. He greeted me with customary warmth. It really did seem as though we had seen each other only the day before. He very kindly gave me a free pass to see a United Artists movie that was then showing in Paris – my first experience of a French cinema house.

The fact that Jean-Paul was connected to the world of movies came as something of a surprise to me. As I now know, he had given classes on French cinema during his time in Newcastle and then at La Trobe University in Melbourne when the Delamottes moved there in 1976. However, this had somehow escaped me as a student at the time. I do recall Monique telling us once that she had been an extra in René Clément's 1966 film *Paris brûle-t-il ?* She had been in the crowd scene showing the soldiers being greeted with great enthusiasm following the liberation of the city. Just being an extra seemed impossibly glamorous. I subsequently learned that Jean-Paul had done the French sub-titles for a number of iconic Australian films, such as Peter Weir's *The Last Wave* (1977) and George T. Miller's *The Man from Snowy River* (1982). Later, he also apparently compiled the sub-titles for *Young Einstein* (1988), whose director and lead actor, Yahoo Serious, was a Newcastle lad. Jean-Paul may well have known this, in which case I like to imagine that it added a sense of connection to the otherwise thankless task of sub-titling. I am fairly certain, on the other hand, that he never knew that I myself had a connection to Yahoo. We both attended Cardiff High School and I admired the antics he and his mates got up to in order to subvert the annual play night performances. He was two years ahead of me so I only really got to know him when his dad gave me my first job, changing tyres and mending punctures after school and on Saturday mornings. Working alongside Yahoo opened a window (or a door) on to his zany universe into which I was sometimes drawn. We developed a strong bond back then and remain good friends to this day. Jean-Paul would almost certainly have been delighted to discover our mutual connection to Yahoo. I wonder what he would have made of those interconnecting doors.

During the four years I spent in Grenoble (1979-1983), I frequently made the journey up to Paris and never failed to contact the Delamottes when I did so. On each occasion Jean-Paul and Monique were quick to insist I visit them at Boulogne-Billancourt. The following entries from my 1982 diary show just how readily they always responded: '*20 juin – tél. à J.-Paul et Monique*'; '*21 juin – déjeuner chez J.-Paul et Monique*'. They always found time for Aussie visitors and those of us who hailed from Newcastle were made to feel particularly welcome. The conversations were always lively and the hospitality generous. On special occasions, Jean-Paul took great delight in bringing out a bottle of Delamotte champagne, though he was quick to add that there was no family connection. Monique's *poulet en gelée* was a special treat – it alone was sufficient reward for hitch-hiking the 560 kilometres from Grenoble to Paris. Monique was taking classes in book-binding at that time and I listened with fascination to her accounts of what this involved. It seemed such an esoteric art, but at the same time an entirely appropriate skill for her to be acquiring, given the place attributed to books in their household.

Jean-Paul, meanwhile, always spoke at great length, over a meal, downstairs in his study or sitting in the garden, of his ambition to raise awareness of Australian culture within France. There was no problem, he would say, in arousing interest in French culture among Australians. He did not appear in the least surprised by the fact that I had crossed the world to undertake a doctoral thesis in Grenoble[2] – on chance and destiny in the novels of Stendhal (it indeed seemed like fate that I should undertake a topic involving a word like '*le hasard*', with an aspirate h). The much more challenging task, which Jean-Paul pursued with missionary-like zeal, was to do the reverse and foster a greater awareness of Australian culture in France. With this aim in mind, he and Monique created the Association Culturelle Franco-Australienne (ACFA) in 1980. Although I only watched from the sidelines in those early days, I felt privileged to witness its genesis. Through the tireless efforts of the Delamottes, this proved to be a great success and their home on the avenue de Lattre de Tassigny in Boulogne-Billancourt quickly became the epicentre for the promotion and celebration of Australian culture in France. To many writers and artists, it came to represent the Australian end of Paris, though, because of our shared Novocastrian history, it always felt more like the Newcastle end of Paris when I was there.

During one such visit, in the summer of 1982, Jean-Paul asked me to help him clean out some rooms in the pavilion or coach-house at the foot of the garden. I was unaware at the time that this was destined to serve as a studio for visiting Australian writers and artists. *La petite maison,* as it was called, also lent its name to the publishing house Jean-Paul launched around that time, under whose imprint he published translations, mostly done by him, of works by

Australian authors of renown, as well as works by up-and-coming new authors and a number of his own writings. He saw this publishing venture as one of the keys to the promotion of Australian literature in France and of French-Australian connections more generally.

Whenever I visited Boulogne-Billancourt, during those years as a postgraduate student or on subsequent trips to France, Jean-Paul would generously offer me copies of the latest such publications. One author he was particularly keen to promote, with a devotion bordering on obsession, was, of course, Paul Wenz. It is not hard to understand why this 'French-Australian' writer struck such a chord with Jean-Paul: not only did Wenz encapsulate the kind of cross-cultural exchange the Delamottes were now actively trying to promote, but I suspect there might also have been on Jean-Paul's part a certain level of personal identification with this intriguing figure of a Frenchman with connections to the Parisian literary milieu (André Gide, in the case of Wenz) who had found his way to Australia and ended up writing stories inspired by his adventures and encounters there. To Jean-Paul's frustration, it proved difficult to generate the kind of interest in Wenz that he would have liked in France. Wenz did have some champions in Australia, on the other hand, most notably Maurice Blackman. In addition to his scholarly work on Wenz, Maurice became founding president of the Paul Wenz Society, which was established in Forbes (where Wenz lived and died) in 2008. Jean-Paul was one of the Society's two patrons. The other was Janet Moxey, Vice-President of the NSW Farmers Association, who at the time was living in the house Wenz built on Nanima Station in the 1890s. As others have noted, Wenz has the particular distinction of being the subject of the first ever humanities PhD awarded in Australia – to Erica C Wolff in 1948 for her thesis 'A French-Australian Writer: Paul Wenz' (University of Melbourne).[3] Several decades later in 1994, Wenz was the focus of another doctoral project, undertaken by an Australian under the auspices of the Université de Paris III. As luck would have it, I happened to be in Paris on study leave when Helen Ledwidge (or Ledwidge-Politi as she was then) defended her thesis entitled *La France aux Antipodes: Paul Wenz (1869-1939) et l'image de l'Australie dans la littérature française'*. Jean-Paul invited me to join him for the *soutenance* and I greatly enjoyed the occasion, though not as much as Jean-Paul himself. His pleasure was impossible to contain. Eight years later in 2002, inspired by Jean-Paul's commitment and enthusiasm, I took the opportunity to make my own modest contribution to Wenz scholarship by presenting a paper on him at a conference on diasporic literature. It is a source of much comfort to know that Jean-Paul was excited to see the published version and that he read it with great relish.[4] It was a rare opportunity to reciprocate, to offer something, however small, in return for the impossibly huge debt I owe Jean-Paul and Monique – for the many doors they opened.

**Notes:**

1. See Tom Thompson's obituary notice published in *The French Australian Review,* no 67, 2019-2020, 67-74 & Guibourg Delamotte's memorial notice published on the Amherst College website.

2. Thesis title: '*Les modes du possible dans* **Le Rouge et le Noir,** *Lucien Leuwen et* **La Chartreuse de Palme** *de Stendhal'*.

3. See, for example, Wallace Kirsop, 'Paul Wenz and Forbes', *Explorations*, 42, 2007, 39-40 (39). See also Natalie Edwards and Christopher Hogarth, 'Wenz Reinvented: The Making and Remaking of a French-Australian Transnational Writer', *Australian Literary Studies*, 36, 1, 2021 (online).

4. John West-Sooby, 'A French Chum in Australia: Readership and Cultural Identity in the Bush Stories of Paul Wenz', in S. Williams *et al* (eds), *The Regenerative Spirit,* vol 2, Adelaide, Lythrum Press, 2004, 65-75.

# Evening Lessons

## Barbara Kelly

In 1974, I was an eighteen-year-old studying French 2, a second-year course covering language and literature, at the University of Newcastle. Towards the end of the first term, I remember hearing that the Delamottes were soon to join the French Department. Students in my year decided that it would be nice to welcome the couple to the city. We organised to greet Jean-Paul and Monique at the Art Gallery and introduce ourselves.

Even though, Jean-Paul was to lecture and Monique was to teach French Language, a less formal relationship than that of student and teacher would soon develop. The Delamottes were very friendly, a delightful couple and always approachable. Before long, they threw their cosy terrace house in Perkins Street on The Hill in Newcastle open to us all. We were invited to visit one evening a month for conversational French. This was a rare opportunity to learn from native French speakers in an era long before the Special Broadcasting Service. At the time, there were less than 2,000 students at the University of Newcastle, television limited to two stations was still black and white, the internet had not been invented and overseas air travel was expensive and exceptional.

That year, the evenings at Perkins Street were as much social occasions as learning experiences. I can remember Jean-Paul explaining that his surname described a person who lived near or around the castle moat. The beautiful Monique wore a Mickey Mouse watch (an unusual item at the time) that had been presented to her by a colleague in the film industry. She made us laugh with her pronunciation of pyjamas. Later in the year, I remember Monique being pregnant with their first child.

Nearly half a century later, I haven't forgotten the warmth and enthusiasm of the Delamottes.

**Note from Monique:**  We were running the Alliance Française which was mainly 'an old Ladies' Club' in June 1974 when we arrived and Jean-Paul and I decided that we would hold *'les réunions' à la maison,* 35 Perkins Street, and we had a growing interest because the atmosphere became theatrical (*lectures de pièces*) and *l'Alliance [française]* became really popular *avec les étudiants* … this person came … John West-Sobby did and many others.

# 'The Paris end of Newcastle' – Perkins Street

## Brian Suters

One of the least known treasures of Newcastle is Perkins Street, brought to light by a Frenchman – Jean-Paul Delamotte.

Early plans of the Port of Newcastle (Stokes map of 1851) and H Dangar's Allotments Plan 1827 show that the street has existed as a residential area since the early 1820s. Perkins Street has a north/south orientation with a steep gradient and glimpses of the harbour. It offered views of the armada of square-rigged sailing ships and steam-driven iron-hulled coal ships. This nineteenth-century fleet of mixed character was serviced by multiple railway lines (some elevated) fanning out to deliver coal to the staithes (coal platforms), creating an ever-changing panorama. At the southern end, above the residential section, stood St Mary's Star of the Sea Church, the Beacon Tower and Newcastle East Public School, master architectural works of the nineteenth century.

Until 1829, Newcastle was known as Kingstown and was a secondary penal settlement – Sydney's so-called Siberia. With coal mining, commercial enterprises, Australian Agricultural (AA) Company Land Management and infrastructure works, Newcastle developed rapidly; the transported convicts were removed and their huts (some in Perkins Street) were demolished. From this time, fine houses and terraces were built – Victorian and Federation style, the terraces stepping up the steep street. The nineteenth century was driven by the needs of industry and infrastructure – essential for a new town.

At this point, there seems insufficient evidence to indicate the place being a Newcastle treasure with Parisian panache. The special quality of Perkins Street has, over two hundred years of European settle-

settlement, attracted many artists, scholars, authors and public figures. Of course over thousands of years the first inhabitants, Woromi and Awabakal people, would have known the area as their homeland. Biraban of the Awabakal clan would have lived with his family learning to fish and retrieve oysters, clams and yams as a hunter and gatherer. Hunting would involve trapping kangaroos, climbing trees, seeking possums and native beehives. As a boy he would have learnt from his elders and mother the dreamtime myths and legends of the region including one which involves the imprisonment of a giant kangaroo in Nobby's Island for stealing a female wallaby by force. The falling rocks from the cliff front represent the kangaroo trying to escape.[1]

Around 1870 following the humiliating defeats of the French in their country by Bismarck's Prussian army, the left-wing citizens of Paris became restive and rebellious. What is known as the Paris Commune resulted in many deaths and exiles to New Caledonia in the Pacific. The Communards, as the rebels were called, attempted to disarm the Republican Guard. The attempt was bungled, resulting in the massacre or exile of thousands. Included among the exiles was Henri Rochefort, a political figure who initially supported the Commune but moved to the political right after exile.

Life as a banished Frenchman in the remote Pacific island New Caledonia, a penal settlement, became intolerable and, consequently in 1874, Rochefort and a couple of other exiles stole a small boat and found their way to Newcastle – quite a journey.[2] Unlike current asylum seekers, many of whom were incarcerated on Pacific islands, 'the Commune' refugees were welcomed by the Novocastrians. One can imagine the festivities which followed the trio who were provided with accommodation in a basic hut, possibly in Perkins Street.

Contrary to the notion that Newcastle was only of British stock, six years later, a young German architect, Frederick Menkens, settled in Newcastle. Menkens left his home in Oldenburg (Varel) in northern Germany in 1876, also fleeing the Franco-Prussian war. Following eight years of training to be an architect and working for the Professor of Architecture on a church in Solingen, he elected to leave Germany and travelled to Adelaide. Like many before and after, he preferred art to war. He became the leading architect in Newcastle. Until his death in 1910 he never regretted his immigration to Australia and contended: 'NSW was the happiest place to live'. Unlike the Perkins Street clan, he lived at The Great Northern Hotel with his best mate Mick (a Weimaraner dog). He designed a major building at the south east corner of Perkins Street – The Lance Villa.

Moving to the twentieth century, Australia had achieved a workable civilisation with all the expected services. Despite two world wars, the Arts grew and were compatible with European endeavours.

In 1974, one hundred years after Rochefort's arrival as an asylum seeking Frenchman, another countryman, travelling by ship from Genoa to Perth, followed on by train across the Nullarbor Plain and the Newcastle Flyer from Sydney and took residence at No 35 Perkins Street, Newcastle. His name was Jean-Paul Delamotte. Accompanied by his wife Monique, Jean-Paul was to teach in the French Department of the Faculty of Arts at the University of Newcastle (organised by Professor Ken Dutton who held the Chair in French), whilst Monique tutored in the French language. Unlike Henri Rochefort, Jean-Paul was not escaping a rebellion. He was seeking to remove himself from bureaucratic constraints and artistic rules. Jean-Paul's main artistic interests were literature and film, which were both expanding in quality and access in Australia. There appeared to be a French indifference and ignorance of Australian creative works. New talent and ideas were emanating Down Under. In film, outstanding directors, such as Peter Weir, Bruce Beresford, Fred Schepisi and films such as *Breaker Morant, Picnic at Hanging Rock, The Devil's Playground,* and *The Chant of Jimmy Blacksmith* were characterised by Australians, providing an antipodean view of the world, as the New Wave. Jean-Paul felt strongly that these Australian films should be distributed to French audiences It was indeed an opportune moment when Jean-Paul Delamotte arrived.

With his scholastic achievements and distinguished contacts, such as Eugene Ionesco, Jacques Chirac (future president of France) and (New-York playwright) Israel Horovitz, he brought a new level of excitement to Newcastle.

In the field of literature Jean-Paul's recognition and promotion of Australian writers was unrelenting. He considered himself to be primarily a writer, however, he spent more of his time assisting both Australian and French writers than developing his own work. The support extended to the creation of the publishing house La Petite Maison in France.

Through distant relatives Jean-Paul had inherited a derelict but elegant 1880 house located not far from the Seine and the Pont de St-Cloud, on the outskirts of Paris. Across the Seine was the glorious Domaine National de St-Cloud where Jean-Paul would later walk and meditate. The park, described as a national treasure, was designed by Le Nôtre – Princess Palatine considered it superior to Versailles. Jean-Paul's mother's side of the family was involved in the coal industry transporting coal, hence their location adjacent to the Seine River transport facilities.

Boulogne provided Jean-Paul with another of his major interests – the film studios. The film industry provided the setting in which Jean-Paul met his beloved Monique. So it came to pass, the lure of Australian literature and film and newly married to Monique, Jean-Paul bought two passages to Sydney and sailed from Genoa to Perth. From there they travelled on the Indian Pacific train across the Nullarbor, eventually completing their journey to Newcastle on the Newcastle Flyer. Unaware at the time, Jean-Paul had taken the first steps in his reciprocity mission between Australia and France.

When Mark Twain arrived at the Newcastle Railway Station at the turn of the century with acute toothache, he was met by a news reporter. Upon their arrival at the same station, the Delamottes were met by Colyn Whitehead, lecturer in the French Department at the University of Newcastle. The next day, Jan Rubenach, another lecturer in the French Department, invited them to her home in Perkins Street. It was a sunny day and from the harbour came the intriguing maritime sounds of ships' horns and seagulls cawing, along with glimpses of the Stockton Ferry and a massive 300 metre coal ship. They were beguiled by the exciting sights and sounds of a working harbour.

It was inevitable for the Delamottes (or fate) that their first Australian dwelling was in an area of creative artists and intellectuals. Number 35 Perkins Street was part of a nineteenth-century terrace which connected, by an archway, to the garden of No 33. Jill Johnston was the owner of Redruth House (No 37). The Delamottes were put up in No 35 thanks to Jill. Often Perkins Street dwellers would drop in, including Jan Rubenach, complete with Great Western champagne and Anzac biscuits. If Chesney Gardner (No 31) turned up with his wife, Nan, the gathering would enjoy Lynch's prawns and oysters. Chesney Gardner was not connected to Peter Seller's Chauncey Gardner. He was with the local radio station and formerly with the ABC. On special occasions John Fenton-Smith (No 39), chef of Approximately Upstairs, would supply foie gras and a carton of Perkins Street Escargot.

The year of 1975 provided the opportunity for full-scale Franco-Australian celebrations. Jean-Paul and Monique had enjoyed life living at 35 Perkins Street in the industrial city of Newcastle for 12 months when, on May 8, Guibourg, their only child, was born at the Royal Newcastle Hospital on the shores of the Pacific Ocean. Although the City Hall was not available, the Perkinites (the friends of the street) gathered in various homes in Perkins Street to celebrate.

In 1976 the Delamottes left Newcastle for Jean-Paul to take a position at La Trobe University in Melbourne for one year. At the end of that year they returned to Newcastle and the stars were in alignment enabling them to rent No 37 – Jill Johnston's Redruth. In April the following year, they returned to Paris with baby Guibourg to attend to family affairs.

Later, towards the end of 1980, Jean-Paul and Monique established the Association Culturelle Franco-Australienne (ACFA). The primary aim of ACFA was to strengthen the cultural bond between

France and Australia. Prior to Jean-Paul and the ACFA organisation, the transfer of artistic endeavour between the two countries tended to be a one-way journey.

In Boulogne, the Delamottes provided accommodation at two locations: ICI-*Aussie* Bedsit and *la petite Maison*. They performed the duties of surrogate ambassadors for Newcastle and Australia. Jean-Paul was well-known at the Australian Embassy, which was beneficial to both Australia and France.

Margaret Whitlam, wife of the former Prime Minister, author and a social worker, was happy to be patron of ACFA. At the Australian Embassy, the personal connection peaked with the well-regarded poet and Ambassador to France John Rowland – who was encouraged by Monique and Jean-Paul to pursue his love of poetry. *Granite Country,* an anthology of verse, was published in 1994. Jean-Paul retained his personal connection with subsequent ambassadors, including Peter Curtis, Kim Jones, John Spender as well as the French Ambassador to Australia, Dominique Girard. These connections reinforced Jean-Paul's goal of reciprocity.

The link with contemporary Australian authors continued fervently with Jean-Paul's French translation of works by Frank Moorhouse and David Malouf. During a trip to Kakadu on the Ghan, Jean-Paul charmed the train guard to allow him space to translate *For The Term of His Natural Life* by the colonial author Marcus Clarke. The guard supplied him with pecan nuts and knowledge of Australian slang. When not translating, Jean-Paul worked to have Australian authors recognised in France.

Through Jill Johnston, Jean-Paul was introduced to Paul Wenz, a French writer, who had migrated to Australia in the nineteenth century.[3] Wenz is the only writer to relate nineteenth-century Australia to the French audience. A keen photographer, he was able to show visual images in both countries. Jean-Paul was struck also by the fact that Wenz, though a friend of André Gide and a translator of Jack London into French, had fallen into oblivion. Jean-Paul soon began a campaign to have him recognised, an ideal example of reciprocity between France and Australia. Journeys from Sydney to Forbes, in the central west of New South Wales, by the Delamottes took on the theme of Rossini's Opera *Journey to Reims* (*Il viaggio a Reims*). Through his journeys Jean-Paul linked up with the locals, including Merrill Findlay, a writer, John and Barbara Bruce, then owners of Wenz' property Nanima, and Allan Wilson, a photographer who had some of Wenz's photographic material. To quote Jean-Paul from his Kelver Hartley Fellowship address (36) in 1997: *'Paul Wenz, formerly the Master of Nanima, is in our eyes the perfect symbol of cultural links between Australia and France'.*

Meanwhile the Delamottes returned to Newcastle regularly. In 1978, they were able to spend some time in No 34, at Jan Rubenach's. In 1980 on their annual stay in Perkins Street, the tenancy was No 39 (the home of Philip O'Brien and painter Aldona Zakarauskus). The ambiance of the street attracted a miscellany of artists, writers, environmentalists, sculptors and Francophiles: Susan Ryman (painter), Ted Prior (children's author and artist) and Susan Prior painter. A notable and controversial 'town crier' was a French teacher by the name of Charlie Goffet. He was loved by the boys at Newcastle Boys High School and feared by councillors, politicians and charlatans. His letters to the editor (*Newcastle Morning Herald and Miners Advocate*) were prolific and often linked to corresponding issues in France. An example was his juxtaposition of a Parisian with a Newcastle fisherman: A Parisian does not want to catch fish, flaying around his immaculate clothes. He is on display – impeccably attired and not wishing to disrupt this by catching a fish; whereas Newcastle anglers at wharves and beaches wear oversized torn flannel shirts with smelly prawns wrapped in newspaper. Charlie became a constant visitor to the Delamottes in Perkins Street and would regularly knock on their door with a bottle of Hunter red, ideas about how snails might be added to Australian cuisine and, on one occasion, a gold-engraved pen which he gave to Jean-Paul.

There is no doubt that the historic nature of The Hill profile, crowned by Christ Church Cathedral and Perkins Street with its cohort of artists and scholars, provides a reflection of Montmartre in

Paris (a place where Jean-Paul lived before coming to Australia). In a sense, Jean-Paul endorsed this by taking up residence at Nos 35, 37, 38 and 39. On shorter stays he lived at 86 Newcomen Street in the Ostinga residence and at 87 Wolfe Street where he stayed many times with the Suters.

The contribution of Jean-Paul to the reciprocity between Paris and Newcastle (and more broadly, France and Australia) was recognised by the Kelver Hartley Fellowship Address 1997. The address fully describes Jean-Paul's work for the cultural betterment of both Australia and France. In retrospect, the farce of the procurement of submarines (in 2021) may have been avoided if Prime Minister Morrison had been a member of ACFA. Perhaps not a silly idea, as Jean-Paul had spent an inordinate amount of time lobbying various ministers for collaboration between our two countries.

Jean-Paul's contribution to Australian culture has been acknowledged by an Honorary Doctorate from Macquarie University, Sydney. In terms of recognition, the apogee came with the award of an Order of Australia in the early 90's by Governor General Bill Hayden, accompanied by Margaret Whitlam. Throughout all these events Monique has been at his side, providing unwavering support, encouragement and love – a true muse.

**Epilogue**

Strangely, it is possible all these great works would not have happened without the "congress" of Perkins Street. The welcome was not unlike the welcome given to Henri Rochefort by the Novocastrians in 1874. I suggest these related events deserve a permanent recognition and what better site than the junction of Perkins and Church Streets.

An opportunity exists, as the current staircase is virtually unusable – a barricade covered in weeds. With a sensitive workable design a small "square" could be incorporated as part of the replacement of existing stairs. A daring and beautiful space which would intrigue both visitors and locals. In my imagination I see The Hill area as an Australian "Montmartre" and Perkins Street as the *butte* (stairs) leading to Sacré Coeur. Perkins Street stairs could be

Newcastle's *butte* leading to the Christ Church Cathedral or St Mary's Star of the Sea. A further benefit could be the inclusion of a traffic calming device for Church Street.

Seriously, it can be said, as in literature, there is poetry and prose: Christ Church Cathedral, St Mary's Star of The Sea and Newcastle East Public School are the poetry, Perkins Street the prose – liveable cities require both.

Note from *Amours de rencontre* (2) : *[Monique] a incarné la douceur de vivre dans une* terrace house *de Perkins street, au flanc de la colline qui domine le port. Notre fille, Guibourg, est née un soir de mai dans un bel hôpital dont les balcons donnent sur la plage de l'Océan Pacifique* (135).

**Notes**
1. John Beach (ed), Biraban's Story, in *To Climb the Hill,* Newcastle East Public School, 2016, 2-5.
2. Jean-Paul Delamotte, Henri Rochefort, *De Noumea à Newcastle (Australie): récit de son évasion* (trans by Ken Dutton).
3. Jill had been a librarian in Orange. 'She asked us: "You must have heard of the French writer Paul Wenz?" Unfortunately we had not.', in *Vivre et Revivre*, 6,936.

# Frank Moorhouse and the Delamottes: A Reciprocity

## Tom Thompson

*You were my French family and you introduced me to France and to French life which found its way into my books and enriched my life.*
                              Frank Moorhouse, 2011

With the passing of Frank Moorhouse on 26 June 2022 we saw many an obituary on the success of his Edith Trilogy, but nothing at all about his lifelong interest in France and his relationships there. As his one-time publisher, who engaged with him in Paris several times, I should record it here for the first time, as a Tale of Reciprocity.

In September 1975, Jean-Paul Delamotte, then attached to Newcastle University with his wife Monique, wrote to Frank Moorhouse via his publishers, Angus & Robertson: 'It would be a great privilege to meet you. Firstly, because I am very fond of your books. Secondly, because I would like to translate & publish in French a short piece by you'.

They duly met at the AGNSW on October 3 and Jean-Paul exuberantly responded: 'My plans are to "read you all" first, but I want to start translating as soon as possible …' Despite the Delamottes' move to Melbourne in 1976, Frank continued to visit and they shared a mutual interest in the new Australian cinema, with Jean-Paul providing the French subtitles for the films *FJ Holden* (Michael Thornhill), *The Last Wave* (Peter Weir, both 1977) and *Long Weekend* (Colin Eggleston, 1978).

The Delamottes returned to Paris, but continued a strong correspondence, creating the Association Culturelle Franco-Australienne (ACFA) in 1980, and Frank became an inaugural member. This developing relationship prompted Frank to revisit his story 'The Girl Who Met Simone de Beauvoir in Paris' (1972) and his screenplay for the film, directed by Richard Wherrett, appeared that year, as well as publishing *The Everlasting Secret Family*.

Frank arrived for his first of one hundred visits to Paris on 8 April 1985, staying with the Delamottes, where he noted: 'A visit to arrange the translation of my SELECTED STORIES by Jean-Paul to be published by Presses de la Renaissance, demonstrating again the great service that the Delamottes are performing for Australia'. His visits coincided with his own adaption of his stories, in the film of the same name, directed by Dušan Makavejev, shown at Cannes in May 1985, with *Coca Cola Kid* appearing in French translation in November 1985. Frank was back at the Delamottes in March 1986, with Jean-Paul introducing him to several notable French publishers who would later take on his work.

In 1987, as publisher for the Australian Bicentennial Authority, I commissioned Frank to select stories for *Fictions 88* and met with Jean-Paul in Sydney where he first voiced his interest in engaging with Australian culture in a spirit of reciprocity. Going to Paris with my own family we could see at first-hand the generosity of the Delamottes towards Australian writers. That year Jean-Paul published three stories by Moorhouse under the title *Un Australien garanti d'époque* (La Petite Maison).

1988. Frank's screenplay of his own stories *The Everlasting Secret Family* is directed by Michael Thornhill and Jean-Paul does the French subtitles. His new novel, *Forty-Seventeen* (Penguin), won the Age Book of the Year award; and Jean-Paul was awarded the Bicentennial Translators Prize for his translations of many Australian writers like Moorhouse and engagement with a developing Australian film industry.

By 1990, Jean-Paul was critical to the organisation of an Australian Writers – *Les Belles Etrangères* program in May 1990 where Frank joined ten other major authors to an even which drew great attention to Australian writing at the time. That year I contracted with

ACFA to produce Paul Wenz *Diary of a New Chum* (A&R, 1990), with a preface by Frank. Frank stayed at the Ici-*Aussie* Studio in Paris in October and December 1990. And Frank wrote for them:

> My first visit to the studio: another site created by the Delamottes for the enjoyment of others; every site is a concept and an act of creativity; every site becomes a repository of human memory, of a community of memory. Thank You. FM

Later that year, Frank again wrote to the Delamottes:

> I have just read the report of the first 10 years of the Association Culturelle Franco Australienne compiled and sent to us. I said to Jean-Paul that he has created from the air, a living work of human art. Unlike the sculpture or the building, the Association is intangible. It is the sum of human contacts and encounters which occur and pass. There are the books published, translated and the articles in journals but the essential work of the Association remains invisible, everchanging, seemingly only of the moment yet it lives in many memories and in the life histories of many of us. It has to be seen, though, as a significant Life Work of JP & M's. It may not be an institution but it is a life work ... JP & M's creativity in this life work is far from exhausted.

In March 1991, Paris again: Jean-Paul and Frank visited the publishers Quai Voltaire to negotiate the French edition of *40/17* and *Sydney Morning Herald* journalist Janet Hawley wrote thus: 'From the Ici-*Aussie* studio as a working base, I've interviewed Frank Moorhouse jogging alongside the Seine and through the Parc de St Cloud, talking about his new book on The League of Nations ... (*Good Weekend,* 30 September).

In 1992 I published new editions of *Everlasting Secret Family* and *Tales of Mystery and Romance* at A&R. Frank also wanted me to produce a limited hardback of *The Americans, Baby,* bound in French silk stockings, but I could only give him a new introduction by Brian Kiernan ... Frank went on via Paris to negotiate the US edition of *Grand Days* (the first in his League of Nations Trilogy), returning to the Delamottes in November for the launch of *40/17 - Quarante Dix-Sept* published by Quai Voltaire Rivages.

In 1993 Jean-Paul drove Frank from Paris to Besançon where he lived with Christine Allsop till 1995, pursuing his work on the Trilogy in Geneva. They made short visits to the Ici-*Aussie* studio in February where Frank noted: 'Once again the studio provided a wonderful refuge and base for a very hectic 4 day stay. Here to present John Tranter reading his poetry at Village Voice.' Jean-Paul supported this by publishing *Amours de rencontre (Papiers australiens)* with photographs of the writers, published by La Petite Maison.

Frank stayed with the Delamottes in September before returning to Australia for the launch of *Grand Days* (Pan Macmillan), returning to the Delamottes in October. In January 1994, he is back at Ici-*Aussie* studio for the 1994 Readings at the Village Voice Bookshop and *Grand Days* won the Adelaide Festival National Fiction award in March.

In 1995 Jean-Paul published *Hors Texte,* my memoir of Australian writers including Moorhouse, locating their recent French publication (La Petite Maison), and this time Frank is at their Ici-*Aussie* studio in August. Jean Paul's translation of Frank's *Grand Days – Tout un monde d'espoir,* would be published by Belfond in 1996.

The writing of *Dark Palace* continued with Frank noting his extended time in Ici-*Aussie*: 'The perfect place to complete revisions of DARK PALACE. I did final work on GRAND DAYS here too, a few years back. I am indebted deeply to Jean-Paul and Monique for their wonderful gift to Australian writers. Thank you. FM' (July 2000).

*Dark Palace* was published in 2000 by Random House and won the Miles Franklin Literary Award in 2001.

As he worked on *Cold Light,* the final book in his Trilogy, he wrote warmly to Jean-Paul on 5 June 2007:

> I have a wonderful tale about the secret workings of literature and our lives and your work. On Sunday I boarded the Bondi Junction train at Kings Cross and sat down (unusual for me because I travel only one stop to the city -- but I had some papers to sort). A young woman next to me looked at me and then she spoke to me in French. I caught your name. She then switched to English and said: 'You are Frank Moorhouse?' I said: 'yes'. She said she recognised my photographs from *Douce Illusion* (sic) – It was *Amours de Rencontre*. She had read all your books and my books through the Alliance (Française). We shook hands and hugged and I got off at the next station. Love to you both, and thank you for all you have given to my life. Frank

In January 2011, before the publication of *Cold Light*, Frank wrote to the Delamottes:

> Edith 3 took 5 years (as did the other two books) – the project has been in my life now for 20 years – really beginning in France after *Les Belles Etrangères* program in 1990 and Geneva when Jean-Paul drove me to Geneva to begin work at the archive. As you know I ended spending 4 years in Geneva and Besançon and then half a year in Normandy and then another in Cannes working on the 1st and the 2nd volume. The Delamottes were always there for support and morale and it was always part of my sense of security to know that you were not far away. You were my French family and you introduced me to France and to French life which found its way into my books and enriched my life.

Jean-Paul's response expresses the purity of his belief in cultural reciprocity:

> I am very moved by your message which I have just read. I don't think I ever received one which could shake me so much. It reaches the deeper and more valuable part of my

conscience, of my memories and my hopes ... I owe you and your writings, not only the joy and pride of being so close to them but also the magnitude, warmth and sincerity of my feelings about Australia and her own cultural dimension ... What a reward your message is for me! I hope and feel confident the coming year will count many Grand Days for you and for Edith. I am going to show your e-mail to Monique now... *De tout cœur*, Jean-Paul

*Cold Light* won the Queensland Fiction Award in 2012.

At *Le Train Bleu,* Paris 2000.

On J-P's crowded pin-board.

# Jean-Paul, *Coonardoo* and me

## Hélène Jaccomard

Around 1985, freshly arrived in Australia, I decided to translate Katharine Susannah Prichard's *Coonardoo* into French. I was studying a BA in English at the University of Western Australia, and the novel was part of the syllabus. I fell in love with the story of unrequited love between a station owner and an Indigenous woman. I heard about Jean-Paul and his 'Petite Maison', his small publishing house through university contacts. His publishing house was indeed small, but it also referred to the little house – in Australia, we would talk of a granny flat, but it was definitely grander than a granny flat! – where so many Australian writers and intellectuals had stayed. Jean-Paul was instantly interested in my translation and, after receiving the manuscript, invited me to work on it together at his home.

When I turned up at his place, Jean-Paul couldn't hide his surprise: 'I expected a little old lady!' I was not quite 30 at the time. Most freelance literary translators are usually retirees with time on their hands and a love for literature. The novel being an Australian classic, Jean-Paul thought it would appeal to a senior person.

Anyway, we got to work: after a couple of hours poring over the translation of the first paragraph, it became apparent that our line-by-line revision would require more than the two or three days I was to stay. So Jean-Paul suggested he'd keep the manuscript, work on it and then send it back to me for a final say. Then he would publish it in the Petite Maison. And this is exactly what happened.

The final translation differed greatly from the draft I had left with Jean-Paul. He had – thankfully – corrected some mistranslations due to my ignorance of the Australian bush, ways of life and ways of saying. The language flowed more naturally. He had added footnotes and a glossary.* In short, he had greatly intervened to make a much better translation than the one I had produced. This is recognised in the fact that the book bears both our names as translators. It was a blow to my ego, but a terrific educational experience. I had no theoretical knowledge of translation techniques and strategies, and very little practice. Like so many would-be translators, I believed that being good at languages and well-read in literature would be sufficient to give me the skills required of a literary translator. Jean-Paul with his gentle and delicate manners had crushed this ill-informed notion.

I had plans to make a living out of literary translation. Armed with this published translation, I could show bigger, more established publishers what I was capable of. Jean-Paul encouraged me in this direction and, once the book came out, did contact his extensive network in the publishing world to advertise it, and advertise me in the process. It didn't quite work out in the end, though through no fault of his.

Big publishing houses were hesitant – this was the 1980s – to commission a translator who would live thousands of kilometres away. They did ask me to suggest authors, write synopses and even translate a few chapters of any worthwhile book. I did – repeatedly, from Thea Astley through Janet Turner Hospital, Shirley Hazzard and Jon Cleary to Elizabeth Jolley – but not one single publisher ever followed up. They would have liked to reiterate the successful story of American author, Paul Auster, who became a sensation in France, in translation, before being recognised in his own country. This confirmed what Jean-Paul lamented bitterly. The interest in Australian literature in France was – and still is – superficial and sporadic. Whenever a book happens to be translated and published, there is no follow up on the author. And if a second or third book of an author is translated, it is often by a different translator, again missing the opportunity for coherence and continuity. In short, there is no long-term strategy to introduce new voices from the Antipodes into the French literary 'polysystem'.

... I never became a literary translator. Instead, I made a career as an academic in French studies and Translation studies: I now teach translation theory, ethics, and practice! Passing on the baton the way Jean-Paul had done with me.

Merci Jean-Paul, for this instructive and humbling experience of translating Coonardoo 'together'!

* See Hélène Jaccomard, 'Translating KS Prichard's Coonardoo into French, The Personal Experience', *Conference Proceedings*, CITAA XV, Perth, 1992, 14p.

***

## La tragédie des Aborigènes**
### Xavier Pons

Victimes de deux siècles de spoliation, les Aborigènes sont devenus la mauvaise conscience d'une Australie blanche forcée de s'avouer qu'elle doit son existence à un acte de piraterie pure et simple. C'est dire si ces Noirs, par leur seule existence, dérangent encore. C'est dire aussi s'il a fallu du courage à Katharine Susannah Prichard pour évoquer leur sort dès 1929 dans son roman *Coonardoo,* dont la traduction française vient de paraître, Ce très beau livre, qui allait devenir un classique de la littérature australienne, eut du mal à trouver éditeur. Son sujet – les amours tragiques d'un Blanc et d'une femme noire – paraissait trop scabreux pour un public accoutumé à voir les Aborigènes représentés d'une forme de sauvages d'opérette abattus par douzaines par les vaillants pionniers. Il n'était pas facile d'accepter leur pleine et entière humanité, présentée sans concession par Prichard.

La romancière avait pris la peine d'aller longuement enquêter sur le terrain, et son livre y gagne un accent d'authenticité irréfutable. L'ethnologue AP Elkin disait que *Coonardoo* était le seul roman consacré aux Aborigènes qui sonnait juste.

(...)

... le roman montre bien que la bonne volonté ne suffit pas pour assurer [aux Aborigènes] un sort décent : dépouillés de leur terre par le colonialisme blanc, ils sont à la merci du paternalisme de leurs conquérants, et tout peut à chaque instant basculer dans la tragédie. *Coonardoo,* œuvre forte et tendre à la fois, conserve une grande actualité. La belle traduction de Jean-Paul Delamotte et d'Hélène Jaccomard lui laisse toute sa saveur. Elle s'accompagne d'un glossaire et de notes où le lecteur trouvera réponse aux interrogations que suscitent les termes aborigènes ou australiens qui parsèment le texte. Quant à l'interrogation majeure – comment réconcilier Blancs et Noirs, comment dédommager les Aborigènes des préjudices qu'ils ont subis – elle reste sans réponse définitive. Mais des progrès ont été accomplis, et *Coonardoo* n'y a pas peu contribué.


\*\* Review of the Petite Maison publication, in *Magazine littéraire*, no 291, septembre 1991, 85.
Back cover blurb : *Première traduction française de ce roman publié en 1929 dont le personnage central est une femme aborigène et le thème l'amour interracial. Ce texte est aussi une peinture quasi-anthropologique de modes de vie indigènes ou coloniaux de l'Australie occidentale de l'époque.*

# Friendship and Remembrance

## Dianne Reilly

Every time that friends ask us where we are going for our holidays, it is always the same reply: Paris, where else?

Of course, we are fortunate enough to travel to other fascinating places in the world too, but in our 34 years of marriage, my husband John Drury and I have visited France many times, creating our own unique and memorable experience every time we are there.

It is the combination of history, beauty wherever one looks, culture – music, art, theatre – and the food and wine that attracts us all to France. But for us, it is the wonderful people we have met over the years and who are now our friends, who keep us returning.

For any Australian with a strong interest in the cultural relations between Australia and France, the Association Culturelle Franco-Australienne (ACFA), and the Atelier Littéraire Franco-Australien (ALFA) with its publishing arm La Petite Maison, all established by Jean-Paul and Monique Delamotte, are natural attractions.

For Jean-Paul and Monique, the Association Culturelle Franco-Australienne which they founded in 1980 has been an all-consuming passion which emanated from their years as academics in New South Wales and Victoria. A not-for-profit organisation, their inspiration was to foster cultural and educational exchange between Australia and France, specifically in the fields of literature, art, the performing arts and historical research. With numerous distinguished Australian writers and others in public office as members, the Association has had marked success in generating many publications through La Petite Maison, including works by Paul Wenz, Frank Moorhouse, Geoffrey Dutton, Katharine Susannah Prichard and Jean-Paul himself.

I first met Jean-Paul Delamotte in the early 1980s when, as La Trobe Librarian at the State Library Victoria, I corresponded with him before arriving in Paris for a conference and he graciously invited me to visit. The work that Jean-Paul and Monique were carrying out from their home at Boulogne-Billancourt was respected in French circles in Australia and I was very keen to know more about this cultural centre they had established.

I arrived for lunch with other guests at their charming home on the Avenue de Lattre de Tassigny in Boulogne. I was greeted by the friendly and immediately hospitable Monique who took me through to the delightful library where the elegant Jean-Paul was offering delicious Delamotte Champagne as the *apéritif*. Immediately impressed, I asked him if it had come from his own vineyard! He laughed and hastened to assure me that he was not the owner of that Champagne house which is one of the oldest, established in 1760; he simply enjoyed the product and always served it at his many parties.

Over the years, John and I have visited the Delamottes many times and we have met numerous French and Australian writers around the Delamotte table, as well as those whose interests in the liaison between our two cultures have led them to Jean-Paul's door. The conversation was always stimulating!

In 1977/78, I had been the recipient of an exchange fellowship from the French Government to work in the Bibliothètheque Nationale de France and in the Bibliothèque Publique d'Information at the Centre Pompidou. At the Bibliothètheque Nationale, I had the privilege of working with Claude Bouret, the Conservateur of the Cabinet des Estampes, and I benefitted enormously from his generous supervision. For some time teaching as Professeur d'Histoire de la Gravure at the Ecole du Louvre, on his retirement from his substantive position at the Bibliothèque Nationale in 2005, he was recognised as honorary Conservateur-en-chef in the Département des Estampes et de la Photographie at the Bibliothèque Nationale.

I had the pleasure of introducing Claude and his wife

Blandine to the Delamottes, this occasion marking the beginning of an enduring friendship. Of course, they all had much in common, including books and libraries, publishing – Jean-Paul through his small publishing house La Petite Maison and Claude, a talented designer and wood engraver himself, was co-founder and long-time President of the art journal *Le Bois Gravé* – and Monique as a renowned designer of fine book-bindings and Blandine as an art historian. Added to which all had enjoyed travels to Australia at various times. When the Bourets' second child, Hermance, was born in 1983, I was honoured to be invited to become her godmother. Since I was unable to return to Paris for her christening, Monique kindly acted as proxy godmother for me.

Among the many delightful celebrations hosted by Jean-Paul and Monique was a wonderful cocktail party at their home, attended by many guests, Australian and French, in September 1999. Among them were Frances Awcock, then CEO and State Librarian of Victoria, and her husband Chris Awcock, and Claude and Blandine Bouret.

In their quest to promote cultural relations with Australia, Jean-Paul and Monique would invite successive Australian Ambassadors to their home to learn about the activities of ACFA and to enjoy the Delamotte hospitality. As it happened, John and I were invited to join Jean-Paul and Monique at a cocktail party at the Australian Embassy when a reciprocal invitation was issued by Ambassador Alan Brown and his wife Gillian Triggs.

In 1996, Jean-Paul and Monique arrived in Melbourne for a few days after visiting their many friends in Sydney, Newcastle and Forbes. Jean-Paul had asked me to make a reservation for them to stay at the Hotel Windsor, their favourite hotel in Melbourne. They had a lingering affection for this old-world hotel, due to its charming ambience and excellent service. Diagonally opposite Parliament House, it features as the Grand Hotel, its original name, in Jean-Paul's book *Un Dimanche à Melbourne* (Paris, La Petite Maison, 1998).

As the Vice-President of the Institute for the Study of French-Australian Relations (ISFAR) at the time, I took advantage of Jean-Paul's presence in Melbourne to invite him to be guest speaker at a special cocktail party held for members in the hotel. Gracious as always, he very kindly agreed and gave a delightful presentation which introduced many of us to the French writer Paul Wenz and his life and career near Forbes in New South Wales, about whom he was such an expert.

The Institute for the Study of French-Australian Relations was founded to stimulate research into French-Australian relations at Monash University in 1985 by three scholars, the late Dr Dennis Davison, senior lecturer in English, the late Dr Colin Nettelbeck and Dr (now Adjunct Professor) Wallace Kirsop, both senior lecturers in French. Along parallel lines to ACFA in Paris, its purpose is to act as a forum for those from academia and the wider community, francophone and francophile, with an interest in French-Australian matters, for discussion and exploration of the diversity of links between the two countries. Its twice-yearly journal, *The French Australian Review* (formerly *Explorations* to 2007), records the results of much literary and historical research and investigation carried out.

Given the similarity of vision and purpose, I was pleased to be able to present Jean-Paul with an honorary life membership of the Institute, its publication *Explorations* (now *The French-Australian Review*) being a bulletin devoted to the study of French-Australian links.

It was on their visit to Melbourne in 1996 that John and I took the Delamottes to the Melbourne General Cemetery to see the recently restored gravesite of Comte Lionel de Chabrillan, Victoria's First French Consul (1852-1858). They were suitably impressed by the careful restoration of this historic monument which had been organised by ISFAR in 1994. The memorial was originally installed in 1858, according to the instructions of his wife, Céleste de Chabrillan, and the restoration had been made possible with the financial assistance of the French government and the support of the Alliance Française de Melbourne.

Jean-Paul and Monique fondly remembered having seen, during their year in Melbourne in 1976, a remarkable portrait of a young woman by a renowned French artist. We took our visitors to the Young and Jackson Hotel opposite the Flinders Street Railway Station and they were delighted to see an 1875 oil painting by French academic painter Jules Joseph Lefebvre. This is *Chloé*, long thought of as an icon of the city where, since 1909, she has been viewed by countless Melburnians and visitors alike.

This nude portrait was exhibited at the Paris Salon of 1875 and was highly praised. After winning awards at the Sydney International Exhibition in 1879 and the 1880 Melbourne International Exhibition, *Chloé* was purchased by a local surgeon, Thomas FitzGerald, for 850 guineas. Loaned briefly to the Melbourne Public Gallery in 1882 by its new owner, its propriety was vigorously debated. Upon Fitzgerald's death in 1908, the exquisite painting was purchased at auction by Henry Figsby Young, owner of the Young and Jackson Hotel where it has been on display ever since, and where it is destined to remain permanently. Despite controversy and the sneers of art critics, Melburnians' sentimental regard for the painting earned it heritage protection in 1989. In 1995, as the centrepiece of a National Gallery of Victoria exhibition of French art, *Chloé's* aesthetic quality was reaffirmed.

The archives of Jean-Paul and Monique Delamotte and of the Association Culturelle Franco-Australienne (ACFA) 1975-2015, were presented to the State Library of New South Wales by Jean-Paul in September 2015. This wise decision, no doubt reassuring to the Delamottes, ensures that these invaluable research records are held in a secure and appropriate home where they will be accessible to researchers in perpetuity. With the kind permission of the Delamottes, the index to this collection has also been reproduced online since 2017 on the ISFAR website, for the benefit of members and researchers.

**Conclusion:**

For the establishment in 1980 of the Association Culturelle Franco-Australienne (ACFA), for his constant efforts in the promotion of Australian literature and culture in France, and to mark his outstanding service for over twenty years to Australian/French relations, Jean-Paul Delamotte was justly made a Member of the Order of Australia in 1992.

Over the decades of Jean-Paul's long and distinguished career as scholar and as an academic in Australia and in his determination, despite some set-backs, to promote Australian literature and culture in France at the highest levels, it was the successes and the support of Monique and many friends that inspired him to continue in his invaluable efforts. He is remembered for his talent in building lasting friendships in France and Australia, for his generosity, his determination and his enormous contribution to the development of strong French-Australian cultural relations, an enviable reputation indeeed!

# HOME: Paris 1988

# Allan Chawner

Our son Thomas took his first steps in the studio apartment, *la petite maison*, in 1988. He also learned to make a funny face at the old ladies who smiled at him in the Metro. We were able to stay in the apartment at the rear of the home of Jean-Paul and Monique Delamotte in Boulogne, Paris, as guests for an exhibition. Carol and I were there to install a photography and text exhibition in the Australian Embassy titled: 'Hunter Valley People'.[1] Brian Suters was the instigator and curator of the work in collaboration with the Association Culturelle Franco-Australienne; Paul Kavanagh as writer/poet, my wife Carol as editor and myself as the photographer. Jean-Paul coordinated the French connections and Monique welcomed us into their home.

Jean-Paul worked hard to arrange meetings and promote the exhibition in Paris. The freight and permissions had to be organised through diplomatic channels. The embassy is not the easiest place to have a public exhibition and Paris was having some issues with bombs in the Metro so there were some protocols to work through. Jean-Paul worked tirelessly to facilitate a successful exhibition in difficult circumstances. He was behind the scenes.

> **1st of February 1988**. Jean-Paul went with us to the Australian embassy to begin installing the exhibition and we had celebration drinks here at the Delamottes tonight. The opening was planned to be tomorrow but had to be delayed till later in the exhibition period. Jean-Paul and Monique asked us to dinner and that was very nice of them as Carol would now miss the opening as she had to return home for work.

The exhibition was well received and Jean-Paul was integral to making the experience successful. It was 1988 and Australia was celebrating the Bicentennial, so the embassy was busy.

We had some time before the show was set up and I took the opportunity to photograph Paris. Jean-Paul would greet us in the morning with a list of suggestions for the day. Where to eat what to see and where to go. I think a list can be seen in one of the photographs taken in the kitchen lying beside his plate. In another photograph you can see I went shopping with Jean-Paul, buying flowers for a lady who loaned us a cot for Thomas. I was shocked at the cost of the flowers and we thought we might have bought a cot for the price of that bunch. Nonetheless, we dutifully delivered the flowers and returned the unused cot as Thomas always slept with us. Protocol was a learning experience in France.

Jean-Paul loved Chartres Cathedral and this was the first tour on his list. We are still grateful for his introduction. I made a photographic book of images of Chartres and that is included in Jean-Paul's collection. We visit Chartres every time we visit France, the most recent in October 2019. He also directed us to Versailles and I believe he drove Thomas and his musician friend there some years later when Thomas visited with the Australian Youth Orchestra.

> **30th of January.** This morning Jean-Paul kept us, and made us late again, to say we could go to Compiegne but also recommended Saint Denis Basilica and the flea market in that general direction. Jean-Paul was our tour guide. I imagine he must have made these suggestions for many people who visited Paris. The list got longer while our time in Paris diminished quickly.

**Home**

The darkness of the house surprised me. In the evening the lighting comes from lamps in preference to ceiling lights. The effect is much more cinematic with lighting as part of the compositional arrangement of an image. In the day the window light reached into the rooms creating high contrast that was also stark and back lit. The camera I used was made for landscapes, but I loved my Widelux and used it for portraiture. The camera sees 120 degrees so I can describe the contents of the room. The camera does not care for light coming directly into the lens and flared strangely as the lens revolved. The camera also blurred anything that moved and consequently people often had parts that disappeared. Chance plays a part in describing the space and the portraits are part of the contents of the room. I must wait for the film to be processed to see the results, so I am in Australia before I see that someone has lost their head.

We sat in the kitchen with Virginie Lenoir, Monique and Jean-Paul. Monique has a quizzical expression and Jean-Paul with awaiting gaze. Virginie is also waiting on Monique as a question floats across the table. Like a scene in a silent movie awaiting text. A photograph of an ordinary lunch in the home of extraordinary people. I stand back also waiting. I am looking for an opportunity to record the everyday. This is a welcoming home.

I can hear Jean-Paul speaking. His French accent is marked and the language is precise. He is arranging. There is a library, a study and vase of daffodils. The window light overcomes the darkened room. Monique receives something from Jean-Paul. She is dressed to leave, perhaps to shop or perhaps to send a letter. I stay in the room and move to see Jean-Paul against the bookcases around the room. There are many books in the room. Jean-Paul draws my attention to a small book on the desk, something he is working on. He is on the phone in French, of course, but I hear the tenor of his voice and see his relaxed state. He is at home.

Monique allowed me to accompany her to the butcher shop, not far from the house. The butcher collects clocks. The shop is so different to Australian butcher shops as it is filled with other objects.

We had dinner with Monique and Jean-Paul. There were other friends invited as well. The guests included a librarian, a photographer and Virginie who lives there while writing her PhD.

We are brought together over food. Jean-Paul said that we should meet as many people as possible and remember them and stay in contact with them. Guibourg is there too, growing with this stream of people, seen having breakfast with Virginie or downstairs rocking in the chair. She was unwell that particular day, but her books are open on the table. Virginie too is downstairs studying her research in the lamplight with Jean-Paul's journals behind her.[2]

Carol and I had tea with Monique in the kitchen. This was in 1995. She's seen smoking a pipe. Monique has a studio downstairs where she binds books. These are not just bindings, but wonderful presentations of the idea of a book.

\*\*\*

**4th of March 1988:** I saw Jean-Paul this afternoon, he is a funny man, always running up and down in his mind to search for other avenues to investigate what has not been done, up five tracks at once, a very sincere and deep-thinking man, well worth knowing. If I have learned anything from this trip it is to open up again and try to be more thoughtful about questions and answers to fully understand the question.

**Notes:**
1. *Hunter Valley People,* Exhibition catalogue: images & words of … *mots et images de* Dawn Brooker; Skye Cassidy; Steve & Helen Dunn; Marie-Anne Hockings; Bernie McClintock; Maureen Tredinnick; Ray Kelly. In Paris, Grenoble, Newcastle-upon-Tyne, Muswellbrook, Newcastle, 1988.
2. Viginie Bauer-Lenoir, *'Le cinéma australien contemporain 1975-1988 : reflet d'une société'*, PhD *en langue et littérature anglophone,* 1992. Monique: 'I remember that during a whole year, she was coming every day to work from Jean-Paul's personal archives collected on Australian cinema from Charles Chauvel on … Virginie was the second person to use JP's private collection', 30/09/22.

**Note de Monique:** photo taken early March; the path that runs from *La Grande Maison* to the *petite* is unpaved. Denis Wenz called it the Southern Cross path because Australian hosts stayed there. It reminded us of our Newcastle garden. I planted the *primevères* (primroses) alongside. *Je crois bien que nous allions à l'Ambassade.*

1. Home

2. In the kitchen with Virginie

**3. Buying flowers**

**4. Jean-Paul on the phone in his study**

**5. Formal dining room 1993**

# The Studio Ici-*Aussie*

# John Emerson

In 1995 I started a PhD at the University of Adelaide, comparing French and Australian representations of colonial history in contemporary cinema, and went to Paris twice.

During my first stay that year, like any student with no connections living in Paris, I ended up in a tiny attic room under the slates of a cheap rundown hotel with no lift. It was probably an old *chambre de bonne* carved into two even tinier rooms. It was in the Place Dauphine, beautiful outside. There was no telephone, no radio, no television, no bathroom, no toilet, no cooking facilities and the single window looked down a narrow lightwell. The City of Light was just crossing twelve million residents, but turned out to be lonely for the outsider.

Apart from meeting passing residents at breakfast, I discovered an American student who was renting his room by the month while doing a Master's degree. It was barely big enough for a single bed and he had crammed in books, a computer and a printer. It looked like a prison cell. I left in February hating Paris and never wanting to return.

A few months later in 1995, the French Department at Adelaide offered me a three-month research trip in Paris. Long before university I had been learning French with the dream of one day living in Paris, reading and speaking in French, gazing out from café terraces. With my recent memory of the lonely attic with the toilet down the hall and the bathroom off the landing at 14 francs a use, I was initially not keen to spend three more months in a grim cell. Before the days of Airbnb it was very difficult to find affordable accommodation for medium-term stays. Three months was too long for a hotel and too short for a lease. The French preferred minimum terms of three years and to get them you needed to be related to André Gide.

The Head of French, Professor Jean Fornasiero, advised me to get in touch with Jean-Paul and Monique Delamotte, who ran the Association Culturelle Franco-Australienne (ACFA) from a Parisian suburb I had not then heard of, Boulogne-Billancourt.

Without hesitation, they offered me the three-months stay in the 'Studio Ici-*Aussie*', set up just for such a purpose. I didn't know then, but that was the start of fifteen years when the Studio Ici-*Aussie* would be my *de facto* home in Paris, as it was undoubtedly for all the lucky people who stayed in it.

On a chilly November day in 1995 I arrived at Roissy airport and made my way to the avenue de Lattre de Tassigny in Boulogne-Billancourt. Jean-Paul had alerted me not to get off the métro at Porte de Saint-Cloud but at *Pont* de Saint-Cloud. British Airways had left my suitcase at London, which made the métro turnstiles much easier to navigate. I found the house, pressed the '*gardien*' button and a new world opened up.

Jean-Paul and Monique welcomed me like old friends into their polished marble hall and Jean-Paul drove me to the studio not far away. It was in a post-war apartment complex. I was happy not to be in a classic old Parisian building after my experience on the Place Dauphine. Light freely streamed in through the studio's full-length west-facing windows that looked out onto a large open space of lawn and garden beds.

An exercise book sat on a shelf with handy suggestions from past visitors for where to shop and find a coffee. There were nine boulangeries within a five-minute walk. The kitchen was fully equipped and the cupboards full of non-perishable cooking ingredients. Books lined the shelves, many were by a publisher I was to become familiar with, La Petite Maison. Reading Jean-Paul's *Amours de rencontres*, I began to learn about his and Monique's time in Newcastle and Melbourne in the mid-1970's, their discovery of Australian literature and culture, their daughter Guibourg and the busy cultural hub they had established so Australians and French could meet.

That first stay I also got a firsthand extended experience of the longest transport strike since 1995. All the métro lines and all the buses stopped running for six weeks. I ended up stocking up on snacks and water and walking all the way into the centre of Paris every second day to find the libraries and archives I needed. It was zero, freezing, but always welcoming to return to the warm studio with its underfloor heating.

From time to time Jean-Paul and Monique would invite me over for a coffee or lunch and over Christmas I looked after the house and the pet cat when they were away. In the fridge they had left me a bottle of champagne and smoked salmon.

With Jean-Paul and Monique having such a vast network of often prominent and highly placed friends, I did not expect an opportunity to impress them. But one day just after Christmas, I did. I had found a copy of Bertrand Tavernier's 1981 film set in 1930s colonial Africa at the film archives and told Jean-Paul that I wished I could interview the director to find out why he chose that setting. The book he had adapted the film from, Jim Thompson's *Pop. 1280*, by contrast was set in Texas.

One of the members of the ACFA, Jean-Paul told me, was a young woman called Virginie who was married to a cinematographer Denis Lenoir, who had worked with Tavernier. Through her I managed to get Bertrand Tavernier's address and I wrote to him asking for an interview. I expected to hear nothing back.

One day the studio telephone rang and an unknown deep male voice asked for 'Monsieur Emerson'. I was suspicious and replied, *'C'est moi'*. The reply caught me off-guard: *'C'est Bertrand Tavernier.'* He explained that he was filming the last few scenes of *Capitaine Conan* out at Aubervilliers and that, if I could get out there on Thursday, he could give me twenty minutes. To help me find the studio, he suggested sending me a fax with directions, so I gave him Jean-Paul and Monique's number.

About half an hour later the studio phone rang again. This time it was Jean-Paul. He was ecstatic about a fax coming from Tavernier's Little Bear film company, addressed to me. Even more so after I ended up spending a day on the set with Tavernier's son Nils filming the whole day for his film on the film. I stayed for lunch with not only Bertrand Tavernier, but the producer Alain Sarde and the mayor of Aubervilliers, Jack Ralite, a former Minister of Health under Mitterrand. The following year *Capitaine Conan* won the César's Best Director and Best Actor for the lead male, Philippe Torreton,

My supervisor back in Adelaide had also put me in touch with some French doctoral candidates studying colonial cinema who based themselves in the library at the Maison des Sciences de l'Homme (MSH) on the boulevard Raspail. The library at the MSH turned out to be an international hub of researchers from Romania to India to South America. It became my regular working spot, especially as it had early access to internet and email. I returned from the three-month stay in the studio to Adelaide feeling that I now had some friends in Paris, Jean-Paul and Monique and some colleagues in my field of study.

I had been back barely a month when I received a scholarship from the French government to spend a year at the Sorbonne starting September that year, 1996. I contacted Jean-Paul and Monique, but a year was too long to stay in the Studio. I spent months negotiating student accommodation with the Cité Universitaire and finally found a room in the Maison de Monaco.

I lasted there about two weeks and began to pine for Boulogne. The spoiled-brat Monegasque students turning up in their Monaco-plated sports cars stacked with stereos were not interested in meeting an Australian. The Maison de Monaco was also right on the ceaselessly roaring boulevard Jourdan. I rang Jean-Paul and told him how miserable I was feeling. By chance the studio was vacant and he offered it to me on a month by month basis, alerting me that I might have to occasionally spend a week or two in the Noël studio on the rue de Silly, on loan from kind friends (Gabrielle Lord was the Noël's first guest in June 1993).

I moved out of the grand but stuffy Maison de Monaco and met Jean-Paul at the Studio Ici-*Aussie*. It was like returning home. The cane furniture, the round dining table, the familiar books on the shelves, the television with France 2's *20 Heures*. That day was one of my happiest in Paris. As it turned out, I was able to stay there all the way till the following September in 1997, other guests of the French Australian Cultural Association staying in the Noël Studio.

Being there for much longer, I developed an increasingly stronger friendship with Jean-Paul and Monique. They generously asked me to many of their sumptuous lunches and dinners and there I met Australians such as Carla Zampatti and her husband, Australia's Ambassador John Spender, Marie Ramsland and Ken Dutton from Newcastle University; an exhilarating range of accomplished poets, writers, academics and artists. And of course, Guibourg, who was then living in a restored coach house at the other end of the garden known informally as *la petite maison*. Its name is the source of Jean-Paul and Monique's publishing house, La Petite Maison and a sketch of the coach house appears on the back cover of its titles.

On Monique's advice, I also volunteered every Friday at Elaine Lewis's Australian Bookshop on the quai des Grands Augustins. Jean-Paul and Monique's La Petite Maison had a corner there for their titles. There I would meet visiting Australian writers like David Malouf and Nicholas Jose. I also got to know some neighbourhood Parisians of the *6ème* and found myself one night having drinks in a bar along from the bookshop with a group of postmen. It was an insight into a real working Paris life I treasure. With the benefit of these expanding networks and with the friends I was making at the Maison des Sciences de l'Homme, I soon began to develop my own friendships, most of which last until this day.

One hot morning in summer 1997, Monique called me at the Studio and asked me if I was free for lunch, she was one short. I was and to my surprise ended up having lunch in the garden in a small group including her and Jean-Paul, Helen Garner and Carla Zampatti.

I also got to meet French writers that normally would not have met many Australians. One Saturday night with my friend Jackie Dutton, now a professor of French, we attended dinner at the Delamottes with Serge Doubrovksy among the three eminent French literary figures at table. We all had to wait until nine-thirty to eat as Serge wrote in the early evening and would not allow a dinner invitation to break his schedule. Jackie and I heard tales going back decades of Parisian literary life, including a ranking of various publishers, some with scorn and some with reverence, and of their opinion of the selection process for the Académie Française.

In September I was awarded my *Diplôme d'Études Approfondies* and I packed up and went back to Adelaide to continue my PhD.

The reciprocity spirit of course was not limited just to France. Jean-Paul, Monique and Guibourg visited Australia regularly ever since their return to France in the late 1970s after the death of Jean-Paul's parents.

Still a PhD student in 1999, I was thrilled to welcome them to Adelaide twice, once in 1999 and again in 2008. Both visits led me to new friends and connections that I would have missed.

During that year-long stay in 1996-1997, Jean-Paul was translating part of South Australian born Geoffrey Dutton's autobiography *Out in the Open*. Geoffrey had stayed at *la petite maison* in May 1985 (1st-12th). Jean-Paul published his translation with La Petite Maison with the title *Et Voilà!* in 1998. He became interested in the Dutton family's grand old homestead, Anlaby, located in South Australia's mid-north and wondered if I could arrange a visit.

On hearing of the connection to Geoffrey Dutton, the owners were very happy to welcome Jean-Paul and Monique and myself. The Duttons had sold all their belongings and the property in 1977, but Hans and Gill Albers had managed to fill the 34 or so rooms and the corridor that linked them with magnificent furnishings, statues and artwork. I ended up spending every second weekend at Anlaby helping out with the 10-acre garden and sometimes a week at a time to advance the writing of my thesis.

I got to know Jean-Paul and Monique even better during these Australian visits. I would meet them in Sydney or Melbourne and we would race around from place to place. Their enthusiasm for putting people in touch initiated many a friendship or acquaintance.

During the times I was back in Boulogne, I also got to know one of the Studio's upstairs neighbours, Sasha Vitkine. Born in Berlin in 1910, Sasha was Jewish and spoke eight languages. A survival of both world wars, he went on to various creative careers combining art and technology. He built his first computers in the 1960s and 1970s which are now in the Cité des Arts. He was a photographer of industrial settings that were exhibited in the Pompidou Centre next to Salvador Dali. From the 1970s he began to specialise in digital sculptures, designing them on computers he built, connected to a wood lathe.

In 2005-2006 when I was there, people were still using dial-up for internet connections. I was longing to be able to maintain email contact with both my European and Australian friends without having to go to an internet café with French keyboards. Jean-Paul kindly offered me the use of his computer, but I had the same problem. Tackling a French keyboard is not something easily done on a casual basis. Sasha offered me his Wi-Fi connection. I knew my Macbook had the built-in tool and soon I had a new window to the world.

I had been already in awe at Sasha's technological skills. He was then 95 and had kept up with technological developments around the world. One day he asked me about the wind farms in the mid-north of South Australia. I was embarrassed to show my almost complete ignorance of them, apart from having noticed them in the distance.

He had a studio in the building on the other side of the garden, crammed with computers, cameras, printers and a computer-controlled lathe. When he was 98 he bought a new lathe and set to work writing a new software program to control it. Two years later Jackie Dutton was again in Paris and I proudly introduced her to Sasha, who had just turned 100. He lived almost five years more.

In the late 2000s Jean-Paul and Monique let out the Studio Ici-*Aussie* to more permanent tenants. There was in fact a huge amount of work behind the scenes greeting the visitors and cleaning up after them.

I was very fortunate in later years to stay a few times in *la petite maison* after Guibourg moved to her own place. On these stays I spent some time almost every day in Jean-Paul's office on the garden and became more involved with the administration of the Association's book stock and archives. Jean-Paul and Monique have always kept meticulous records. Their work over the decades was quite visible in the vaulted room downstairs through the hundreds of labelled folders of correspondence with people from Australia and Europe.

At one point Jean-Paul showed me one of his references for the lectureship he had applied for back in 1974 at the University of Newcastle, New South Wales. It was by none other than Eugène Ionesco. I had many years before on that first 1995 trip to Paris gone to Ionesco's famously (and still running) *La Leçon* and *La Cantatrice chauve* at the tiny Théâtre de la Huchette buried in an alley off the Boulevard Saint-Michel.

Of course, there was much documentation about Paul Wenz. I think Jean-Paul saw Paul Wenz as the ultimate incarnation of French-Australian reciprocity. Wenz was the first and perhaps only French writer to write stories in French, set in the Australian bush. It stands in contrast to the crowds of Australian writers who have written stories in English, set in France, both fiction and non-fiction. In 1948 the University of Melbourne awarded the first PhD in Australia to Erica Wolff, for her thesis entitled 'A French-Australian writer: Paul Wenz'. Jean-Paul and Monique never missed an opportunity to promote Wenz and freely gave away copies of Wenz books he published through La Petite Maison.

There also were boxes of signed guest books, showing who had stayed at *la petite maison* in the 1980s, the Studio in the 1990s and 2000s and the Noël studio in the rue de Silly. The early 1980s guests in *la petite maison*, as well as Geoffrey Dutton, included Peter Weir, Colleen McCullough, Frank Moorhouse and Nancy Cato – just to name a very few. Then there were boxes of the signed books of lunch and dinner guests. There must be thousands over the years. All lucky beneficiaries of Jean-Paul and Monique's forty-plus-year-long project to welcome Australians to France and – in the name of reciprocity – connect them to their French peers.

**We could not underestimate the legacy.**

# Jean-Paul Delamotte and I: outline of a thirty-year collaboration

## Maurice Blackman

In the early 1980s I was settled in to my academic career and I decided to strike out on a new area of research: I began to explore the domain of French-Australian cultural contacts and exchanges. I commenced work, with the help of some colleagues, on a bibliographical project listing works of all kinds written in French about Australia and Australian topics. Based in Sydney, I worked mainly in the Mitchell and Fisher Libraries and also at the Australian National Library. At first the listings comprised mainly historical scientific works and accounts published by the early explorers, but I soon discovered increasing numbers of literary works and memoirs published during the nineteenth century as curiosity about and exchanges with the Australian colonies increased, particularly after the gold rush of the 1850s. In 1984 I happened upon some works written by a more modern French writer living in Australia who was completely unknown to me: Paul Wenz. Fascinated, I quickly read as much of him as I could find and began to do research about his life.

As luck would have it, in 1984 I also came across a long article in *Le Monde* written by Jean-Paul Delamotte, a Frenchman who had recently been teaching in Australia and who had also discovered Paul Wenz here and been fascinated by him. I decided straight away to focus my interest on this new discovery. In 1985 I was in Paris on a long study trip which was mainly going to be about Wenz. I contacted Jean-Paul and Monique and was warmly welcomed by them at their home in Boulogne and so began thirty years of friendship and a true working relationship.

Jean-Paul immediately began sharing his knowledge and contacts with me and my great project was launched. Over the next ten years I would meet at regular intervals with Jean-Paul and Monique, either on their visits to Sydney or on mine to Paris. In Sydney he introduced me to Tom Thompson, who was then a commissioning editor at Angus and Robertson, and we discussed plans to publish a translation of some of Wenz's early short stories together with his only work written in English, *Diary of a New Chum*. Through Jean-Paul, I also met the author Frank Moorhouse who was then working in Paris on *Grand Days,* the first volume of his Edith Trilogy. My translation *Diary of a New Chum and other lost stories* would be published by Angus and Robertson in 1990, with an Introduction by Frank Moorhouse. Meanwhile, Jean-Paul republished Wenz's final novel *L'Echarde* in 1986 through his publishing venture La Petite Maison.

In 1989 I was once again on a major study trip to Paris. Jean-Paul introduced me to Wenz's great-nephews Claude Gonin and Denis Wenz, who would both be extremely helpful to me in my researches on Paul Wenz's life, and I became friends with both. I was also able to meet other relatives of Wenz through them. Jean-Paul and Monique came again to Australia in 1991 and we all made a visit to Nanima, Paul Wenz's home in Forbes, and organised a launch of my newly published *Diary of a New Chum* in Forbes. During this time in Sydney, Jean-Paul, Tom Thompson and I discussed plans to publish a translation of *L'Echarde*.

In 1992 and 1993 I found myself once again in Paris working on my research project. Jean-Paul had recently established the Association Culturelle Franco-Australienne which was designed to assist visiting Australian artists, writers and academics during their stay in Paris. During my visits I was able to stay at the Studio Ici-*Aussie*, sponsored by the Association, and attend some of the inaugural meetings. Jean-Paul and Monique made further visits to Australia later in the 1990s and I would catch up with them also during several short stays in Paris. By this time I had been able to publish several articles on Paul Wenz and had written a short biographical sketch of him for the

*Australian Dictionary of Biography*. I had also finished the first draft of my translation of *L'Echarde*. Angus and Robertson had ceased its activity as a publisher, but Tom Thompson and Jean-Paul were determined to see it published. Jean-Paul established a new publishing venture in 1995 called the Atelier Littéraire Franco-Australienne and carried on producing a number of works about French-Australian connections.

As it happened, that publication of my translation of *L'Echarde* would have to wait until 2004. That year saw a great celebration of Paul Wenz both in the city of his birth, Reims, and in Australia. Jean-Paul and I attended civic ceremonies at the beginning of the year as guests of honour to inaugurate a street named for Paul Wenz in Reims. Later in the year my translation, *The Thorn in the Flesh*, was published in Sydney by Tom Thompson through ETT Imprint in association with the Atelier Littéraire Franco-Australienne. It was graced with an elegant Foreword by Helen Garner. This was to be followed in 2005 by a superb artistic book-binding project co-ordinated by Monique Delamotte. The book in question is a small bilingual publication entitled *Paul Wenz Français & Australian* containing two short stories by Paul Wenz in the original French and their Australian translations, accompanied by eight original etchings by the Australian artist Daniel Pata. Each of the 150 limited edition copies is printed on hand-made paper and each is uniquely bound by the artisan members of the publisher, Bookbinding Exhibitions Australia Inc.

I retired from the University of New South Wales at the beginning of 2007. I continued to make annual visits to France after my retirement and I naturally maintained my contacts with Jean-Paul and Monique. They made a last trip to Australia in 2011 and together we drove out to Forbes, where we visited Nanima once again and also visited the Forbes cemetery to pay our respects at the grave of Paul Wenz and his wife Hettie. My last personal contact with Jean-Paul Delamotte came in 2014 in Paris, thirty years after my first contact with him in the pages of *Le Monde*. For me, and many others, he was indeed the ideal embodiment of French-Australian cultural exchanges.

# The Thread of Friendship

## Joanna Murray-Smith

It was Frank Moorhouse, dearest family friend, huge champion of young writers as I was then, who first introduced me to the Delamottes. It is fitting that our subsequent friendship across hemispheres came about through such a charismatic and deeply loved link. When I recently heard of Frank's death, it was of the Delamottes that I first thought. He was an indefatigable spruiker of their charm and importance in the literary relationship between France and Australia.

The Delamottes are interwoven in the fabric of my life with Raymond Gill. We first met them in Paris and their beautiful little apartment for visiting writers was the setting of my honeymoon. We woke up on the second day of our marriage on a spring day in Boulogne, excited by the journey we had just commenced, already somehow different to the years spent together pre-marriage in student houses.

The Delamottes invited us to dinner and, as impoverished newlyweds not long out of university, we were overwhelmed by the beauty of their house and garden, Monique's exquisite cooking and the conviviality of their love for Australia. The elegant Jean-Paul, a shawl casually thrown around his neck, the kittenish charm of Monique, their impeccable sense of beauty and spirited engagement with writers and writing composed a rarefied, but completely unstuffy version of what life should be all about.

Subsequently, we invited the Delamottes to my childhood house in the Melbourne seaside suburb of Mt Eliza for lunch with my mother. With its floor-to-ceiling bookshelves overflowing with my parent's 30,000 odd books, the Delamottes seemed perfectly at home.

As Raymond said in his obituary: 'Jean-Paul Delamotte became a pioneer in the move to open literature to otherness. He became a staunch promoter of cultural reciprocity' and as such he shared the same passions as my father, Stephen, whose library they sat in and from where they looked out into our wildly Australian bush garden. It was wonderful to be able to reciprocate their astonishing generosity to generations of Australian writers in France. Years later in Paris, Monique still remembered the details of that lunch with remarkable accuracy.

Every time Ray and I went to Paris, the Delamottes met a new member of our family. From the honeymoon to stopping off in Paris after a year studying at Columbia in the writing program, with first son Samuel whom Monique insisted on babysitting so we could have a night out. After a production of my play *Honour* at the National in London, a momentous event in my writing life, we flew to Paris and introduced them to the forcefield that was two-year-old Charlie, watched intently by us as he investigated every nook and cranny of their magnificent sitting room. And finally on a five-week sojourn in the 11th arrondissement, we took a metro to Boulogne and introduced them to our little Lucie, received rapturously by Monique. I'll never forget the refuge of that house and their warmth on that trip as we tried to recover from the horror of the attack on the office of *Charlie Hebdo,* which happened around the corner from our apartment near the Bastille.

And just as they watched our family grow, so we watched Guibourg emerge from childhood, this remarkably poised, beautiful and ferociously intelligent young woman, whose own little girl we were so thrilled to meet in more recent years.

There was no formality to our friendship. It was ignited by literature, but flourished in the atmosphere of family, of camaraderie in a life dedicated, sometimes with great difficulty, to the arts. Jean-Paul with his vast catalogue of books and translations never tired of his conviction that our countries were united by more than what separated them. But behind his commitment was a loyal and ardent partner. Monique facilitated so much of the warmth that embraced Australians when they crossed the threshold, an effervescent presence, an intellectual powerhouse, an adoring mother, an extraordinary cook, a passionate advocate of friendship, a tastemaker in her home, a natural ally of children, a vivacious conversationalist and a champion of her beloved Jean-Paul and his endeavours.

I'll never forget her taking me aside one evening and into her little workroom where she showed me the exquisite book-bindings she had made by hand, each one a work of art. All the years before she had been too modest to show me what an artist she was, her own creativity eclipsing so many self-proclaimed artists like me.

Ray and I speak often of the Delamottes. We drank a toast to Jean-Paul when he died, for his eccentric and wonderful belief in the giving and getting of words and cultures. And Monique remains for us both, one of the world's great women, a star in herself.

# Two Extracts from *Les Amours de rencontre (1)*

## Jean-Paul Delamotte

### Les jardiniers de l'Université

L'Université de Newcastle a été construite en forêt. Elle recouvre une centaine d'hectares dont les deux-tiers demeurent plantés. Les arbres sont, en majorité, des variétés d'eucalyptus et les arbustes appartiennent à la famille ultra nombreuse des mimosas.

Une route circulaire entoure la partie centrale du campus. Les bâtiments de briques, largement espacés, n'abîment pas le paysage. De grands troncs s'élancent à une vingtaine de mètres des pelouses. Tantôt leur écorce est tombée, laissant le fût lisse et clair. Tantôt elle persiste et les traces d'incendies passés s'y voient encore. Parfois elle est fibreuse et comme velue. Souvent, des dédoublements, des fourches, des écarts de conduite sylvestres trahissent les origines modestes d'anciens rejetons qui ont poussé après les coupes destinées au boisage des galeries minières. Des galas (*sic*) blancs, des roselles multicolores ont leur nid dans les parages.

Quand on s'enfonce vers l'extérieur des terres, on franchit un pont qui enjambe la route circulaire et surplombe un ruisseau. Certains coins donnent une petite idée de la rain forest, la forêt tropicale, et nul ne s'y aventure. Les térébinthes imputrescibles dont le bois servait aux pilotis des appontements, tordent leurs branches. Les opossums strient de leurs griffes les eucalyptus gris au sommet desquels, pendant la nuit, ils grimpent dévorer des feuilles.

A Paris, j'aimais beaucoup Bagatelle ou, dans un autre genre, le Père-Lachaise. Lorsque l'idée de me promener sous les frondaisons de Nanterre m'est venue, je l'ai écartée comme déraisonnable. Ici, nous explorons le parc. Flamboyants, figuiers, chênes de marais, magnolias, fougères, acanthes se succèdent. De curieuses fleurs rouges, des liliacées, poussent au bout de leur pique, à quatre mètres de haut. Le sentier goudronné s'incurve par pure courtoisie autour d'un gommier gris. Nous dépassons le domaine des ingénieurs, qui se sont installés à l'écart, en pleine nature, et se sont offert une jolie fontaine, entourée de gazon et de Westringia (buisson aux ombelles blanches). Nous atteignons la clairière où le bétail venait paître autrefois et les hommes s'assemblaient en cachette, postant des guetteurs dans les branches (les « cacatoès », parce que le signal d'alerte était leur cri), pour pratiquer un jeu de hasard et d'argent interdit par la loi, le *Two Up*, que je rattache, sans m'embarrasser de nuances, à l'antique pile ou face. Plus loin, dans le vallon, jaunissent les roseaux de l'étang. Sur l'autre versant, commence le golf des aciéries. Nous sommes au vert.

Deux grues grises s'envolent, de la droite vers la gauche, et se posent paisiblement dans les plantes aquatiques. Vision ... visionnaire, dans un contexte universitaire.

Je lisais récemment les Petites Annonces, pour me délasser de Barthes et Foucault, n'est-ce pas, et j'ai remarqué aux offres d'emploi : Jardinier de l'Université. À Newcastle, c'est un métier d'avenir (35-37).

## The University Gardeners

Newcastle University was built in the bush. It covers a hundred hectares, two-thirds of which remain planted. The trees are mostly varieties of eucalyptus and the shrubs belong to the very large family of mimosas.

A circular road surrounds the central part of the campus. The widely-spaced brick buildings do not mar the landscape. Large tree trunks rise up about twenty metres in the lawns. Sometimes their bark has fallen off, leaving the bole smooth and clear. Sometimes the bark remains and traces of past fires can still be seen. Sometimes it is fibrous and hairy. Often, splits, forks and sylvan deviations betray the modest origins of old shoots that grew after sections cut off so as to form wooden props in the mines. White galahs and multicoloured rosellas nest in the vicinity.

As you go further inland, you cross a bridge over the circular road and over a stream. Some corners give a hint of the rain forest and no one ventures there. The rotting terebinths, whose wood was used for the piles of the wharves, twist their branches. Possums streak the grey eucalyptus trees with their claws and at night they climb to the top of them to devour the leaves.

In Paris, I was very fond of Bagatelle or, in another genre, Père-Lachaise. When the idea that I was walking under the foliage of Nanterre came to me, I dismissed it as irrational. Here we explore the park. Flame trees, fig trees, swamp oaks, magnolias, ferns, acanthus follow one another. Curious red flowers, lilies, grow at the end of their spikes, four metres high. The tarmac path curves around a grey gum tree as a courtesy. We pass the domain of the engineers, who have set up shop in the middle of nowhere and have given themselves a pretty fountain, surrounded by grass and Westringia (bush with white umbels). We reach the clearing where the cattle used to graze and men used to gather in secret, posting lookouts in the branches ("cockatoos", because the warning signal was their cry), to play a game of chance and money forbidden by law, Two Up, which I link, without bothering with nuances, to the ancient game of heads or tails. Further on, in the valley, the reeds of the pond turn yellow. On the other side, the steelworks golf course begins. We are out in the country.

Two grey cranes fly from the right to the left and land peacefully in the water plants. A vision ... visionary, in an academic context.

I was reading the Classifieds recently, to take my mind off Barthes and Foucault, wasn't it, and I noticed in the job ads: University Gardener. In Newcastle, that's a job with a future.

Translation by Marie-Laure Vuaille-Barcan & Ken Dutton

# Le *Vaucluse*

(*Newcastle, 25 juin*) Pour la première fois depuis des années, un cargo français, le *Vaucluse*, est amarré dans le port de Newcastle. Rentrant de l'Université, je longeais le quai en voiture et ai failli ne rien remarquer, tant le décor portuaire m'est devenu familier. Soudain les trois couleurs, à la poupe, m'ont sauté aux yeux. Elles sont par principe voyantes, mais on ne saurait le leur reprocher, surtout à vingt mille kilomètres des sous-offs, sous-fifres et grippe-sous qui risqueraient de vous en dégoûter. Sans hésiter, j'ai fait demi-tour, parqué la Mini au pied du colosse et je suis monté à l'échelle de coupée.

Mes pensées n'étaient guère maritimes : j'évoquais Samuel Beckett, Roussillon (le village au sol rouge où il s'est réfugié pendant la guerre) et l'allusion à un certain Merdecluse d'*En attendant Godot*.* Aussi Gordes, que j'ai beaucoup aimé jusqu'à sa conquête par l'inquiétant Vasarely. Bon, j'ai offert mes services terriens au commandant, puis aux officiers réunis dans leur carré.

Malheureusement, c'est un naufrage survenu juste à la sortie de Nouméa qui a conduit le bateau ici, pour évaluer les dégâts en cale sèche. Par curiosité, j'y suis descendu le lendemain, en pleine nuit, avec un de mes nouveaux amis. A la lueur de grosses lampes, suspendues loin au-dessus de nos têtes, nous avons examiné la coque bosselée. J'avais l'impression de violer l'intimité d'un être surnaturel. Un navire, généralement, est vêtu – revêtu – d'eau en partie, jusqu'à la ceinture, le bas-ventre au moins caché. Celui-ci était nu. Les blessés échappent communément aux règles de la pudeur. L'hélice jaillie de l'étambot où s'incruste du corail, semblait insolite et vulnérable comme un organe génital énorme. Nous nous sommes faufilés entre les gros blocs de bois sur lesquels repose, en équilibre théorique, la quille, faussée par endroits : la ligne de tins, symbole de rectitude et de résistance à l'écrasement. L'argot résume justement d'un mot le conseil que la Société donne à l'homme : « Ecrase ! » (33-34)

# Le *Vaucluse*

(Newcastle, June 25). For the first time in years, a French freighter, the *Vaucluse*, is moored in Newcastle harbour. Coming back from the University, I was driving alongside the wharf and almost didn't notice anything, the look of the harbour having become so familiar to me. Suddenly, the three colours at the stern jumped out at me. They are conspicuous by their very nature, but we can't blame them, especially when they're 20,000 kilometres from the non-commissioned officers, underlings and penny-pinchers who might make you sick and tired of seeing them. Without hesitating, I turned around, parked the Mini at the foot of the colossus and climbed the gangway ladder.

My thoughts were far from maritime. I thought of Samuel Beckett, Roussillon (the village with its red soil where he took refuge during the War) and the allusion to a certain Merdecluse in *Waiting for Godot*.* I thought too of Gordes [in the Vaucluse Department], which I loved until it was overtaken by the disquieting [artist] Vasarely. Anyhow, I offered my terrestrial services to the commander, then to those gathered in the officers' mess.

Unfortunately, it was a shipwreck as the boat was leaving Noumea that had brought it here to assess the damage in dry dock. Out of curiosity, I went back the next day, in the middle of the night, with one of my new friends. By the light of large lamps hanging high above out heads, we examined the dented hull. I felt as though I was violating the privacy of a supernatural being. Generally, a ship is partly clothed – clad – water up to the Plimsoll line, with at least its lower abdomen hidden. The latter was naked. The wounded are usually not subject to the rules of modesty. The propeller, springing coral-encrusted from the stern, seemed as out of place and vulnerable as an enormous genital organ. We crept between the large blocks of wood on which the keel rested in theoretical balance, distorted in various places, whilst the straightness of the line of wooden blocks seemed to symbolise their uncrushable nature. Slang sums up precisely in a word the advice Society gives to mankind: "Crush!"

Translation by Ken Dutton & Marie Ramsland

\* At the beginning of Act II of *Waiting for Godot*, Vladimir and Estragon are discussing whether or not they are in the Vaucluse region. Estragon transforms *Vau*-cluse into *Merde*-cluse, and says he's spent his whole life in it.

*Monsieur* Charles Goffet (Hunter Living Images).

# How One Man Sparked My French Revolution

## John Beach

If it's true that we can never escape our childhood, then the shadowy figures looming in those memories of youth are always with us, for better or worse. Perhaps our pessimistic nature draws us back to the blackest of them, but we can never overlook the rare gems of our past who played a positive role in determining our pathways in adulthood.

*Monsieur* Charles Goffet was such a gem. *Vraiment, il était génial, brillant et drôle !*

Dressed in his only green suit, waves of grey hair flowing back over his head, he presented a formidable and perplexing figure to first year students of French at Newcastle Boys' High School, as he rained down on our heads chains of impossibly complex verb conjugations, some highly inappropriate jokes and embellished tales of French bucolic life. Only later did we find, and it didn't matter, that he'd not left Australia and wouldn't until his retirement.

His presence found in me a love of all things French – and it's lasted a lifetime. Charlie, as he was called, inspired generations of boys to aspire to *la vie française* and he is still spoken of in reverential whispers whenever his ex-students meet!

Initially, M. Goffet generated a range of *nouvelles émotions* in his young and culturally-deprived students. His attempt at getting his charges to nasalise their vowels often ended in his immense frustration. His modelled *exemplars* to show how to produce a peculiarly French honking sound lead quickly to complete dissolution in the room. Tales of Parisian life and *la rive gauche* created in my mind a fantasy world which I wanted to be part of!

With us he shared his hatred of anything mechanical, anything smacking of authority and his love of race horses. He worked tirelessly to convince us of the beauty of the French language, the richness of French culture and, *au contraire*, the barren nature of our own. His world was a kind of 1950s version of *la belle époque* of French life, of Jacques Tati, Jean-Louis Trintignant and Louis Renault. He presented to us his Gallic Utopia, into which we entered willingly. Many of us never came out.

And yet Charlie's *traits de personnalité* were diverse and curmudgeonly. An un-reconstructed contrarian, even the merest rumour of a visit by his Nemesis, the School Inspector, forced him into a mental space where he was on the barricades of the *Commune de Paris* once more, fit and ready to repel any external forces, but especially those sent to check and report on him.

His frequent letters to newspapers, often published, revealed a man opposed to entrenched authority, especially if it came from *la droite* of politics. His frequent burst of hot outrage at civic affairs came in contrast to his daily *insouciance*, his classroom manner a *quotidian* application of *laissez-faire* economic theory to the world of pedagogy. His casual stroll into the room, invariably late, was quickly forgotten as he launched immediately into a lengthy account of why French is the universal language, used by diplomats to ratify important treaties, noted, he said, for its precision and lack of ambiguity.

Expansive, too, the subject matter of Charlie's letters. Recounting his encounter with a particularly thick student, he recalled:

> But it was in his French studies that his genius for mistaken identity reached its apogee, leading to mistranslations that did not amuse the Head Teacher. For example, the modest French '*Tant pis, tant mieux*' was boldly expanded by Alister into 'Having relieved herself, the aunt felt much better'.

Then came the jokes, often *risqué*, usually anti-British, quite punny and mostly inappropriate but fascinating for pubescent boys. One day he described for us a situation from the banks of the Seine, when an amorous couple was observed by a concerned walker, the supine woman seeming to be quite lifeless. When a gendarme was called to investigate, he reported back: '*Ce n'est pas grave monsieur, la dame est anglaise.*'

His wit extended to other staff members. Charlie always addressed fellow French teacher Kelver Hartley as 'Kelver, *en deux mots*' (Kel ver, in two words), because this was the pronunciation of the French '*Quel ver*', meaning 'What a worm'. And of course the hierarchy of the State Department of Education deserved his intense scorn and derision, which he happily shared with us each lesson.

This pattern of hilarity and anarchy went on for decades, each new batch of first-year students in turn were charmed, frightened, awestruck and finally succumbed to the Charlie legend. He saw off many headmasters, saving his respect for only one, Harold Beard, who won Charlie's admiration because he replaced Scripture lessons with sex education, a substitution of which any Frenchman would approve.

But how could this endearing revolutionary's tale come to its end?

Charlie's *coup de grace* was his sudden and untimely death, though even that he delivered with *panache*. As he sat down after completing an hilarious after-dinner speech to a dinner of Old Boys of the school which he loved dearly, Charlie had a massive *crise cardiaque* and died right there.

His legacy? He had sown a seed in the minds of hundreds of boys, awakening in us alternative ways to look at life, a *style de vie* in which humour sat beside a questioning of authority, where French cinema exposed us to a complexity and aesthetic which was not present in TV's *Skippy*, and in which Peugeot had a heritage richer than Holden's. His irreverence and boldness, summed up by the Napoleonic phrase he often quoted – *Impossible n'est pas français* – became part of us.

But our French revolution lasted all our lives.

# THE EARLY YEARS: JEAN-PAUL
## *par lui-même*
## Ken Dutton

For most readers of this volume, particularly Australian readers, the Jean-Paul they remember will be the man they knew in the years following his and Monique's arrival in Australia in 1974 – the soft-spoken, serious but amiable *littérateur* and *cinéaste*, the promotor of cultural reciprocity, who had played host over the years to thousands of Australian authors, academics, publishers, film-makers, artists, musicians, politicians and diplomats.

But there is another Jean-Paul of whom we knew little until his widow Monique transcribed and released a number of extracts from his *carnets* – the diaries that he began writing on 25 January 1948 at the age of 16 and continued to write uninterrupted until his death. This massive work, in the form of a *journal intime,* runs to 160 volumes over 7,300 pages and countless words.

I must admit to a certain hesitancy about opening this very personal, indeed intimate, autobiographical document to a wider audience, feeling at times almost a kind of voyeurism in reading Jean-Paul's very frank accounts of, for example, his amorous adventures. Knowing, however, that Monique had given her blessing to such a project, I have pressed on, in the hope of revealing something of the intellectual and emotional development of the man we knew.

The account of Jean-Paul's childhood and adolescence which follows is based on a document written by his mother which Monique came upon only recently, along with a commentary by Monique herself.

\*\*\*

Jean-Paul was born on 21 October 1931, the second son of François Delamotte and his wife Yvonne, *née* Guibourg. An older son, Yves, had been born to François and Yvonne in February 1922. In the intervening years, Yvonne had suffered a miscarriage and the birth of Jean-Paul was the result of a successful medical intervention.

Whilst the birth of her second son was warmly welcomed by Yvonne, it appears that the reaction of François was, to say the least, somewhat less enthusiastic. This difference would be mirrored in the parent-son relationship, Jean-Paul and his father never having the same degree of intimacy as that between Jean-Paul and Yvonne. This was even more so in the case of his paternal grandfather: Monique would later write: 'Jean-Paul had no loving feelings towards this tight-fisted grandfather who once, as a gift, offered him his calling-card.' Jean-Paul once told her that François and his father worked facing each other for 30 years, seated at a large oak desk, running the family coal business. The desk would end up some years later in Jean-Paul and Monique's home in the Avenue de Lattre de Tassigny in Boulogne-Billancourt.

With his maternal grandparents the opposite was the case. Paul and Marie Guibourg lived in a large house in Boulogne, to which they welcomed writers, musicians, academics, artists and clergy. Jean-Paul's letters to his grandmother Marie refer to her as his 'darling, adored granny' (*la mémé chérie, adorée*). She died in 1965.

By the age of four, Jean-Paul had learned the alphabet and was starting to read. The following year, he was having pre-school lessons at home twice a week and a certain Miss Hill was coming to the house to teach him English. In 1938, he was enrolled as a correspondence student in the *Cours Hattemer*, a private, secular school independent of the State education system. Founded in 1885, it is still in existence, operating two schools in Paris as well as providing distance learning from kindergarten to senior level. It was already clear that Jean-Paul was a gifted student, as he took first place in Spelling and Mathematics at the annual exams.

Then came World War II and a period of enormous disruption in the life of the Delamotte family. François (born in 1895) had already served in the First World War, but was now called up again as a captain in the army; taken prisoner by the Germans, he spent most of the war years in captivity.

For Yvonne and Jean-Paul, it meant a series of hurried moves: first to stay with Jean-Paul's aunt Adèle in the little village of Andelu in the Yvelines Department (where the family pig was called Adolf); then to the village of Gerson in the Ardennes, where Jean-Paul briefly attended school, again taking first place in the exams. From August 1941 till the end of the war, they shuttled between Andelu, the Loire Valley, Boulogne (where Jean-Paul received some private tutoring in addition to his *Cours Hattemer* correspondence classes) and Brittany. His brother Yves, meanwhile, had joined the Swiss maquis.

In the summer of 1946, after seven years of an anxious, unsettled, chaotic life, the 14-year-old Jean-Paul opened a notebook into which he transcribed his favourite poems. It was the harbinger of things to come.

The following year, his education was at last able to resume a normal path. He was enrolled in one of the best high schools in Paris, the Lycée Janson-de-Sailly in the 16th *arrondissement*. Founded in the 1880s, it was dedicated to the training of the future scientific, literary, military, industrial, diplomatic and political élites. Its alumni include major political figures such as Prime Minister Laurent Fabius and Presidents Lionel Jospin and Valéry Giscard d'Estaing, as well as the military aviator Roland Garros, who was to give his name to Paris's main tennis court.

It is at this point that we start to hear the voice of Jean-Paul himself. On 25 January 1948, he begins the first of his *carnets* and opens with one of the great themes that would recur regularly in the years that followed: Love. The 16-year-old Jean-Paul has already experienced the hormonal rush of adolescence and is beginning to wonder what it must be like to fall in love, while suspecting that it isn't how his romantic mind imagines it:

> *Je me demande ce qu'au fond peut être l'amour : sans doute pas tel que je l'envisage avec un certain espoir, romantique. Mais plus ordinaire, avec cette différence qu'il y a entre ce qu'on sent et ce qu'on exprime. En tout cas, on doit aimer L'AMOUR !*

He continues, tantalisingly: '*Heureux d'avoir vu cette jolie jeune fille blonde et bleue, ses yeux sur moi. Soyons naturel, charmant, heureux*'.

The identity of the pretty young blonde is unknown – perhaps all that Jean-Paul knew of her is that she had her 'eyes on him' – but Monique would later comment that the state of being natural, charming and happy 'is a state of mind that Jean-Paul will stick to until the final day'.

On 4 July that year, he passed his *baccalauréat*, coming First in Latin translation, Second in Greek translation and Third in English. He referred to this period as an *époque merveilleuse. La plus heureuse. Divine!* The reason – at least in part – is not hard to find: he had his first kiss! On 25 August, he writes:

> *J'ai pour la première fois embrassé une femme. Je sais maintenant qu'un baiser n'est que poser les lèvres. Par le plus beau matin du monde, l'ouverture de 'Rosamonde' m'enchante.*

He took advantage of the school vacation to spend September in England, where he was 'ecstatic' at the beauty of some of the works in the National Gallery, and he was able to see Laurence Olivier as Hamlet in film. Then back to Boulogne for the *rentrée* at Janson in October.

The summer of 1949 found him dreaming of love: *Chaque instant de la journée et mes rêves sont pénétrés par l'attente de l'amour ... Plaisir de penser à ce rêve d'amour fait cette nuit ... amie blonde.* Not only in his daydreams, then, but in his sleep as well (*cette nuit* means 'last night'). A visit to his brother Yves in Tunisia was a temporary distraction.

At the *rentrée* in October 1949, the now 18-year-old Jean-Paul undertook what is known as the *hypokhâgne* – the first year of the *khâgne* or preparatory study for entry into one of France's *Grandes*

*Ecoles*. Jean-Paul now transferred from the Lycée Janson-de-Sailly to an even more prestigious institution – the Lycée Henri IV. Founded in 1796, it is situated in the rue Clovis in the very heart of the Latin Quarter and shares with the Lycée Louis-le-Grand the distinction of being recognised as one of France's two most highly-regarded secondary education establishments. Its alumni include Jean-Paul Sartre, President Emmanuel Macron and the developer of the Suez Canal, Ferdinand de Lesseps.

In the extremely competitive environment of the *khâgne*, success was measured by one's place in a *concours* (in which the number of successful students was determined in advance) rather than by one's grades in an examination. Jean-Paul learned in June that he had been one of the successful ones. He also learned that he had been awarded a Fulbright Scholarship to take up a position as Assistant at Amherst College in Massachusetts.

He spent time before his departure attending the Festival d'Aix-en-Provence. Deeply impressed by a performance of *Don Giovanni* and by Aix itself, he would return there regularly over the years that followed. Monique later explained that what drew him there – in addition to the Opéra – were what she called his *rencontres amoureuses*.

On 15 August 1950, he set sail on the steamer *Scythia*, arriving in Amherst via Canada on 14 September. A private liberal arts college founded in 1824, Amherst College was an all-male establishment until the 1960s. Jean-Paul's role was to teach French language, both written and oral. Extra-curricular activities also loomed large, however, particularly once Jean-Paul discovered the recently-introduced phenomenon known as the blind date. On 29 October, he would write: *Je vis, j'écris, et le monde est mon jardin !*

His time at Amherst completed, he left on 4 June 1951 to hitch-hike from Boston to New York and then all the way to San Francisco. The secret to his success in being picked up was his display of a large sign reading 'French Student'.

As it happens, one of the visitors to the home of his grandparents Paul and Marie had been the composer Darius Milhaud, later to achieve fame as one of the influential group of composers known as *Les Six*. Of Jewish parentage, Milhaud had emigrated to the United States at the outbreak of World War II and took up a teaching post at Mills College in Oakland, California. From 1947 to 1971, he divided his time between Mills College and the Paris Conservatoire. Darius and Madeleine Milhaud arranged for Jean-Paul to teach a six-week Summer School at the College. After that, it was the boat to Le Havre on 21 September 1951 and back to Paris.

On his return, having been successful in the *khâgne*, he was admitted to the Paris Institut des Sciences Politiques (commonly known as Sciences Po), where he was selected to form a *Groupe de Travail* with future French President Jacques Chirac. It was the beginning of a long-standing friendship.

Having passed his First Year exams at Sciences Po in May 1952, he spent the month of July hitchhiking across northern Europe, taking in Brussels, Bruges, The Hague, Amsterdam, Elsinore, Oslo and Stockholm. Once back in Paris, his *rencontres amoureuses* resumed – and redoubled. The *carnets* tell the story:

> *30 août : Rencontres de jeunes filles agréables et douces. Les femmes adorent qu'on leur parle lorsqu'on a l'air gai.*
> *28 septembre : …ces filles qui passent si rapidement dans mes bras melaissent un peu de tristesse …*
> *11 octobre : Besoin de quelques mois de chasteté …*
> *12octobre : Pour m'amuser, je me demande si je ne suis pas ce qu'on appelle «un séducteur». «Séducteur», non sans doute mais «coureur de filles» ['a womaniser'] assurément … et avec succès. Je ne vois personne autour de moi qui ait dû prendre autant de caresses, aborder autant de filles … mon caractère libertin …*

A libertine, a womaniser, a Don Juan! Perhaps it should not come as a surprise that Jean-Paul had (if readers will excuse the cliché) a 'very French' attitude to sex. But to those of us who knew only the Jean-Paul who had arrived in Newcastle in 1974, happily married to a charming young wife, it comes, to say the least, as something of a revelation.

His life took a very different turn in October 1952. With the Cold War well underway, the 21-year-old Jean-Paul was called up for military service.

In the aftermath of World War II, Germany had been divided by the conquering powers into four zones: English, American, French and Soviet. The French Occupation Zone was in the south-west of Germany, including the area of Baden-Württemberg. Jean-Paul was sent first to Boot Camp in the town of Schramberg on the edge of the Black Forest, then to Freiburg im Breisgau where a French barracks had been established in the district of Vauban (named after Sébastien Le Prestre de Vauban (1633-1707), a military engineer who had built fortifications in Freiburg while the region was under French rule).

Life in the Vauban barracks was a new and not particularly pleasant experience. Jean-Paul's time was taken up with what he called 'ridiculous chores'. He wrote to his beloved grandmother: *Je perds mon temps car il est certain que l'esprit ne s'enrichit guère ici.* To his mother he wrote of his melancholy at being reminded of his comfortable earlier life by the sight of a familiar painting (*Le Printemps* by Paul Chabas) on the wall:

> *Je viens de nettoyer la chambre de deux sergents. Ce qui m'a amusé, c'est que ton portrait «Le Printemps», très joliment encadré, décorait le mur. Ce rappel d'une existence presque fastueuse m'a rendu mélancolique.*

He resolved to make the most of things by studying German and learning morse code – both of which he felt might prove useful to him later on.

In January 1953, he was laid low with mononucleosis (grandular fever) – an infectious virus which saw him hospitalised for some weeks. In typical fashion, he used his time in hospital to write poetry.

Fortunately, there were periods of leave. At Easter, in uniform, he spent his six days' leave to travel to Vienna with a friend. Also in the travelling party were two young women - one would play a major part in his life throughout the months and years to come. Her name was Françoise.

The Vienna trip left him ecstatic. They were *les plus beaux jours de ma vie passée*. He wrote to his mother that Vienna had 'saved his life' by letting him re-discover everything he loved in life. He contrasted this experience with that of the barracks:

> *Pendant six jours j'ai retrouvé tout ce que j'aime le plus et été très heureux. A la caserne Vauban, la seule chose qui soit terrible est l'inaction. Traîner ses jours dans la paresse et la bêtise …*

He 'had it up to here', he wrote, with this stupidity and lack of meaningful work. As well as truck-driving and loading and unloading coal wagons, there was the attitude of his senior officers, the kind of reverse snobbery of professional or regular soldiers towards those conscripted 'intellectuals' who thought themselves so superior: *Mon commandant m'a dit «Je vais t'en faire baver. Tu n'as pas encore compris. Tu es l'étudiant qui se croit supérieur ! Parce qu'on est étudiant, on doit être maté !»*

His reaction to these threats to "break him" and "give him a hard time" was to turn inwards, to engage in a process of introspection: *En se cherchant, on trouve bien le 'moi', unité confuse mi-organique, mi-spirituelle qui sous-tend chacun des aspects du caractère.* Finding this inner self (*le moi*) was the key to what he called *une grande vie intérieure … et un parfait accueil réservé à autrui*. To get the inner life right was to condition for the better one's relationships with other people.

On 5 June 1953, after a second stay in the army hospital, Jean-Paul was granted 20-days' leave, which he spent in Paris ('and with what pleasure!'). The following month, back in Freiburg, his life began to change for the better and he began to study German in greater depth. Not only that, but the *Chef de Cabinet* of the General commanding the Southern Zone of Freiburg, General Schlesser, appointed him as an interpreter in headquarters, a position he took up on 4 August. He wrote to his mother: *Tout a changé et la vie est devenue bien agréable …* We may assume that at least part of the reason for this pleasant change relates to an otherwise unexplained comment on Page 836 of his *carnets: rencontres amoureuses*.

Even Freiburg took on a more agreeable aspect, as he now had an independent room opening onto the river Dreisam and was free between midday and 2.30 pm every day to walk around the town. On 9 August he wrote in English: 'Breakfast in my room. More freedom. Happiness. Discovery of sensibility and imagination. Writing also German.' By 4 September, he was writing of *des jours ... passés à être heureux et à aimer.*

On 15 November, at the age of 22, he could write to his mother:

> ... *en ce moment, je suis tout-à-fait content. Pas mal de choses intéressantes: synthèses de presse allemande, beaucoup de traductions; vois de nombreux Allemands ... les journées passent avec rapidité. Enchanté de faire du Droit et de l'allemand et ne vois pas les heures disparaître.*

He had made up his mind to waste none of his life and he listed the things that mattered most to him: *réussite, bonheur, beauté, fierté, intensité, grandeur, travail, amour, affection, foi.* The last-named attribute should not be overlooked, as his faith endured into his final days: colleagues whom he took on a visit to Chartres will remember his taking a few moments to pray in the Cathedral.

In early January 1954, buoyed by the fact that he had only another four months of military service ahead of him, he was able to spend three days in Paris. Love was, of course, in the front of his mind: *L'amour, le vrai, à rechercher ; le faux ne pose pas de problems ...* And again: *Savourer à jamais les visages des femmes, leur compagnie, leur gaîté, leur amour. N'oublier pas combien elles me manquèrent.* Nor was religion forgotten: *Il vaut mieux vivre de la façon la plus favorable, c à d [c'est-à-dire] en accord non seulement avec Dieu ou soi-même, mais avec la société !*

By February, he was already thinking about study at Harvard and was gathering his strength to *vivre le mieux possible les quelques semaines d'avant le retour.* On 1 March, in Paris, he listed the causes of his happiness:

- *Admirables réussites*
- *Joie du retour*
- *Joie de la liberté actuelle et future*
- *Souvenir du malheur*
- *Charmante Peach*

This last, enigmatic, item is only moderately explained in a later note which lists what he calls 'all the elements of happiness': *L'approche de la liberté, la rencontre de Peach, le souvenir vivace des moments affreux que j'ai vécus et le goût du travail.* It would appear that he had met Peach during this brief (three-day) sojourn in Paris.

He made up his mind to take full advantage of his last few weeks in Germany to consolidate friendships he had formed, to improve his German, to establish contacts which might prove useful to him in the future and, perhaps, to obtain whatever assistance he could from General Schlesser. The latter in fact provided him with a letter to the Office des Universités recommending him as a participant in a seminar to be held in Berlin.

His military service completed, his mind now turned to two matters in particular: his interrupted studies at Sciences Po and his *rencontres amoureuses*. With regard to the former, he had reached a point at which he needed to find a thesis topic. This became his preoccupation during the final months of 1954 and, by January 1955, he had decided on a topic: India.

In February, he attended a lecture by the Hungarian-born journalist and essayist Tibor Mende, a specialist in Third World countries, whose book *L'Inde devant l'orage* had just been translated from English and was published in Paris by Le Seuil. On 1 March, he met with Mende at the Café Royal in Saint-Germain and, on the 17th, met with the Indian Ambassador.

Narrowing down the possible fields of study, he eventually settled on a thesis concerning Tata Enterprises, nowadays known as the Tata Group. Based in Mumbai, the Tata Group now consists of 29 publicly-listed companies with a combined market capitalisation of $311 billion. A letter dated 13 March 1955 from what was then Tata Enterprises was presumably sent by sea, as it did not reach Jean-Paul until 20 July. It was clearly supportive of his project, as it gave him *un immense plaisir*. His eventual topic was: 'The Contribution made by Tata Enterprises to Indian Economic Development'.

Two subjects now dominated his thoughts: *Tout ce que me donnent les femmes, seul intérêt de ma vie avec le voyage aux Indes, me fait plaisir, je m'en réjouis.* As to the first of these interests, the *carnet* entry for 29 September says it all: *Hier soir, Hélène*. On the other hand, such casual relationships were ultimately unsatisfying compared with his grand amour :

> *15 octobre. Tristesse et dégoût des amours faciles. Comme toujours dans ce cas, je pense à F. Oh Françoise, seul amour, amour rejeté ! ... Je pense à Dieu! Mon Dieu que je me rapproche de vous ... Je pense à la femme que j'épouserai, si Dieu le veut.*

On 1 November, he left for India.

On his return to Paris in early 1956, he found that the company of his fellow-students at Sciences Po fell far short of what he had experienced in the USA and India. On the other hand, he believed he had found his vocation as a writer, with some interesting implications for his romantic life:

> *Je suis mécontent de mon travail, d'être au milieu d'élèves de ScPo qui ne m'intéressent pas, de ne pas retrouver les sommets de San Francisco ou Bombay ... Pourtant ... équilibre parfait grâce à une activité créatrice qui donne un but à ma vie et à une décision sage. Le rejet du mariage parce que je ne suis heureux que si j'écris.*

To the question of marriage we shall return. To complete the story of his academic work, he believed that the presentation of his thesis on India meant that he had met all the requirements for graduation from Sciences Po. In the words of Guibourg in her obituary of Jean-Paul, 'Upon his return [from military service] he had thought to apply for the degree, and when the Head of the school refused, ... Jean-Paul proceeded to say *"Je me considère comme diplômé de votre école, Monsieur"* and left.'

Returning now to Jean-Paul's *rencontres amoureuses*, the years 1954-1955 as reflected in his *carnets* reveal a long list of women's names – some with a comment, some without. Set out below are the relevant entries:

> *12 mars    J'avais besoin d'un réconfort physique et sentimental, je l'ai eu (Margot)*
> *17 mars   Je suis tendu vers l'avenir. Adieu Margot. Adieu Nelly. … Nelly, Margot, Marika, Gabriele … quelle chance que les femmes soient si faciles à convaincre … Dorine … Sylvia …*
> *20 février 1955   Tout est parfait. J'ai reconnu la duperie – agréable d'ailleurs – de l'amour physique. Je me suis passablement amusé cette semaine (Elisabeth, Claudia …)*
> *29 avril   Françoise … de retour*
> *11 mai   Françoise abandonnée. Il y a des moments où je crois que l'amour n'existe pas.*
> *27 juin   Sur près de 60 femmes que j'ai connues un peu intimement, je n'ai fait la cour à aucune, je n'ai espéré d'aucune un baiser, bien trop vite accordé. Aucune ne m'a ému, aucune ne m'a fait penser à elle. Sauf F. Moi, qui me crois si malin, j'ignore tout de l'amour. Quel péril que la facilité !*

Just what are we to make of these entries? Readers will make their own judgment, but it is hard not to observe what might be called a Don Juan syndrome – better still, perhaps, a Don Giovanni syndrome. The Mozart opera that had so impressed Jean-Paul at Aix-en-Provence would become almost the sub-text of his *rencontres amoureuses* at this stage of his life: women, he says, are 'easy to convince'; he might 'passably amuse' himself with them; he has known around 60 women intimately (one is reminded of Leporello's Catalogue Aria) – but as to love, either it does not exist, or he knows nothing of it: physical love, ie sex, is nothing but a *duperie* – a deception (though, he concedes, a pleasant one).

One wonders, indeed, whether the 'obsession with the external world' to which he refers on 13 July 1955 is a reference to his amorous encounters, as he comments: *Je crois que la hantise du monde extérieur me conduirait à la tristesse de Don G[iovanni]*. Though, he adds: *Bien sûr, c'est amusant d'attirer à soi quatre ou cinq femmes par jour ...*

To the above array of easy conquests, however, we observe that he makes one notable exception: F[rançoise].

By April 1956, he suspected that he would soon be called up again. For the previous two years, the (then) French colony of Algeria had been fighting for its independence, a National Liberation Front (FLN) having been formed to take up arms against the locally-born French *colons* (popularly known as *pieds-noirs*). Some 350,000 French troops were sent to Algeria, in an attempt to put down the insurrection, fighting the 150,000 strong FLN combatants.

And once again, Jean-Paul's education would be disrupted. On 12 May 1956, he heard that he had been granted a Foreign Affairs scholarship to study at Harvard for 10 months, beginning on 1 September. Having received confirmation that he had indeed been conscripted into the army, he was obliged to approach the Harvard authorities with a request that his scholarship be held over.

Certain by now that his vocation was to be a writer, he wrote on 5 August 1956 on his arrival in Algiers: *La seule chose qui me soutienne et me donne même par moments une véritable joie est la vocation d'écrivain*. His service in Algeria would be quite unlike his stint in Germany; since June he had been in an office job in Orléansville (now known as Chlef), west of Algiers: *Mon travail consiste à préparer les dossiers d'avancement des officiers, les punitions, les décorations ; les moments + ou − désagréables ont leur intérêt ...*

On 11 August he was posted to the Dar el Alia area of Algiers.

Reading Jean-Paul's *carnet* entries for this period, one feels as though he seemed completely unaware of the bloody conflict taking place all around him. His grand obsession lay elsewhere: *La seule chose qui me soutienne et me donne même par moments une véritable joie est la vocation d'écrivain,* he wrote on 5 August. And again, a week later:

> *Depuis hier après-midi, je suis heureux, non plus par le seul espoir d'écrire un jour mais par la réalité. La chance m'a conduit à Dar el Alia. De ma table, je peux contempler toute la Baie d'Alger. Je retrouve tout ce que j'aime, les parfums de la vie. Je sais depuis longtemps ce qui me procure le bonheur. Il suffit de peu de choses : une table et un papier blanc ... Quelles bonnes journées !*

Something different now began to fascinate him. On 15 August, he wrote: *Tous les gens que je croise un instant me passionnent, je voudrais en choisir un certain nombre et sans les connaître, parler d'eux.* This was indeed something new: instead of writing about people who knew one another, what if one were to write about the relations between strangers? *Il me semble que la littérature est un exposé de rapports entre humains : jusqu'à present, seuls les rapports entre humains qui se connaissent ont été décrits.*

He set to work immediately on exploring his new idea: *J'ai écrit ce matin une petite nouvelle qui ebauche l'un des sujets qui m'intéressent le plus: comment décrire les liens qui existent entre des gens qui ne se connaissent pas ?* The result would be *La Communauté*, published in 1962 by Gallimard to huge critical acclaim.

Something else, however, was never far from his mind – or rather, someone. Françoise. The matter had to be brought to a head. Of all the women he had known, she was the exception, the one for whom he had experienced true feelings of love. But marriage was another matter entirely: *Je refusais de prendre le terrible risque de vous épouser car je crains le mariage et, de ce qui en fait la réussite, je n'avais que l'amour. Vos sautes d'humeur, votre absence de confiance en moi et d'abandon me faisaient peur.*

He continues:

> *J'ai tenu plus de cent femmes contre moi* [shades of Leporello again: 'cento in Francia…' ]. *Aucune ne semble avoir vécu lorsque je pense à vous. L'amour ne peut être qu'exceptionnel. On ne collectionne pas les passions ou bien elles perdent tout leur sens.*

Still she continues as one of his two great obsessions:

> *Pour un de vos regards … dédier cette matinée algérienne à vos yeux et à la mer, puisqu'enfin je suis écrivain.* And next day *(24 September): Je pense à écrire, à F et à la mer. Je souhaite revoir F à Paris. Je l'aime et elle m'a certainement oublié … Je n'ai pas envie d'aimer une autre femme que F. Pourtant, je n'ai pas voulu d'elle.*

On 30 September, he writes: *Je songe à F avec ferveur, je lui envoie une carte. Hier soir, je pleurais en pensant à elle et en demandant à Dieu la force d'être écrivain.*

And finally, on 9 October: F *est à Lyon. Je ne regrette pas d'avoir renoncé à elle en refusant à tout prix de l'épouser.* At this point, it seems that he had finally exorcised this demon: Françoise now all-but disappears from his *carnets*.

On 3 October, he learned that he could return to civilian life. On 20 October, the eve of his 25th birthday, he left for New York on the steamer *Flandre*, arriving on Sunday 28 October. Three days later, he was in Cambridge, Massachusetts, ready to take up his scholarship at Harvard. He was enrolled for a Masters degree in the School of Public Administration, finding its Dean to be *un Professeur très aimable.*

By November, he had found a small apartment in Kelly Road. But he felt a twinge of homesickness, heightened by a suspicion that this was not a country in which he would find love. He in fact asked himself: *Mais qui prendra en moi la place de F ?* And he added: *Je crois, au fond, que je regrette toutes mes amies autant qu'elle. Il n'y a vraiment pas de raison que je ne rencontre pas ici une gentille fille.* He would be disappointed.

At a dance on 1 January 1957, he observed only *filles laides, espérant une tentative, mâles esseulés, aucune finesse, aucune noblesse …* He decided to look for accommodation closer to Harvard Square, even if it was too small for him to invite women back. After all, he added, *Ce ne sont que des femmes que je n'aime pas.*

Meanwhile, he had his studies – and his writing. He was sending articles to a number of journals in France, doing translations, reading Thomas Wolfe, lunching with Serge Doubrovsky and Claude Vigée, listening to Mozart.

On 4 January he left for Florida via New York. *Libre, je vais vers le soleil,* he wrote. Arriving in Miami on 8 January, he was delighted by what he found: *Découverte véritablement enthousiaste de la Floride, pays des couleurs chaudes et du soleil où je suis arrivé au sortir d'un Boston enneigé.* But his stay was brief and, by 14 January, he was back at Harvard.

His view of American women had not changed. He wrote of *la femme américaine, ennemie de l'homme, luttant contre lui par tous les moyens. Mon opinion des femmes américaines est devenue sévère.*

Having sat his First Year examinations, he flew back to Paris for the summer. In his room in Boulogne, he contrasted the wives of his French friends with the American women he had met: *Je suis ce soir dans ma chambre, sans amour, sans amie (les femmes de mes amis sont belles, non comme des mannequins ou des vedettes mais comme des femmes …).*

By 18 July he was back in his beloved Aix-en-Provence, where a performance of Mozart's *Marriage of Figaro* left him struck by the magic of this *œuvre géniale.* On 25 August, back in Paris, he wrote: *Je reviens avec quelque travail accompli, de beaux souvenirs d'amour, des projets, un équilibre parfait des trois dimensions du Temps.* It seems that at least part of his happiness was due to his having met some worthy successors to Françoise:

> *Que j'ai été heureux ici ! Avant tout, j'ai préparé les livres que je veux publier à partir de l'année prochaine et j'ai été heureux. Puis j'ai rencontré quelques femmes, soit que nous ne faisions ensemble qu'une simple promenade, soit que nous faisions l'amour*

> *et j'ai été heureux. J'ai retrouvé ma ville, j'ai retrouvé Aix, soirées de joie, instants d'émotion; j'ai vécu chaleureusement, humainement, j'ai été heureux. Il me reste mes souvenirs. Il me reste le bonheur.*

On 15 September 1957, he flew back to Cambridge. His friend Claude Vigée was now teaching French language and literature at Brandeis University in Waltham, Massachusetts, a private research university founded in 1948 as a non-sectarian, co-educational institution sponsored by the Jewish community. Vigée invited Jean-Paul, who was three years his junior, to give three lectures a week at Brandeis; another friend, Serge Doubrovsky (who was also Jewish and would himself later teach at Brandeis), drove Jean-Paul to meet up with Vigée there. The three friends would often dine together in the weeks to come. By January 1958, Jean-Paul had 70 student assignments to mark. In April, the fine weather allowed him to give his lectures in the open air: he and his students were reading Françoise Sagan's novel *Bonjour Tristesse*, which had been published four years earlier.

Jean-Paul was now beginning to think about a future career. On 22 March, he wrote to his father: *Le vrai problème est de choisir entre une situation bien rémunérée et une situation où l'on ait davantage de liberté. Je ne te cacherai pas que je penche vers la seconde solution.*

Having completed his Masters course at Harvard, he left Cambridge for New Orleans, making up his mind to settle the question of future employment on his return. From New Orleans he flew to Mexico City, where he stayed until 17 June before beginning a tour of historic sites, his aim being to remedy what he called *l'étroitesse de ma culture*. First was Chichen Itza in Mexico, a large pre-Columbian city built by the Maya people between 600 and 1200 AD. From there it was on to the Yucatan Peninsula, with a *journée très agréable* at Uxmal, a Mayan city in Yucatan State. On 19 June, he stopped over at Havana before leaving the next day for Port au Prince in Haiti. On 23 June, he arrived in Martinique, staying first in the cultural capital Saint-Pierre (*[où] je vais m'installer tranquillement dans un hôtel au bord de la mer*) before spending a week in the administrative capital, Fort-de-France.

By early July he was back in France and, later that month, travelled to a favourite city of his – Aix-en-Provence, where the Festival d'Aix was in full swing. What should be on the Festival program but a performance of *Don Giovanni!* Together with *The Magic Flute* and *The Barber of Seville*, Jean-Paul was able to attend these performances thanks to the generosity of his grandmother Marie Guibourg, who had bought him tickets.

The end of summer came all too quickly and the question of finding employment now became urgent. In late September 1958, as he approached his 27th birthday, he accepted the offer of a position with the *Service d'études législative*s of a body known as the CNPF (*Centre national du patronat français*), which represented French employers. It would be hard to think of a body less suited to Jean Paul's character and interests.

It was not long before he realised that, as he put it, *je ne me sentais pas dans mon élément.* He informed the Head of his Department, who asked him to give the position a six months trial. He was using his every free hour to engage in the activity he knew he was born for: writing. On 7 October, he discussed his dilemma over dinner with his friend Jacques Chirac. In November, he noted in his *carnet: Chaque soir, de 9h à minuit: ÉCRIRE … Il faut quitter le CNPF.* And he missed the company of women: *S'il se présentait un véritable amour, ce serait bien, ce serait apaisant. Je me sens mourir.*

By now, a new interest had entered his life: cinema. He decided to enrol at the École Pratique des Hautes Études, with a view to undertaking a doctoral thesis on the film industry. *Je pense*, he wrote, *aux Relations de l'Industrie du Cinéma avec le Gouvernement.*

The École Pratique des Hautes Études (abbreviated to EPHE) is known as one of France's *Grands Établissements*. Highly selective, it is counted among France's most prestigious research and higher education institutions. Within the École, the sociologist Georges Friedmann had founded the Centre d'études de communication de masse (CECMAS) whose early participants included the celebrated semiotician Roland Barthes. Friedmann would become Jean-Paul's thesis supervisor.

On 1 March 1959, Jean-Paul noted in his *carnet*: *Encore au CNPF (de 9h du matin à 9h du soir). Comment faire pour m'occuper de ma thèse et écrire? Je fais bien de vouloir me dégager.* The next day, his frustration had reached boiling point and his language became uncharacteristically (to put it mildly) colloquial: *Je n'ai jamais vécu de façon aussi conne. C'est pitoyable !* It was the last straw: he resigned.

He wasted no time. The following day, 3 March, he met a Monsieur Rimette, Director of the Boulogne film studios, to discuss his thesis topic. Rimette, in turn, put Jean-Paul in touch with the film producer and production manager Julien Derode, who would later work as co-producer with David Deutsch on the 1973 film *The Day of the Jackal*, directed by Fred Zinnemann. (In 1963 Derode, by now the official representative in Paris of Seven Arts Studios, would invite Jean-Paul to become his 'right-hand man', a proposition which Jean-Paul eagerly accepted.)

From now on, Jean-Paul would divide his time between his creative writing and his doctoral thesis. On 29 April 1959, he noted: *Depuis lundi je me lève à 7h, me couche tard ; je poursuis un double but : Littérature et Thèse.*

The next relevant extract from Jean-Paul's *carnets* reproduced by Monique is also the last. It reads: *Thèse soutenue le 20 décembre 1960 à l'École Pratique des Hautes Études – Section Sciences Économiques et Sociales – sur « LES RELATIONS DE L'ÉTAT ET DE L'INDUSTRIE CINÉMATOGRAPHIQUE EN FRANCE DEPUIS 1945 ». Travail de 500 pages.*

***

Monique would later comment on this final entry: *Après sa soutenance de thèse, Jean-Paul entre par la grande porte dans le monde du cinéma tout en gardant à l'esprit ce qui est essentiel pour vivre sa vie : L'ÉCRITURE, son monde secret.*

To conclude this account, there is one more quotation from Monique which I must not omit. Writing of the early years of the relationship between Jean-Paul and herself, she comments: *Cette époque marque la fin de la vie libertine de Jean-Paul.*

Of course! He had at last found the love of his life.

JP (6) with mother and brother Yves (16)

Father on leave WWII

With his maternal grandparents

Amherst College 1950

Right: Hitchhiking in the US 1951

Spring 1966 at 34 years old – taken when *Sans hâte : cette nuit* (Plon) published.
NOTE de Monique :
   C'est ce doux visage que j'ai aimé at 1st sight.
   Nous travaillons ensemble aux studios de Boulogne depuis juillet 1965.

JP & Monique 1967

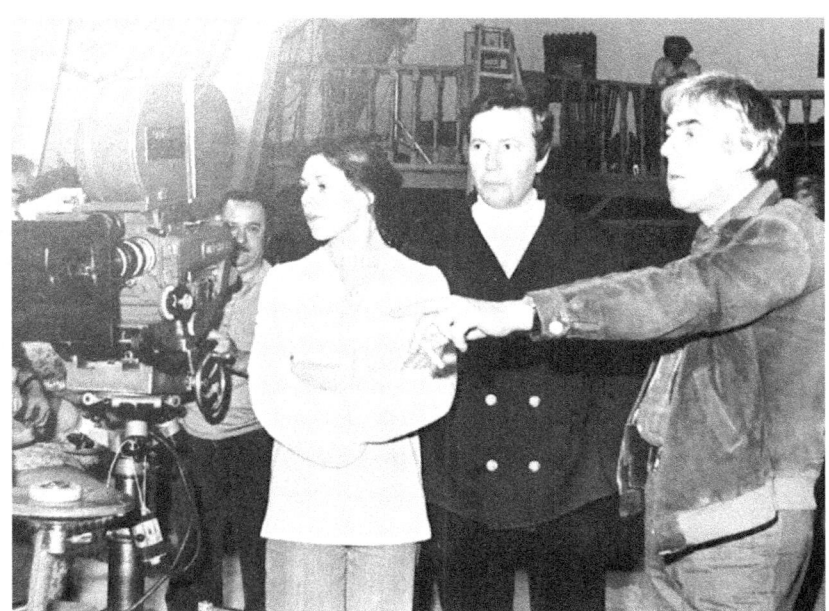

With cameraman Raoul Coutard on film set 1972

# An Unforgettable Moment
## Gionni Di Gravio

I only have one tiny story about him, and only met him once. That being around the time we were uploading the University photographs to our flickr site. I will never forget that moment.

On that day, which I believe must have been around 14 December 2007, we were uploading the photographs of Jean-Paul and Monique – here:

https://www.flickr.com.photos/uon/2275973796 and

https://www.flickr.com/photos/uon/2275973656

I was sitting at my desk thinking 'what a beautiful looking man; what a lovely woman' and then, who poked his head round the corner and door to my office but Jean-Paul himself! I said: 'I've just been looking at the historical you and now here you are, conjured from the past to now emerging in the present.'

Many years later, he responded: 'I have never forgotten our encounter, some three years ago, and I am sorry I put your card so carefully aside that I have not been able to find it!'

He requested our services in archival expertise for a period of one to two weeks, staying in Paris, as their guest, to view his papers and advise on whether we would be interested in accepting his archives for use by future researchers at this University. He was also happy to contribute towards the cost of an airline ticket from Australia should we choose to proceed.

I excitedly wrote to our University Librarian telling him of Jean-Paul and his wife Monique's long association with the University of Newcastle since 1974; our surprising and synchronistic meeting them in person just as we had uploaded images of them both to our flickr site.

Jean-Paul was in the process of ordering his archives particularly those relating to the Franco-Australian Cultural Association which he established in 1980 after his return to France and continued up until 2000. In addition there were papers relating to the Atelier Littéraire F-A, a small press dating from 1995. He had translated some of the major Australian writers, such as Marcus Clarke, Frank Moorhouse and Geoffrey Dutton, into French.

He had also promoted Paul Wenz, the French writer of stories which are authentically Australian, as well as material relating to former legendary Prime Minister Gough Whitlam and wife Margaret. Our University Library holds some of the titles (and we recently accepted a further consignment transferred to us through Professor Dutton).

Jean-Paul's work has supported the cause of Franco-Australian 'cultural reciprocity', which we have also been involved with, through the years with Emeritus Professor Ken Dutton and [the editor's] research projects involving Ludovic de Beauvoir, Henri Rochefort, Francis Barrallier and the Jarry/Gray Manuscript Diary.

My University Librarian used 73 words to say: 'No'

In the *University Gazette*, September 1974 (5):

AU REVOIR MONTMARTRE
    Jean-Paul Delamotte, who holds a PhD degree from the Sorbonne, and his wife Monique lived in Montmartre before coming to the Department of French at the university. Dr Delamotte has taught at colleges in the United States, is a novelist, scriptwriter and playwright and has had considerable experience in the motion picture field as a producer. Madame Delamotte worked for MGM as European publicity assistant. Here as long-term visitors, they say they enjoy learning about Australia. Jean-Paul, who has also worked as a translator (adapting in French a play by Tennessee Williams), is looking forward to meeting Australian writers and film people.

***

**Note** from Monique:
Tutoring program for Jean-Paul, Newcastle, included Samuel Beckett's *Watt*; Eugène Ionesco; Roger Martin du Gard's *Jean Barois*; Victor Hugo's "La Tristesse d'Olympio".
11 October 1974: Venue du Professeur Onimus – conférence sur Beckett. '*Je me souviens avoir été assez fier de sentir que mes élèlves étaient bien préparés.*' (Diary entry, 2,978)
1st term 1975:   Jean Paulhan's *Les incertitudes du langage*; Boris Vian
2nd term:        Honoré de Balzac's E*ugénie Grandet* ; Pierre Corneille *Le Cid* ; Jean Racine *Britannicus* ;  J-P Delamotte's *La Communauté*

7 avril 1975 : Arrivée de David Stratton à Newcastle in view to organize a film festival.
13 August 1975 :   'French writer says GO', *Newcastle Herald Tribune*, (2)
16 August : 1ère soirée du Festival with *The Cars that Ate Paris*, Peter Weir

# Memories of Good Friends

## Peter Weir

I was fond of Jean-Paul and Monique and was saddened to hear of his passing. I hope these few words may be of interest.

We spoke on the phone and occasionally met over the years, both in Sydney and Paris. He was a kind and thoughtful man and our conversation, as you can imagine, was mostly about films and books. Europe was somehow further away in the 1970s! We still had a trace of the 'cultural cringe' and that such a sophisticated and elegant Frenchman took enough interest in our cultural life, to move here! And teach! That was impressive.

Our major involvement was with my then recently completed film *The Last Wave,* which was to have its European debut at the Paris Film Festival. It was 1977. Jean-Paul, who was working on the French sub-titles, kindly let me stay at his and Monique's apartment. What a hectic few days! Jean-Paul became my guide/translator/and host, he even helped me with my French!

At the time I was planning a film on the Australian forces serving in WWI (later to become *Gallipoli*) and wanted to visit the battlefields in Northern France. Jean-Paul got to work, booking me by train to Amiens where he arranged for friends to show me around. A very powerful experience which further inspired me to keep going with that planned project.

JP and Monique were wonderful. They helped me through the rigour of press conferences – arranged dinners – introduced me to friends and fellow film lovers and wined and dined me in fine style. Lots of conversation, lots of laughter. They made me feel at home.

Just writing these few words and looking in my diary of that year has swept me back to that exciting time and unlocked the memories of two good friends.[1]

**(From Weir's Diary** – transcribed)
**Monday** 31 October 1977
Hotel too expensive + go to J's office. Ring Jean-Paul Delamotte + he is happy to put me up for the night! Jeanine + I lunch with Pierre – H Deleau after a visit to his cinema . V luxurious home
**Tuesday** 1 November
Good sleep. JP and I go through key subtitles (All Saints Day here is public holiday).
I go to Hôtel Des Invalides, which is closed, J-P to pick up Monique at the station.
We all meet back at the apartment for lunch. What a lunch! Have roast beef, salad, savoury eggs etc etc (mousse au chocolat) – friend of Delamottes from Australia there, Gay [Reeves], French teacher.
**Thursday** 3 November
Up early to catch the train from Gare du Nord .. Blank day, … excellent weather for a … Somme. Met at station … + sister Agnes (our driver … wonderful day, so good to … Paris + away from … talk. They are both good company + speak English. We visit Syndicat at Albert + talk to one of the Anciennes. Escape him after ½ hour and on to 11am meeting with Max Boret at Dernancourt. Desolate feeling in this village. Boret is rough character, brusque at first + v suspicious. His yard a tangle of rusting iron. Took some moments for the eyes to adjust to the war relics. At first seemed like any junk yard then the brain began to sort out the shapes. Horror. Almost all the junk was war material twisted into grotesque shapes. Barrells [sic] full of bullets, bomb-shells – some live. Bonet's hand is mangled – A shell blew up on him not so long ago. (A good friend of his had died collecting the stuff.) Pastis with him in village – he gives me helmet bayonets bullets buttons in a …

**Saturday** 5 November
1st Screening Today "PREMIÈRE MONDIALE" !!! 11.00h – 15h30 et 22h.
8am to L'Empire. Sound check, good, but hope I haven't made it too loud. Jean-Paul coming at 9.15 or so for French version in preparation for Le [*sic*] Conference du Presse ! … work on that – together and sometimes overlapping – form a powerful portrait suggested answers, words that I don't know. To theatre. I stay for beginning (tell Jacques I don't want to introduce it). Good attendance he says (critics & press only for the 11AM)/ while its on I wander to a bar drink 3 cognacs in a row. End of screening. End of screening – watch last reel in projection …

***

**Addenda to Peter's entry** : In Jean-Paul's diary *VIVRE ET REVIVRE* (3,749)

***Samedi matin*** *5 XI 77 dans la chambre de Peter au Royal Monceau : Enseignements sur les rituels et traditions aborigènes (a whole page of notes).*

*La Lorraine (famous brasserie), vers 3h et demi, après la première projection mondiale de THE LAST WAVE. Très heureux que le film soit un vrai film et Peter aussi vrai que tout ce que j'aime. Je crois que le public a achevé le film: c'est un film qu'on achève. Mais on n'achève pas les films comme les chevaux, du moins aujourd'hui. On les achève comme une BELLE ŒUVRE.*

*Très content que Costa-Gavras [Greek-French director], que j'avais appelé, soit venu, ait rencontré Peter, le revoie lundi avec moi au Royal-Monceau [Hôtel].*

*Et très heureux d'avoir déjeuné ici, à La Lorraine. Par hasard, à une table juste à côté de celle de Jeannine (Seawell) et Peter.*

Récapitulons (3,750)

***Samedi soir****, revu The LAST WAVE, qui a été applaudi. Les gens ont ri à "Charmant" dit par l'aborigène à propos des tableaux, des œuvres de la jeune femme (Annie, femme de David).*

***Dimanche****, Peter et Jeanine sont venus déjeuner.*

***Lundi*** *à 5h. j'ai retrouvé Costa Gavras et Peter à l'hôtel Royal Monceau : j'étais content de les avoir fait se rencontrer. Ils ont parlé de musique ...* ***Mardi*** *: Le soir, on apprend que Peter a le Prix Spécial du Jury alors que je m'apprêtais à le conduire à Roissy ! Nous retournons à L'EMPIRE, assister à 'la remise des prix'. (Malgré la lamentable performance du minable directeur général d'Antenne 2). Enfin, on était très content et notre Peter très beau avec sa petite casquette et Claudia Cardinale. Quelleréussiteducinéma,notrePeter!*
***Mercredi*** *: L'après-midi, j'aborde le travail ('Julia') en salle de montage et comptais rester le soir, mais en téléphonant à M j'apprends que Peter n'était toujours pas parti et qu'il se trouvait avec Jeanine chez nous. Je rentre donc pour dîner avec eux, très content. Dernière bouteille de champagne. Peter, très content, passe la nuit ici. ( nous habitions alors 5 rue Vital, Paris)* ***Jeudi*** *: Je dis au revoir à Peter et retourne à mon doublage de 'Julia'.*
**Le 24 Octobre** *JP avait noté : 'Plongé dans les sous-titres de THE LAST WAVE' et au 31/ 10 'Je viens de voir Peter WEIR'.*
**Le 8 Nov. 77** *: Monique a noté : Achat de petits cadeaux pour Ingrid et Julian Weir.*

\*\*\*

In fond memory of Early Days, warm admiration of the Present
and enthusiastic faith in the Future,
BRAVO PETER WEIR!
Many sincere thanks to you, Wendy, Ingrid and Julian
for your visit to Boulogne on July 10, 1991.

*... en honneur de Peter, Wendy, Ingrid & Julian WEIR.* Janine Seawell, Anne Sauvêtre, Jean-Michel & Claudine Thoridnet, John McManus, Eileen McManus, Bill & Nadja La Ganza, Helen Wadlington, Tony Maniaty, Claire Clouzot, Eliza McDonald, ... Hulin, Dorothée & Jacques Pinoir.

**POSTSCRIPT**  (by John Ramsland)

Peter Weir was born in Sydney, Australia on 21 August 1944. He was educated at Scots College, Vauclused High School and Sydney University. He left university without completing his degree and hit the road for Europe. Later, he worked in the TV industry and began making short films. He has frequently been called Australia's 'master of mystery and imagination' and some of his feature films are beautifully bizarre and discreet artistic horror – *Gallipoli* (1981) is an exception.

The idea Weir had for *Gallipoli* as a feature film was reinforced as a practical project in 1976 when Jean-Paul Delamotte organised a trip for him to visit and study the northern battlefield cemeteries that included Australians in France and Belgium. He returned, very much moved and immediately wrote a preliminary outline for a film that would put Australia cinema on the international map, reinforcing what was called the 'Australian New Wave', together with his earlier period and mystical film *Picnic at Hanging Rock* (1975). For *Gallipoli,* he asked popular and highly successful Australian playwright David Williamson to develop his outline into a full screenplay. For four years, Weir and Williamson went through many drafts trying to penetrate the myth of the 'glorious defeat' of the Anzac forces under British command.

In 1980, sufficient financial backing came when Rupert Murdoch and Robert Stigwood formed a film production company Associated R&R Films. Murdoch's father Keith had been a significant wartime foreign journalist who exposed the failings of the Dardanelles campaign. Weir was provided with a modest budget of AUS$3 million – nevertheless, it was the highest of any other Australian film to that date. Weir took about four months to shoot in coastal South Australia and Egypt and came in just under budget. It was released in August 1981 in Australia and the United States of America with a huge success in both countries and, one month later, in Britain.[2] Weir's *Gallipoli* became one of the most evocative anti-war tracks on a par with Lewis Milestone's Oscar-winning *All Quiet on the Western Front* (1930), the greatest war film ever made along with Kubrick's *Paths of Glory* (1957).

By the time *Gallipoli* came into being and with *Picnic at Hanging*

*Rock* under his belt, Peter Weir was at the forefront of the 'new wave' directors and was one of early Australian directors to gain widespread international recognition and close attention. Not just a superb storyteller, but a great stylist who filled the screen with rich colours, memorable panoramas and powerful thought-provoking imagery and sparse dialogue. He learnt his craft by directing impressive short features before making his feature debut with *The Cars that Ate Paris* (1974). Soon after, he attracted universal attention with *Picnic at Hanging Rock*, an eerie, atmospheric elegant slow-burner about three schoolgirls who mysteriously disappear on a picnic jaunt in the bush. The beautifully shot, mysterious thriller *The Last Wave* (1977) is set, unusually, in urban Sydney.

Peter's wife Wendy Weir, as a costume designer, enhanced Picnic's luminous appearance by designing crisp white costumes to contrast with the monumental landscape of Hanging Rock. She also designed costumes for *Gallipoli* and *The Year of Living Dangerously* (1982) that brought him to America where he immediately struck gold with *Witness* (1985), a beautifully-written mystery about the Amish puritan society. It aptly demonstrated Weir's ability to combine dramatic storytelling, beautiful visual artistry and the elements which have dominated all his future works, like alienation from the mainstream society and turmoil in an impoverished country. His uniquely poetic visual and mystical style continued to be alluring to moviegoers. [3]

*Filmography*
1967 *Count Vim's Last Exercise;* 1968 *The Life and Times of the Rev Buck Shotte;* 1970 *Three to Go;* 1971 *Homedale;* 1972 *Incredible Floridas;* 1973 *What Ever Happened to Green Valley?* ;1974 *The Cars that Ate Paris;* 1975 *Picnic at Hanging Rock;* 1977 *The Last Wave;* 1978 *The Plumber;* 1981 *Gallipoli;* 1982 *The Year of Loving Dangerously;* 1985 *Witness;* 1986 *The Mosquito Coast;* 1989 *Dead Poets Society;* 1990 *Green Card;* 1993 *Fearless;* 1998 *The Truman Show;* 2003 *Master and Commander: The Far Side of the World;* 2010 *The Way Back.*

**Notes:**

1. Transcription of handwritten letter sent to editor, dated 25.x.22 & signed: 'Best wishes, Peter Weir.
2. Taylor, Downing reviews a Classical War Movie, *Military History Monthly,* June 2015, issue 57, 60; David Quinlan, *Quinlan's Film Directors*, BT Botsford Ltd, London, 1999, 360.
3. Derek Winnert (gen ed), *The Ultimate Encyclopedia of the Movies*, Carlton Books Ltd, Museum of the Moving Image, London, 1995, 175.

Top: JP and Peter Weir. Above: Making of *Gallipoli*.

# Reciprocity in the cinema of David Gulpilil: Fables of friendship and cultural exchange
## John Ramsland

> There can be no qualification about my Government's commitment to the cause of the Aboriginal people. We are determined that the long record of injustice, repression, neglect, the record that has marked our treatment of Aboriginal people for two centuries of white civilization on this continent, will be brought to an end.
>
> EG Whitlam, Prime Minister of Australia[1]

[Craig] Ruddy ... said that while he was from a vastly different world to Gulpilil, the experience of painting the actor had been rewarding. 'It was fantastic although I was told I would find it difficult to get him to stay for very long'.

'But he was beautiful, so warm and so friendly. David is a man who crosses the lines that still divide two contrasting worlds. One is an infinite world of spiritual connection with the land and universe as a whole and the other a materialistic conformation of Western civilisation.'

> Craig Ruddy, 2004 Archibald Prize Winner [*Two Worlds*][2]

Jean-Paul Delamotte became a close friend of ex-Australian Prime Minister E. Gough Whitlam when Whitlam was installed as Australia's Ambassador for UNESCO and the Whitlams lived in Paris from 1983 to 1986. They shared views of 'Rapprochement' and 'Reciprocity' as philosophies and frequently discussed such matters with their wives, Margaret and Monique.

Jean-Paul took a sophisticated interest in the development of Australian feature films and the literature they were based on. He published on the subject in depth.[3]

After taking office of the Federal Australian Government back in December 1972, Whitlam announced that there would be a royal commission on the granting of Indigenous land rights. Negotiations soon began on issuing a lease to the Gurindji people at the Victoria River of the Northern Territory. Their land had been appropriated since the 1850s by the Wave Hill pastoral station, later owned by Vestey Ltd, the giant international British pastoral company.

In 1966, Aboriginal elder Vincent Lingiari (1908-1988) had led his people off the station to a nearby river bed. The prolonged strike was concerned about the refusal of Vestey to pay the stockmen $25 a week in wages, instead of little more than mere weekly rations. It soon transformed into a much wider demand for their ancestral land to be returned.

After a prolonged struggle, the Gurindji were granted a land lease to 3,250 square kilometres of the old Wave Hill station with several important sacred sites enclosed and protected. On 16 August 1975, the Prime Minister, known as 'Jungarni' (meaning Big Man) to the Gurindji, took a theatrical part in a ceremony to return the land to the Gurindji people. Whitlam famously picked up a handful of soil from the ground and poured it into Lingiari's hand, symbolising the handover of the Crown lease: 'I want … to acknowledge that we Australians have still much to do to redress the injustice and oppression that has for so long been the lot of black Australians'.[4]

For Whitlam and the Gurindjii, it was an unforgettable moment, combining rapprochement and reciprocity with the strong possibility of reconciliation. As Whitlam admitted, there was much left to do.

A year before Whitlam had begun his campaign, British cinematographer Nicolas Roeg's poetic odyssey *Walkabout*, filmed on location, was released in 1971. Like Whitlam's gesture at Wave Hill, the film was about the need to establish harmonious and trusting relationships. Yet the story climaxes in a tragic misunderstanding.

More significantly, it made a film star of Gulpilil, a sixteen-year-old tribal dancer from a community in Arnhem Land making him a celebrity for the rest of his life. He became a determined campaigner to preserve traditional culture.

Back in 1977, Vincent Lingiari was generous in replying to Whitlam in his own language – translated as : 'Let us live happily together as mates, let us not make it hard for each other'. But feature films as complex narratives, like *Walkabout*, set out to show that it was difficult to achieve Lingiari's wise and considerate philosophy. After all, most films until recently were directed from a white perspective.

After reading the novel by James Vance Marshal, Roeg was deeply impressed by its central theme; he wrote a screenplay and began planning to film on location in Australia. It wasn't until playwright Edward Bond rewrote it that American sources funded the cost of filming it. For the leading roles, Roeg chose a relatively unknown British female, his own son John and, importantly, Gulpilil.[5]

Roeg chose his cast skilfully. Jenny Agutter played a fourteen-year-old school girl and Lucien John (or Roeg, in reality), her six-year-old brother. Their deeply depressed father, played by John Meillon, appeared in a brief but frighteningly brilliant cameo at the beginning.

The story begins when the disturbed father drives his two innocent school children in uniform into an isolated place in the semi-desert pretending it is for a picnic. Unknown to them, he had decided to kill himself and them as well in a horrifyingly realistic scene. He succeeds with the former, but not the latter. He fires a revolver at them, but they are at a distance and he misses. He desperately throws petrol over the car and, as it burns fiercely, he shoots himself in the mouth, falling backward into the fire. After witnessing this terrible scene, the children crawl away and soon get hopelessly lost in desert country.

They wander aimlessly; the boy falls into a dream world, as he plays with his toys; the more mature girl struggles with him over sand dunes and Namatjira-type red rock-faced hills of harshly beautiful landscape. They reach a small waterhole, shaded by a single tree, where they are able to refresh themselves until the spring water mysteriously dries up.

Gulpilil makes a sudden appearance on the adjacent high sand-dune hill, almost dancing down it, imagining he is hunting with two long spears. At first, he doesn't notice the desperate children, but then begins to approach them. He is about the same age as the girl and is going through a tribal ritual towards manhood – a survival test – sent by his people alone in the desert. It is an important *rite de passage*. When he reaches the children, communication seems impossible. He speaks no English. He carries a dead lizard he has recently speared.

As a debut for Gulpilil, the part is a rare gift; he carries it out with panache and deft physical movement due to his ability as a dancer. He is naked, apart from a loin cloth; he has a magnificent and compelling screen presence.

As he doesn't understand they now desperately need water, he walks slowly away until the boy solves the problem by gesturing with his finger to his open mouth. Gulpilil stops, makes a straw with a reed and they are able to draw water from the subterranean spring source at the waterhole. Thus, with a gesture of friendship and concern for their safety, the three become travelling companions across an almost magical landscape with the Aboriginal lad leading them.

Gradually, sexual tension grows between the girl and the Aboriginal boy. On the physical, spiritual and emotional journey the two lost children pass from innocence to experience becoming aware of their own sexualised bodies. The Aboriginal's hunting ability provides food cooked on an open fire which keeps them healthy over their long journey through wilderness.

When the trek nears its end, they find shelter in a derelict abandoned farmhouse on the margins. The Aboriginal lad performs a night-long ritual courtship dance outside – brilliantly handled by Gulpilil in a disturbing climax sequence. The girl refuses to acknowledge its meaning while the dancing becomes increasingly fast, violent and desperate. He remains outside the house, symbolising cultural divide. In the morning light, the children find the young Aboriginal's decorated body dead, hanging from a tree. He has sacrificed his life. Quickly, the girl turns away and the two white children, so well cared for and healthy by the Aboriginal youth's leadership, set off on their journey to reach nearby civilisation.

Roeg symbolically ends his film with a dream sequence of the girl's imagining. The girl, now married and living in a small modern unit, suddenly pictures in her mind an undisclosed part of the journey; we see the three independent travellers happily naked swimming and playing in a beautiful poetic setting of a large waterhole towards the end of their epic journey. Their very nakedness indicates the disappearance of two rival cultures: the tribal and the Western worlds. Instead, they now belong to a beautiful natural environment they can innocently enjoy.

*Walkabout* disturbs and Gulpilil's performance remains magnetic. Several decades later it is still one of the most imaginative films ever made in Australia. It is a most potent distillation of the threats of the desert landscape that can be overcome only by the Aboriginal tracker's role, skills and knowledge. Part myth and part fact, the figure of the Aboriginal tracker has continued to fascinate and beguile white filmmakers.[6] *Walkabout* was much admired by Jean-Paul Delamotte – and rightly so – in his studies of Australian film.

A film of visual beauty and power in the portrayal of desert landscape, *Walkabout* has the Aboriginal tracker (Gulpilil) ebulliently at home on the ochre rocks and vast sun-baked spaces while the cityscape is full of robot people and modern glass skyscrapers inhabited by anonymous middle-class denizens. Nevertheless, the Aboriginal youth fatally becomes aware of the girl's attractive body and decorates his body with white clay to perform his tribal dance to woo her. Her eyes show fear and he takes it to mean rejection and a portent of his own death as a sacrifice to white civilisation.[7]

In 1976, Gulpilil went on to score another major success in

*Storm Boy* (1976), directed by French-born Australian filmmaker Henri Safran, set in a magnificent coastal seascape in stark contrast to the desert of his first film. In the critically acclaimed film version of Colin Thiele's novel, Gulpilil plays the solitary Aborigine Fingerbone Bill who teaches a lonely boy how to deal with the natural environment. He almost becomes a surrogate father as the boy has a somewhat difficult rapport with his actual father, who is reclusive and bitter and angry about his marriage breakup, working as a lonely fisherman. In this film, Gulpilil emerges as an actor of mature charismatic presence.

Mike and his son live in a fisherman's shack near the 90mile beach on the edge of an isolated nature reserve which the boy explores in play by himself during the day. He is too far away from the small town to have playmates. His father Mick shuns the materialism and gossip of small country town society. His life changes for the better when he meets Fingerbone Bill who has been banished from his people. He lives alone and hidden on the reserve. Aided by Fingerbone Bill and Mike, the boy rescues three pelican chicks orphaned by a gang of reckless bird shooters invading the reserve. There are overlapping themes of alienation, marginalisation and loss connecting *Storm Boy*, the outcast Fingerbone Bill and the pelicans that the boy raises with Fingerbone's wise assistance.

*Storm Boy* is a powerful allegory of the potential relationship of rapprochement and reciprocity between Black and White as well as respect for the natural environment. Everything ends hopefully. The film was one of the Australian feature films chosen to be shown at the Centre Georges Pompidou in Paris. Other films about Aboriginality shown there were *The Chant of Jimmy Blacksmith* (Fred Schepisi, 1978); *Dingo* (Rolf de Heer, 1992); *Jedda* (1955) directed by Charles Chauvel and *Walkabout* (1971). Delamotte was excited about this exposure in the City of Light.

David Gulpilil had a sustained career as one of Australia's best-known actors at home and in France with more than a dozen major feature films to his credit. In 1977, he appeared in Peter Weir's *The Last Wave* as Chris Lee, an urban Aborigine who still sustains and belongs to a hidden ancient culture that exists beneath the city streets.

> *Comme les autres ? Non, sans doute. Richard Chamberlain* [American star] *y incarne un jeune avocat de Sydney, confronté inopinément à l'univers aborigène, ressuscité grâce à un acteur étrange et remarquable de cette ethnie : David Gulpilil, membre d'une tribu de la Terre d'Arnheim, l'immense région protégée du Territoire du Nord. Un passé immémorial dont les origines remontent au dreamtime* ...[8]

Weir develops an imaginative coherence full of dreams about the city rather than a linear narrative. Gulpilil responds well to these ideas with a subtle nuanced performance that heightens the tension in the scenes he appears in. As Chris Lee, he intones: 'Dream is a shadow of something real'. *The Last Wave* is a haunting science fiction journey into the unknown where dreams and nightmares conspire as one. The film did well in the box office.

While at La Trobe University as a senior tutor in media studies at the Media Centre, Jean-Paul Delamotte became absorbed in New Wave Australian cinema. He wrote a review of *The Last Wave* for a prominent French newspaper among several other Australian films. As a professional subtitle-writer, Jean-Paul completed worked on this film and several others for French release.

On the wake of his success with *Picnic at Hanging Rock*, *The Last Wave* was the next directional effort by Weir. It had a budget twice that of *Picnic*. The script was derived from the director's own mystical experience. Weir visited Pompeii and then Tunisia and, on a walk, found a carving of a child's head that he imagined he had seen in a dream before finding it.

The conversation he had with Gulpilil helped to form the narrative of the disaster movie. Weir could not avoid racial and cultural tension – his location shooting was picketed by Aboriginal protest groups. But he had the support of tribal elder Nandjiwarra Amagular who appears briefly in the film as Charlie.[9] Jack Clancy, in a review in *Cinema Papers*, wrote:

> ... two contemporary issues force their way into our conscious through all the teasing mystery – the place of

>Aboriginal culture in a materialist, rationalist Christian culture, and an uneasy sense ... of a physical and spiritual environment violated by that materialist, rational white culture.[10]

The previous year, Gulpilil appeared in Philippe Mora's underrated bushranger saga, *Mad Dog Morgan*, as Morgan's companion and only friend. The film holds up better now, but didn't receive much in critical acclaim when it was released. As Billy, Gulpilil enjoyed the free-wheeling quality of the direction and responded well with a subtle backdrop performance as one of the oppressed in a brutal colonial convict society. Filmed on location in the beauty and wilderness of landscape, the performances of Dennis Hopper and Gulpilil, the main actors, stood out. Gulpilil added to his personal persona and status as an actor in *Mad Dog Morgan*.

The so-called childsaving institution, in which the three young girls in Phillip Noyce's magnificent *Rabbit Proof Fence* (2002) were forcefully placed (by steamer and not train as in the film) in the remote Moore River Native Settlement which was deliberately isolated from both white society and their own traditional country. The English-born Chief Protector of Aborigines in Western Australia, AO Neville, favoured the state-run settlement over Christian missions for the reception of "half-caste" children since these allowed the "half-castes" to marry "full-bloods". He believed absolutely in breeding out the colour.

The Moore River Native Settlement was established north of Perth in 1917 on about 600 hectares of infertile ground. It served as an 'Aboriginal dumping ground, where Indigenous or those white society wished to drive away could be sent under a legal warrant. The three girls found themselves in a prison-like, barracks-style compound which was fenced off from the Aboriginal camp surrounding. It was a place where they were to be prepared for work in European society: boys as manual labourers; girls as domestic servants for whom there was an insatiable demand in middle-class white society.[11]

The Moore River inmates were provided with a rudimentary elementary education to grade three. The sewing room for girls provided the only real vocational education. They were fed a poor diet : meat broth, dripping, jam and bread. They ate with their fingers. Discipline was harsh with capital punishment or fourteen days in solitary confinement. All of this was historical reality. Noyce's film about a real incident of three girls escaping back to far home country has been frequently described as a journey into the nation's soul and an outback odyssey. It was an emotional tour de force and gripping entertainment.

In *Rabbit Proof Fence* Gulpilil was cast as an outstanding but ageing government tracker, living in the Aboriginal camp beside Moore River institution. The film was a rare combination of a thrilling chase and poignant social drama about institutional treatment of Aboriginal children in the first half of the twentieth century. The acting of Gulpilil is unforgettable. The film entertains with a tense, breathtaking game of cat-and-mouse of the tracker's work while engaging the conscience of a terrible legacy of injustice that Whitlam had spoken about when Noyce was an impressionable youth. Noyce had now returned from a significantly successful Hollywood experience to make the film.

To the viewer, the tracker (Gulpilil) seems strangely half-hearted in his efforts to recapture the absconders. Gulpilil gives a magnificent nuanced performance using his natural screen presence to highlight his character in a series of close-ups capturing his ambiguous facial expressions. His character has been trapped into the pursuit because his own child is an inmate of Moore River; he is fearful that his child will be punished if he does not recapture the girls.

As the tracker, Gulpilil skilfully demonstrates his ability, while finally allowing the girls to return to their homeland. He cunningly rides away with his reputation intact and his child does not suffer.

*Le premier film de l'acteur David Gulpilil,* **Walkabout***, l'a rendu célèbre. Il partage l'affiche dans* **Mad Dog Morgan** *(1976) en tant que partenaire du bushranger violent. Son* *interprétation de Fingerbone Bill (**Storm Boy**), mentor d'un jeune garçon blanc, illettré et solitaire, et de son père, est exceptionnelle. L'intrigue montre l'ambivalence d'une culture colonisatrice et témoigne d'une réelle volonté d'entrer en contact avec la culture aborigène, ... Gulpilil confirme son statut de "star" dans **The Last Wave**, en jouant le rôle d'un Aborigène qui vit à Sydney, loin de son propre pays. Il interprète des rôles dans **Crocodile Dundee** (1986), **Dark Age** (1987) et dans le film science-fiction de Wim Wenders **Until the End of the World** (1992). Puis vient un rôle complexe dans **Dead Heart**. Son interprétation dans **The Tracker**, et celle dans le fascinant **Rabbit Proof Fence** montrent un talent en pleine maturité. Dans ces deux films, il joue un rôle de traqueur de police ... Par sa longue carrière et sa présence impressionnante, Gulpilil personnifie l'histoire des Aborigènes au grand écran.*[12]

While undergoing treatment for cancer, David Gulpilil died in regional South Australia of a heart attack, aged 68. He had been cared for constantly by a live-in nurse in a small cottage. His film roles live on and are a memorial to him. His last appearance was the 'Old Man' in *Goldstone* (2016), a brilliant outback mystery western. In this last performance, he held true to his faith in his traditional culture and the story of his people. Although brief, his performance was magnificent. David Gulpilil Ridjimiraril Dalaithngu had changed the face of Australian cinema.

On the red dirt runway in Ramingining Land, East Arnhem, in January 2022, the fallen film hero was returned to his people in a light aircraft. Gulpilil broke boundaries in his movie roles spanning nearly fifty years. They were, on the main, landmark films.

**Notes:**

1. 'Speech by the Prime Minister at the opening of the National Seminar on Aboriginal Arts', *New Dawn*, September 1973, 2.
2. 'Gulpilil portrait wins Archibald', *Koori Mail*, Wednesday, 7 April 2004.
3. See Jean-Paul Delamotte, *Gough et Margaret*, La Petite Maison, 2020, 16p.
4. Sally Warhaft (ed), *Well May We Say. The Speeches that Made Australia*, Black Inc, Melbourne, 2004, 341-4; Jenny Hocking, *Gough Whitlam. His Time*, Miegunyah Press, Melbourne University Press, 2012, 135-87.
5. Andrew Pike & Ross Cooper, *Australian Film 1900-1977. A Guide to Feature Film Production,* Oxford University Press, Melbourne, 1980, 332.
6. Marcia Langton, 'Out of the Shows', in Peter Minter, *Meanjin. Indigenous Australians*, vol 65, no 1, 2006, 55-71.
7. Anne Hickling-Hudson, 'White Construction of Black Identity in Australian Films about Aborigines', *Literature/Film Quarterly*, vol 18, no 4, 1990, 265
8. Jean-Paul Delamotte, *Amours de rencontre (Papiers australiens) (1)*, La Petite Maison, Boulogne, 1993, 93-4.
9. Johnathan Rayner, *The Films of Peter Weir,* Continuum, New York, 2003, 89-91.
10. Jack Clancy, 'The Last Wave', *Cinema Papers,* 15 (1978), 259.
11. Robert Manne, 'The Colour of Prejudice', *Spectrum. Sydney Morning Herald*, 23-24 February 2002, 5.
12. John Ramsland, 'Les Aborigènes et le grand écran', *Correspondances Océaniennes,* vol 4, no 1, octobre 2005, 35.

# Mentor and Friend :
# Journeys through Australian Cinema
## Virginie Bauer

The first time I rang the doorbell at no 11, avenue du Maréchal de Lattre de Tassigny I had no idea how much my life would change. After writing an extended essay on 'The Contemporary Australian Cinema 1975-1985', followed by a Master's thesis on the same subject under the supervision of Professor Michel Fabre at the Paris III Sorbonne-Nouvelle University, I was now beginning research for my PhD dissertation. Professor Fabre had given me the name and address of someone who would be able to help me, which is why I was standing on that doorstep in Boulogne-Billancourt.

A tall, grey-haired, bespectacled gentleman opened the door and invited me in. That's how I met Jean-Paul Delamotte for the first time. After discussing my work in his office, he took me downstairs to a room with shelves filled with his archives. There were piles of unfiled articles and magazines about Australian cinema. It was agreed and so the deal was done, I would archive all the material and, in return, I could use it for my research.

Thus started a routine that would last for many years: every weekday I would arrive at Jean-Paul's, have a coffee with him and/or his wife Monique then head downstairs where I would work in the room opening onto the garden. This room would play a great part in my life as the visitors staying in *la petite maison* at the end of the garden would regularly come through and talk to me; some of them became friends like Australian photographer Allan Chawner and Brian and Kay Suters from Newcastle. Thus I became a regular at the Delamotte's household.

I had discovered Australia thanks to my father, who visited the country, and to cinema. I was then a young film buff going to the movies many times a week. But unfortunately, few Australian films were released in France in the early eighties. The only ones I saw were *My Brilliant Career* (Gillian Armstrong, 1979) and *Mad Max II* (George Miller, 1981).Then, in 1983, the Cinémathèque in Paris scheduled a film festival dedicated to the new wave of Australian cinema – at that time the films were screened at Palais de Chaillot at Trocadéro and at Centre Pompidou in the Beaubourg area. I discovered *Picnic at Hanging Rock* (Peter Weir, 1975), *The Last Wave* (Weir, 1977), *Breaker Morant* (Bruce Beresford, 1980), *Gallipoli* (Weir, 1981), *The Getting of Wisdom* (Beresford, 1977), *Sunday Too Far Away* (Ken Hannam, 1977) and many more. There was something so fresh, so new in these films which carried me away.

After getting my degree in English (*licence*) at University Paris III, I decided I wanted to write about Australian films and the men and women who made them. That's why I got in touch with Professor Michel Fabre who specialised in English-language literature from countries other than Great Britain and the United States. As Australia was part of his field of research he accepted me as his student.

At the Cinémathèque, during the Australian Film Festival, all Phillip Noyce's films were shown: *Backroads* (1977), *Newsfront* (1978) and *Heatwave* (1982). He was one of the first students who graduated as a director from the Australian Film and Television School (founded in 1973, Chatswood). Reflecting on his body of work, I decided to write him a letter explaining that I was working on Australian cinema for my Master's thesis and asking questions about his work. A year later, I had already defended my thesis when I received a reply from Phillip Noyce with a tape he had recorded with his answers. I went to Michel Fabre and he said I could use this material for a DEA (Master of Advanced Studies). Then it was decided that I would keep on working on Australian cinema for a thesis that was to become '*Le cinéma australien contemporain 1975-1988 : reflet d'une société*'.

Phillip Noyce and I started corresponding – it's difficult to think now of a time without email! Thanks to Pierre Rissient, who selected films from Asia and the Pacific area, many Australian films were presented at the Cannes Film Festival before being shown a few weeks later at the Cinemathèque. That's how I met and interviewed director Frank Shields whose film *The Surfer* (1987) had been shown at the Director's Fortnight. I also interviewed actor Nique Needles who was in Paris with the film *As Times Goes By* (Barry Peak, 1988) for a festival of Australian films at the Publicis cinema. Meanwhile I was still exploring Jean-Paul's archives and my sources seemed to be expended! All the interviews and reviews Jean-Paul had collected were a true goldmine. I was going through *Cinema Papers*, *Encore*, the *Sydney Morning Herald*, chasing news about the Australian film industry in *Variety* and other newspapers Jean-Paul subscribed to.

I also accompanied him and Monique to exhibitions and screenings at the Australian embassy, improving my knowledge about this country I loved, but had never visited. I went with them to a Lloyd Rees' exhibition in Paris; only much later did I discover how important he is in the history of Australian painting. That same day, we all went to a café where Jean-Paul and Monique introduced me to Anne and Daniel Pata, two painters who loved France and Australian art. It was the beginning of a strong friendship which has never ceased. Thanks to Anne, I was able to get in touch with the leading Australian film actor Bryan Brown for an interview. Anne and Daniel visited me the following summer while I was spending my holidays in the countryside in the southwest of France and kindly invited me to stay at their place if I wanted to go to Sydney, which I finally managed to do in 1989.

So for six months, I lived in Sydney with Anne and Daniel, going to the Australian Film and Radio School in North Ryde where I screened at least two films a day. I also interviewed many film people: Margaret Fink, Pat Lovell, Errol Sullivan, David Stratton, David Elfick, Evan Williams, Joan Long, Andrew Urban, Anthony Buckley, Richard Brennan, Ben Gannon, Gosia Dobrowoska, Ken Cameron and Gerard Lee. Phillip Noyce and I finally met after exchanging letters for three years. It was at George Miller's studio in Sydney where Phillip showed me his new film *Dead Calm* (1989) with Nicole Kidman in her first adult role; it also starred New Zealander Sam Neill and American Billy Zane. The success of the film would lead him to expand his career in the United States.

After six months I returned to Paris with a suitcase full of tapes, articles, notes, magazines and books. The most difficult thing to accept was that it was time to stop researching and start writing. I already had so much first-hand material with my interviews, but while I was writing, I was still spending time at Jean-Paul and Monique's meeting new people at the many dinners they organised. One day, Jean-Paul asked me to pick up some of their guests. My heart was beating fast when Judy Davis opened the door; she was Sybylla, the heroine of *My Brilliant Career*, one of my favourite Australian films, and had also played in Phillip Noyce's *Heatwave* (1982). She was in France to shoot *Impromptu* (James Lapine, 1991), a British film where she was playing the part of George Sand. I drove her and her actor husband Colin Friels to Boulogne where Jean-Paul and Monique were expecting us.

Indeed, whenever some Australian people from the world of cinema were visiting Paris, Jean-Paul would ask me to invite them to his place. That's how, one day in 1990, I phoned producer and screenwriter Marc Rosenberg to invite him to a great party Jean-Paul and Monique were hosting for the Australian writers who had been invited to *Les Belles étrangères*, a literary festival celebrating writers from a different country every year. The day was beautiful and we enjoyed the garden where everyone was having lunch, including Peter Weir and his family. Peter Weir was one of the directors I was writing about in that section of my thesis devoted to filmmakers. Talking to him about cinema, even in a casual way, remains a memory I'm very fond of. At the end of the day, Marc Rosenberg invited me to visit the shoot of *Dingo*, the film he was producing, for which he had written the screenplay.

*Dingo* (1991) was the [one of the] first co-productions between France and Australia. It was directed by Rolf de Heer and starred Miles Davis and Colin Friels, with music written by Michel Legrand. So I went to the New Morning, the famous Parisian jazz club where the crew was shooting a scene. I was introduced to the French cinematographer, Denis Lenoir who had been to the outback to shoot the Australian part of the film. *Dingo* remained a unique experience in terms of French-Australian cooperation but, on a more personal note for me too as I eventually married Denis Lenoir. I updated my thesis interviewing writers Marc Rosenberg, Peter Carey and playwright David Williamson while they were in Paris for *Les Belles étrangères*. It was a rare opportunity to include interviews with writers from such varied background. And of course they had to appear in my work.

Writing the thesis proved as hard as I expected, especially as I kept on finding new opportunities to interview filmmakers who were staying in Paris, like Ian Pringle who was directing another Australian-French production *Isabelle Eberhardt* (1992).

The first version was too big, more than one thousand pages, and Michel Fabre asked me to reduce it to seven hundred. It's always heartbreaking to let go of pages of work. Finally, in 1992, I finished it. It was divided in three parts: Part I, 'The cinema industry in Australia'; Part 2, 'Brilliant careers, the men and women who made history in the Australian cinema world' (producers, directors, screenwriters, actors); and the third part could be translated as 'Looking at Australia', where I explored the themes developed in the films from 1975 to 1988.

I defended my dissertation at the Sorbonne University in Paris facing a jury of four persons: Professors Michel Fabre, Xavier Pons, Maryvonne Nedjelkovic and Michel Ciment who was also a film critic and a cinema historian. I had dedicated my thesis to Jean-Paul and Monique who were there, of course, to support me with my family.

Australian cinema remained an important part of my life over the following years. I returned to Australia, to the Australian Film and Television School where Denis Lenoir was invited for a workshop about cinematography and I was invited to talk with students about my thesis and my perception of Australian cinema. I also kept in touch with filmmakers who had become friends like Phillip Noyce, Frank Shields, Marc Rosenberg and Ben Gannon. In Paris, where I lived, I used to meet students and some researchers who were working on Australian films and who sought my advice.

In summer, Jean-Paul and Monique visited me occasionally in my place in the countryside, including the exhibitions dedicated to Daniel Pata's paintings in Rodez and Brousse-le-château, two different places in the Aveyron region. In Paris, I was occasionally seeing friends I had met at Jean-Paul and Monique's, like Allan Chawner.

Then my life changed drastically. I decided to leave Paris, my job as an English teacher and move permanently to the countryside in the southwest of France where I'm still living. I tried to follow what was happening with Australian cinema thanks to the articles that Anne Pata was sending me from Sydney and I watch Australian films whenever they are available. Life takes you on unexpected roads and I've turned to my first love, horses. I became the owner and editor-in-chief of *Arabian Horse Spirit,* a magazine dedicated to Arabian horses in racing, endurance and culture. But Australia is still in my mind. I developed a partnership with the editor of *The Australian Arabian Horse News*, Sharon Meyers, who still writes articles for me and whenever an event or a book about horses and Australia are on the news, I try to report on it.

Writing this paper brings me back to a time which seems to have taken place in another life. I cherish all these memories. Jean-Paul and Monique played a great part in my life. Their generosity and enthusiasm made things which seemed impossible possible. They welcomed me in their family life. I will forever be grateful to them for their friendship and for opening new worlds to me.

Guibourg & Virginie. Photo by Allan Chawner.

Daniel and Anne Pata with Jean-Paul, 31 October 2006.

# Art Exhibitions & an opening in Aveyron
# Daniel Pata

My late wife Anne and I first met Jean-Paul and Monique in 1987 at the '*Expo Australie*' event at the exclusive department store Printemps, near L'Opera de Paris. It was an important Lloyd Rees exhibition that was arranged by Elizabeth Butel with some assistance from the Art Gallery of New South Wales. Lloyd was a family friend, so we were invited to the opening and dinner afterwards. It was a lush and exciting affair and meeting Jean-Paul, Monique and there friend Virginie Bauer capped off an exciting evening, indeed the week. As it was the same week I found an Arthur Streeton painting in the Paris flea markets! But that's another story. Jean-Paul, Monique and Virginie became close friends.

With the assistance of Virginie Bauer, who had been working with Jean-Paul's cinema archives whilst developing a PhD on Australian cinema, we developed the idea of a travelling exhibition of my artwork. It was arranged for the South of France, in the Averyon region starting at Brousse-le-Château and finishing in the city of Rodez. The exhibition was named by Virginie Bauer, appropriately called '*Echo de Lumière*', and was a show of paintings and drawings of France and Australia.

Although my enthusiasm was high for the show, I was to a degree lacking in confidence. Jean-Paul and Monique stepped in with such support, which now I see was something extraordinary. This was typically the way they supported many artists and writers and, indeed, any pursuit in the cause of Reciprocity associated with France and Australia.

Jean-Paul and Monique kindly came down to Aveyron, to Brousse-le-Château to open my Exhibition there. Jean-Paul was wielding a three-page essay which he wrote to open the show! Far and above what was required, but that was Jean-Paul and his exuberant self. I've never forgotten when Jean-Paul came over to our studio in Paris once and saw a work of the Eiffel Tower I painted on the wall. He said: 'I like this work. I will have a love affair with it'. What it does for one's confidence! He had a way about him. His opening speech was phenomenal.

As usual Monique was behind the scenes moving and shaking the whole event. The show attracted five articles in regional newspapers and even rated the evening news on television. It was a wonderful experience coloured by Jean-Paul and Monique.

Monique and Jean-Paul's lives were permeated by such good will and kindness. I count myself fortunate to have been in the orbit of their friends and their friendship.

> I respond to the differences of light, shade and colour giving distinction to various places. Added compositional factors create an alignment with abstract qualities that interest me.

*\*\*\**

***In JP's Vivre et Revivre*** *(p5824) : Samedi 10 juillet 04. vieux village où de petites maisons en pierres à peine dégrossies sont serrées les unes contre les autres au long d'étroits chemins qui montent jusqu'aux énormes tours, à cette gigantesque muraille …. En bas, au premier plan, juste de l'autre côté de la rivière enfoncée dans son lit caillouteux, l'Alrance qui rejoint le Tarn.*
*10h 1/4. Assis de travers sur le rebord du petit mur, quelques mètres en dessous, mini-chute d'eau en filets dont le mouvement semble immuable …*
*Le travail surhumain, cet esclavage dont on admire à présent le résultat ennobli par le temps … Sans doute, aussi, par moments, la fierté des maîtres d'ouvrage, la passion, la confiance … Daniel et Anne sont des amis exceptionnels. Lorsqu'à la Brasserie de la Place d'Armes, à Rodez, assis que j'étais sur une petite banquette surplombant l'entrée, tout à coup Daniel, le visage de Daniel, a surgi à la hauteur du mien, j'ai ressenti l'une des joies les plus vives que l'amitié m'ait jamais procurées.*

*11h20. Nous avons grimpé jusqu'au château par le chemin de schiste, basalte et/ou je ne sais quelles pierres. Et je me retrouve assis dans une des trois salles où Daniel expose 45 œuvres qui me donnent un vrai bonheur.*
*3h05 p.m. Déjeuné avec Daniel & Anne, l'un des plus délicieux de notre parcours à M et moi (peinture, littérature, société, voyage, découverte). Un grand privilège, l'amitié à ce niveau.*
*La joie de pouvoir "se laisser aller" à parler de ce qu'on aime, à tenter de comprendre ce que cela veut dire : peindre, écrire, avoir des amis, ne pas sombrer dans la solitude ...*
*Je suis seul, à présent, la salle n'a plus de convives, sauf moi qui m'attarde ... Le ciel n'est pas bleu, ce n'est pas une très belle journée en termes de météorologie. C'en est une en ce qui nous concerne.*
*(p5828) : Jeudi 15 juillet 04. Daniel ( Pata) est venu déjeuner. Il est peintre et je suis écrivain; il s'intéresse aux autres, moi aussi. Nous nous sentons proches l'un de l'autre, nous nous entendons bien.*

*« écho de lumière : paysages australiens et français », vernissage de l'exposition en présence de Jean-Paul Delamotte AM, écrivain et traducteur, fondateur de l'Association Culturelle Franco-Australienne et de l'Atelier Littéraire Franco-Australien*

*Château de Brousse 12480 BROUSSE-LE-CHATEAU, samedi 10 Juillet 2004*

***

Transcrit de *Midi Libre*, 7 août 2004.

PEINTURE **Paysages australiens et français, à la galerie Foch**
**Daniel Pata, les couleurs de la France vues de l'Australie**

Sous le pinceau de Daniel Pata, les paysages français révèlent tout le charme de leur pittoresque. Depuis qu'il a découvert la France à la fin des années 80, le peintre australien n'a cessé de représenter des paysages de nos régions. Sans délaisser pour autant les espaces si contrastés et quasi vierges de son immense pays, dont il peint le désert ou l'océan, partant jusqu'à six semaines seul, son chevalet sous le bras, avec toujours une bouteille de bon vin. Il a donc aussi arpenté la France, du nord au sud, élisant domicile à Paris, dans le vingtième arrondissement.

La passion de la France n'est pas chose nouvelle chez les peintres australiens. Elle a débuté avec les Impressionnistes, au XIXe siècle. Si Daniel Pata refuse, comme beaucoup d'autres artistes, de voir la spécificité de son travail réduite à son pays d'origine, on ne peut cependant pas occulter ce détail. Car c'est bien un regard neuf sur ces paysages si familiers que nous offre le peintre. De Salmiech, en Aveyron, à la bretonne Belle-île-en-mer, l'artiste donne des couleurs nouvelles aux villages, à leurs clochers et aux ponts de Paris.

Pour cet amoureux de la France, qui lui a rendu hommage tant de fois à l'occasion de nombreuses expositions en Australie, il était essentiel de présenter son travail au public français, et d'abord aveyronnais. L'exposition à la galerie de Foch est l'occasion de rencontrer l'œuvre de Daniel Pata, assurément un grand artiste.

**According to Daniel:** It was a very happy occasion walking over the river at Boulogne and through to the Parc de Saint-Cloud, to an art gallery at Marnes-la-Coquette owned by a friend of Jean-Paul's, Monsieur Vitry. He was an avid collector of paintings. In discussion of art discoveries with him, I recounted a story that happened a year earlier at the Marché aux Puces at the Porte de Vanves in the south of Paris.

I had arrived at the flea market early Saturday morning looking for a treasure, which I did every weekend I was in Paris. In the first minutes I had sighted a painting that looked interesting, but when I noticed a gash of about 50cm in it I decided not to look any closer. Later, walking in the flea market, I noticed a man carrying that same painting. Looking carefully in good light, I realised that I knew the artist – a moderately well-known French painter called Roland Oudot! I was annoyed that I didn't recognise it in the poor light earlier. I couldn't resist and told the man I saw it earlier and asked him did it cost very much. He said, it was '*un prix complètement fou*'. You can imagine my disappointment. To my astonishment, monsieur Vitry said "That man with the painting was me! Such a co-incidence! Needless to say, he sold it for a great profit.

In the last years of Jean-Paul's life he frequently walked this park, which seemed to give him great comfort.

# A Tale of Two Years

## Linda Barcan

1988 and 1989 were years linked by major bicentenary celebrations of two European cultures – the French and the British – in locations on opposite sides of the world. For me, they were two years of intense activity and movement during which I took my first steps towards adulthood and economic independence. They were years in which my joint loves of French language and classical music acted as co-parents, guiding me as I took those steps from my family home to independent living in Newcastle, then to Sydney to further my career, and later to Lyon, France. These three major life events all took place within the space of 18 months.

In 1988, white Australia marked the arrival of the First Fleet to its shores, celebrating the beginnings of European settlement in a country that, 35 years on, is yet to deeply interrogate its history from a First Nations perspective. That year, fresh from my liberal arts studies at the University of Newcastle and armed with majors in French and English, I left home and started work, combining my two areas of specialisation to earn a modest living teaching English to French engineers at a nearby aluminium manufacturing plant, Pechiney at near-by Tomago, and tutoring secondary school students in French.

The following year, in 1989, the French nation celebrated the 200 years anniversary of a key event of the French Revolution, the storming of the Bastille, and the establishment of the Declaration of the Rights of Man. The French Bicentenary's effects rippled across the globe, and reached the shores of Australia. At the start of that year, I moved to Sydney to take up a position as secretary at the French School of Sydney, then undergoing a large-scale removal from Bellevue Hill to

Maroubra, where it was consolidating its primary and secondary campuses. The establishment of a new bilingual school, re-named the Lycée Condorcet de Sydney, was framed as a potent symbol of Franco-Australian cultural exchange. In the publicity surrounding these events, every opportunity was taken to situate the school's move and its re-branding within the context of the 1988 and 1989 bicentennials. Less than a year after I began in this position, my *alma mater* facilitated an appointment as *Assistante de Langue Anglaise*, a role in which I would teach English to secondary students in France. I was seconded to the Lycée Saint-Exupéry in Lyon, located on a high plateau above the city in the suburb of La Croix-Rousse, a neighbourhood once home to the city's famous silk weavers, *les canuts lyonnais*.

At the time, I never stopped to wonder what had led me, a 23-year-old woman from Newcastle, to a city 16,000 kilometres away from home. But looking back, these linguistic, geographic and lifestyle fluctuations – from French to English, from Australia to France, from one job to another – indicate a restlessness of spirit, a split sense of identity and a wanderlust that I now recognise as a consistent character trait. It is beyond the bounds of this reflective essay on French/Australian reciprocity to wonder about the origins of this restlessness. But why did it, in part and for a few years at least, settle on Francophonie and Francophilia to soothe it? The answer does not lie in a cataclysmic event or change, but rather a slow and steady coalescence of activities and affinities that set me on my study and career paths.

In adolescence, my engagement with a local community theatre group, Young People's Theatre, revealed that I had a promising singing voice capable of being trained and, at the age of 15, I began taking private lessons. In the meantime, at school, I had two inspiring French teachers who spotted a budding linguistic ability, and who encouraged me to persist with my language training. At around the same time, I began developing my personal listening habits, as teenagers do, and used my recently acquired bike and a modest amount of pocket money to purchase a monthly magazine that came with a vinyl LP. One of these vinyls was "Stars of The Australian Opera Sing Highlights from French Opera", an awkwardly named yet auditorily satisfying collection of opera-

operatic arias, duets and ensembles, performed and recorded by principal singers of the national opera company, The Australian Opera. As time passed, music and singing began to merge in ways that were unplanned but complementary. My French studies at school and university, and the musical and vocal training in the private studios of my first teachers – Jennifer Ewans, Don McEwan and Mary-Louise Ambler – gave me oral and aural skills, underpinned by declarative knowledge which included reading and writing skills (although there was less if any focus on writing or composition in my singing tuition). Time and again, I found myself relying on my innate aural skills – a musical ear so to speak – to connect the dots. Somehow during my training in the French Department of the University of Newcastle, I had managed to miss Professor Ken Dutton's French Phonetics class, although his book, *Spoken French: A Guide to Phonetic Theory and Practice*, became a well-thumbed volume in my professional library. I was lucky enough to benefit from individual lessons with Ken on French singing diction when our paths later crossed, and I remember with appreciation those sessions in which a reliance on instinct and habit was gently transformed into an awareness of mechanics and their effects. Much of the application of this knowledge to repertoire took place on the job, as I began to get gigs singing French cabaret songs and operatic arias in various venues and forums around Newcastle.

Equipped with this knowledge and experience, and buttressed by the love and support of my family and friends, I set off on my next French adventure, taking up my position as Assistant Teacher at the Lycée Saint-Exupéry in Lyon. There I spent a year making new friends, perfecting my French and gaining on-the-job teaching skills in a manner consistent with what I now realise was an affinity for apprenticeship-style training. At some point during that year of immersion, I became acclimatised to the point where I felt ready to resume singing lessons, and through the recommendation of a mentor, I auditioned for and was accepted into the studio of Franco-Swiss soprano and voice teacher, Evelyne Brunner. Through Evelyne's studio, I met another young singer, Marie-Pierre Jury, and in April of 1990 we performed duets together in a concert at Fontaines-sur-Saône. Serendipitously, Marie-Pierre informed me that the Opéra de Lyon, who had recently appointed a new Musical Director, the Japanese-American conductor Kent Nagano, were conducting general auditions. She was planning to audition and she encouraged me to sign up, which I did. I cannot recall what I sang, but I do remember sharing the Green Room with ambitious and confident young graduates of English and American conservatoria, whom I regarded with awe and admiration, and some of whom made it into the Opéra de Lyon chorus, as did I. The engagement was timely: I was reaching the end of my assistantship contract, and as the time approached I was glad to have some certainty as to my immediate future.

  I returned to Australia for a mid-year visit and, though laid low with winter illness, I felt reinvigorated by the warmth generated by my circle of family and friends, who had received the news of my forthcoming job with interest. My time in Australia reminded me of my appreciation of family, home and friends, but at the same time I was looking forward to a new adventure, enjoying the excitement that precedes a step into the unknown. However, on arriving back in Lyon, I was relieved to experience a sense of comfort and familiarity. In the previous year, I had discovered many aspects of the city during my time off from teaching duties. The assistantship schedules were specifically designed to allow foreign-language assistants, of whom there were five at our school, to immerse themselves in the culture, history and lifestyle of the host city. And so, individually and as a group, we had time to explore the Croix-Rousse with its *traboules* (hidden passageways secretly connecting buildings and streets) and its pastel-coloured buildings, the Old City (the *vieux Lyon*) with its medieval history, the Cathédrale de St Jean with its Romanesque and Gothic architecture, the nineteenth-century Basilica at Fourvière with its funicular railway linking the hill to the city below, the Roman amphitheatre, where I would later perform in the opera company's production of Verdi's *Il Trovatore*, and the Presqu'île, situated between the two rivers which so defined this multi-coloured and multi-layered town. The historic Opera House sat on the island, but for the time I was in Lyon it remained silent, as it was undergoing an extensive refurbishment. I was to be a part of the first opera season presented *hors les murs*. The new job saw me move to a less familiar part of town, across the rivers Saône and Rhône to number 46, rue Raulin, an apartment in a narrow street directly opposite the rehearsal studios. Every day, my newfound colleagues and I would rehearse from 9 to 6, with a three-hour lunch break in the middle. As employees of the city, we were entitled to a book of lunch vouchers that allowed us to enjoy some of Lyon's famous cuisine, in true French leisurely, sit-down fashion. Thanks to my proximity to the workplace, there was even time for a siesta before rehearsals resumed in the afternoon!

  The building where the Opéra de Lyon had found its temporary home was first described to me as *l'ancienne école du service de santé militaire*. More recent history had given it more infamy, and whispers from the older choristers to the new arrivals soon communicated its secrets. During World War II the imposing building, first built in 1894 in the form of three large pavilions constructed around a large courtyard, had been occupied by the Gestapo, led by the so-called "Butcher of Lyon", Klaus Barbie. These were the spaces in which the chorus, orchestra and principal singers of the Opéra de Lyon rehearsed, in large, reflective rooms that for me not only resonated with the harmonious sounds of vocal, choral and orchestral music, but also with the imagined echoes of the horrible deeds committed under Barbie's regime. On our way to costume fittings in an upstairs room, we would pass through a stairwell with bullet holes visible in its walls. The hall where the orchestral *sitzprobes* were held was known to have been a place of execution, and the locked rooms beneath the chorus rehearsal room were, by some accounts, unopened torture chambers. Those dark and musty rooms, viewable only through grated windows in their doors, were redolent of sombre times that seemed not so distant, especially upon learning that Barbie himself was incarcerated in a nearby prison. Shortly after I left Lyon to live in Cologne, Germany, the Opéra renovations were completed. The new building, with its award-winning design, including an impressive semi-cylindrical dome atop the original neoclassical walls, was once more the natural home of the opera company. The site the company left behind is now the *Centre d'histoire de la résistance et de la déportation,* a museum which aims to ensure that the awful history of Lyon's subjugation by the Nazi regime will never be forgotten.

The performance program we delivered outside the walls of the opera house in various venues around Lyon was rich and wide-ranging, with concert stagings privileged due to the company's nomadic status. My contract began with a recording of Poulenc's *Les Dialogues des Carmélites,* which had been produced onstage during the previous season. The original cast was reassembled, and I was brought in as an extra chorister to replace a house mezzo-soprano who had been tragically killed in a car accident. The new Musical Director, Kent Nagano, was an enterprising, up-and-coming young conductor, as ambitious as he was charismatic, and he brought with him several record deals from which we all benefitted. Other recordings we made under the auspices of the opera company were Rossini arias sung by established soprano Katia Ricciarelli, and a production of Hector Berlioz's opera *Béatrice et Bénédict,* based on the Shakespearean play "Much Ado about Nothing", with rising star Susan Graham in the female title role, and fine French tenor and Opéra de Lyon regular Jean-Luc Viala as her male counterpart. This opera was also performed in concert as part of the 90/91 season. Other concert performances were of Wagner's *Parsifal,* Busoni's *Turandot,* and the oratorio *Gilgamesh* by Czech composer Bohuslav Martinů, whose works were being foregrounded during the centenary of his death. *Il Trovatore* and *La Bohème* were fully staged, presented in the city's Roman amphitheatre and at the Auditorium Maurice Ravel respectively. The company took advantage of its peripatetic condition to tour concerts to surrounding regions and cities and so, as a working musician, I visited Provence, Paris, Toulouse, Clermont-Ferrand, Montpellier and Avignon as well as the beautiful town of Annecy, which I was able to introduce to my father, Alan Barcan, and my step-mother, Margaret Barcan, when they came to stay with me in 1991.

Although I was offered a second contract, personal circumstances led me to resign and move to Cologne, where I stayed for two years before returning to Newcastle. Back in my hometown, I undertook further studies at the University of Newcastle, gaining my Honours degree in my other major, English, before taking up a position in the chorus of Opera Australia in Sydney. This last event came about on the advice of a fellow singer who was also auditioning, paralleling my Lyonnais experience.

\*\*\*

It is now time to return to the question I posed at the start of this reflective journey: how and why did a young woman's restless spirit come to roost in Francophonie and Francophilia?

As I was studying singing at precisely the same moment I was learning French, it seems to me that part of the answer lies in the intersection between music and language, in the way in which melody and rhythm thread their way through both music and language. There is little doubt in my mind that my acquaintance with the prosody of the French language, its melody and rhythm, benefitted me as a young, emerging singer of classical vocal music. At the same time, coming to grips with notes on the staff and the way in which they interacted with sung syllables and words, helped me with my singing studies and, especially, with singing in French.

Although at the time I didn't make the connections, as a Lecturer in Voice at the Melbourne Conservatorium of Music, now teaching diction to students of singing, I am more fully aware of the native characteristics of spoken French that make it so pleasing to sing. These include its open-ended syllable structure; the long, monophthongal vowels; the relatively equally accented prosody; the final tonic accent, and the tendency towards liaison and elision between words. These linguistic features combine to encourage the student of French lyric diction to sing towards the end of the line, to engage the breath for the full length of the phrase, to elongate and purify the vowel, and to think in phrases rather than in words or syllables. Learning to speak French as an adolescent and young woman and applying this knowledge to repertoire in my own lessons, practice and performance essentially also taught me how to sing, training me unconsciously in the techniques of breath support and legato, in the musicianship of phrase-shaping, in the craft of the storytelling in the form of thoughts. As a lifelong student, teacher and singer, the inherent singability of the French language is a topic that I am keen to explore more deeply in my musings and writings, but that will have to wait for another time and place!

*Il Trovatore* at the Roman amphitheatre, Lyon.

# How a Chance Discovery led to a Treasure Trove of French Literature

## Gerry Collins

Merewether Beach and its ocean baths have been like a spiritual home for me.

Wonderful memories of holidays spent at my grandparents' place on Ridge Street as a boy and regular swimming training sessions on Wednesdays at the ocean baths as a teenager have been with me all of my life and keep drawing me back.

However, at just 20 years of age I left Newcastle and returned only sporadically over the next forty years. When I retired in 2010 and came back "home", I quickly made regular visits to Merewether a part of my routine and it was one of those visits which was to start a chain of coincidental exchanges which took me unintentionally, but joyfully into a fascinating world of French literature.

A part-time job as a presenter on ABC Radio Newcastle was a perfect way to slowly step away from my long career with the ABC as a sports broadcaster, spent mainly in Brisbane. I was filling in for Carol Duncan in July 2012 on her afternoon program that concluded at 4.00pm each day and had developed the habit of heading to Merewether after each shift. Just being there was a perfect way to unwind. At the same time I needed to be constantly on the lookout for possible interviews and there it was sitting looking at me as I sipped a coffee from the espresso bar on the beach.

In a copy of the local newsletter *Making Waves*, there was a headline 'Skye Cassidy – Fully Tubed'. Underneath was a photo of that young local surfer, Skye Cassidy, and the following fascinating information:

> In 1988 this photo, taken by well-known local photographer Allan Chawner, was seen by people in Paris, Grenoble, Newcastle-upon-

Tyne, Muswellbrook and Newcastle in the *Hunter Valley People* exhibition under the auspices of the *Association Culturelle Franco-Australienne* (founded in Paris in 1980 by Jean-Paul Delamotte).[1]

Jean-Paul Delamotte – there it was – a side reference (in brackets) in a free neighbourhood community newsletter a long way from Paris! It was a name which meant little to me at the time I read it and yet within 48 hours I was to be enlightened about one of the most amazing culturally-aware French citizens to have ever come to our shores.

I had a strong hunch that here really was a story that I could use. Little did I know what it would lead to, nor the many coincidences which would follow.

In addition to the photo of Skye Cassidy was a poem, attributed to Skye and called "Fully Tubed". It had been put together by Newcastle writer, Paul Kavanagh who had cut and re-arranged her words from an interview he had done with her.

As I read aloud that poem I could see that here was a chance for some experimental but interesting radio. I had done enough surfing to recognise that any of the many people who have ever been propelled on a surf-board by Mother Nature could relate easily to this original piece of literature.

Firstly, though I needed a contact for this story and there on the bottom of the article was a contact name: Marie Ramsland. A quick phone call the next day and I had the first of many, many conversations with Marie and we have subsequently become good friends. Indeed Marie became my mentor as I prepared my memoir *A Fortuitous Foray into France* for publication.[2]

It was Marie who enlightened me on Jean-Paul Delamotte and she described a man I not only wanted to meet, I wanted to interview. Fortunately she had a phone number for me and soon I was calling Paris and meeting over the phone this amazing Jean-Paul Delamotte.

The first thing that struck me was his enthusiasm and his determination that literary relations between Australia and France should continue to be promoted for the good of both countries. I was to find that few people had done more for that aim than Jean-Paul Delamotte himself and it wasn't surprising that he often used the word "reciprocity", his French accent giving the word almost exactly it's French form, *ré-ci-pro-ci-té*.

Each interview would be allotted a five to ten minute slot on the program, but I was to find when I reluctantly brought this interview to a close that it was close to a half-hour in length! Hence a major editing job had to be done. I had been so taken in by my fascinating guest that time had flown.

Not surprisingly that interview included so many of the topics covered by other contributors to this book, including the *Association Culturelle Franco-Australienne* and its significant backers, Gough and Margaret Whitlam, the awarding of an Order of Australia medal to Jean-Paul and, of course, Paul Wenz whose wonderful writing gave a new perception of our own country. I am only one of an enormous number of people indebted to Jean-Paul Delamotte for alerting us to the writing of Paul Wenz.

Not only did the finding of the Merewether newsletter open up a new world for me, it came only a matter of months after I had started a Diploma in Languages at the very university which had managed to attract Jean-Paul Delamotte when he decided to head for Australia – the University of Newcastle.

It was the initiative of Emeritus Professor Ken Dutton, then the Head of the French Department of the university and he obviously saw something very appealing about the application from the young couple, Jean-Paul Delamotte and his wife Monique. In acting decisively and quickly, he opened the way for Newcastle to become their Australian home.

Naturally in the interview we spoke about Jean-Paul's time in Newcastle and I find now that whenever I see the sign for Perkins Street at its junction with Hunter Street, I still hear the voice of Jean-Paul with his distinctive accent saying what sounded to me like 'Pairkeens Strreet'. There is little doubt that he and Monique enthusiastically embraced this city which to other French people may have seemed like '*le bout du monde*'. Jean-Paul spoke glowingly of his neighbours in that little *quartier* and I recall him speaking in particular of a woman, who said – on hearing that he was French and that he was here to work at the University of Newcastle teaching French literature and film – he should promote the work of Paul Wenz. Was ever a challenge taken up with such enthusiasm and how fortunate are we that she alerted him to the skills of his countryman, who had also made a home in Australia?

Certainly I wasted no time in obtaining my first Paul Wenz book after the interview, *L'Écharde*. Purchased online, it was a new print of the original published in 2010 by the original publishing house Zulma. I was enthralled by Wenz's observations of '*la vie de bush*'. Of course I had read many books about the Australian bush and had lived for 14 years in western New South Wales but here was a different view of those familiar scenes. No Australian author would have written of a ram: '*Il possédait peut-être parmi ses ancêtres un sujet qui fut admiré par Louis XVI à la ferme nationale de Rambouillet*' (Il, the ram possessed perhaps amongst his ancestors a subject who was admired by Louis XVI at the National Farm of Rambouillet). Interestingly that farm still exists in Rambouillet where it was established by Louis XVI in 1783. The first sheep there were imported from Spain and were merinos, the same breed which was so popular in Australia and which Wenz undoubtedly would have raised on his farm at Forbes.

On the completion of the interview Jean-Paul invited me to their home in Boulogne-Billancourt and I said that I would love to do that if the opportunity arose.

The year 2012 was unfolding in an interesting manner for me. I was enjoying doing the Diploma of Languages course and the opportunity that came with it to improve my French. My studies were to be interrupted, though, by a request from ABC Television to return to work as the swimming commentator for their coverage of the London Paralympic Games. I was able to obtain leave from the university but naturally had to do some work while I was away. That included an essay on the renowned French novelists, Jean-Paul Sartre and Albert Camus.

As always during my career, I found it impossible to pack up and come home after major events were finished, knowing how close I was to France. So my partner Robyn and I headed for France, maintaining my custom of going there whenever I was working in Europe. It was my constant visits to my daughter Cathy's exchange student host family in Le Puy-en-Velay in central France which had driven me to go back to university to study the language because I found that my schoolboy French wasn't good enough. *La famille Gaillard* were wonderful people and they always made me most welcome.

I studied French at the University of Queensland for three years until I retired in 2010 and moved to Newcastle. I started the Diploma in Languages course at the University of Newcastle at the beginning of 2012, not knowing that it was possible to complete the Diploma course with a semester as an exchange student at La Rochelle. It wasn't until I had completed the assignment on Sartre and Camus that I discovered that I was not only eligible to go to La Rochelle, but that I could also apply for a Kelver Hartley Scholarship to help cover the costs. That called for a celebration and where better to celebrate than lunch at La Coupole Restaurant in Paris? It was a place frequented by Sartre and where Camus had celebrated his Nobel Prize for Literature.

So I had been back into the world of French literature with another Paris appointment coming up – to visit Jean-Paul and Monique Delamotte at their fascinating house in Boulogne-Billancourt.

Before that I had time to research La Rochelle and the intriguing Kelver Hartley, who had retired in 1969 and lived like a pauper while building an amazing nest egg of money to enable students of the University of Newcastle to study in France.[3] It was an extraordinary gesture and I still find it hard to believe that I was able to benefit from the generosity of this amazing man and his determination to leave a legacy from his time as the inaugural Professor of French at Newcastle.

While studying in France, Kelver Hartley had met the famous French writer and publisher André Gide. Years later when he was living in poverty in Sydney, his star student of previous years Grahame Jones proposed a meeting with Hartley for his own star student Hilary Hutchinson and her description of that meeting makes fascinating reading. She was deep into her doctoral studies on Oscar Wilde and Grahame Jones took her to Sydney's Central Station where he had organised to meet Hartley, 'an eminent scholar in this field'. Among the things that they discussed was the influence of Wilde on the works of André Gide with Hartley adding that he had once taken afternoon tea with Gide. Obviously that experience would have been a long way from the life that he was leading at that time in poverty in Sydney.

André Gide, a controversial character, had been awarded the Nobel Prize for Literature in 1947. Prior to that he had become infamous for his refusal of the manuscript of Marcel Proust of the first work of his *À la recherche du temps perdu,* while working for the publishing company *La Nouvelle Revue Française* – a refusal that was to lead to a famous apology from Gide and an equally famous reply from Proust.

Meeting Gide had obviously meant a lot to Kelver Hartley. Similarly Gide himself was overwhelmed when he first met Oscar Wilde.

Little did I know when I discovered this link between Gide and Kelver Hartley that Gide would continue coming back into my life for years to come as I was to get deeper and deeper into the world of French literature.

A trip which Robyn and I had planned for the south of France had to be cancelled and so suddenly we realised that we had the opportunity to go almost straight to La Rochelle, to have a look at this city which could provide an unexpected and exciting experience for me in just 12 months time.

I had contacted Jean-Paul Delamotte and we had organised to go to their Parisian home on a Monday evening and so we found ourselves on the Paris Metro 10 line bound for the final stop of that line, Boulogne Pont de Saint-Cloud.

To say that the welcome we received was warm is an understatement. Both Jean-Paul and Monique welcomed us as if we were close friends and the fact that we were from Newcastle appeared to make them feel that we were. I loved that close association they had with my home town and realised that we were experiencing the energetic enthusiasm that they devoted to people who they met and that enthusiasm was also there for literary pursuits and, of course, they had the talent of being able to transfer their enthusiasm for authors such as Paul Wenz onto others.

Their elegant home with its full bookshelves provided an appropriate backdrop to our discussions of their life in Newcastle and of Jean-Paul's impressive career. Having read as much as I could about Kelver Hartley, I was well aware that it was his replacement at the University of Newcastle, Ken Dutton, who had lured the Delamottes to Newcastle. I had heard a lot about Ken Dutton from Doctor Bernie Curran, who had become a good friend after I met him at a University of Newcastle Alumni event in Brisbane and I was well aware of the high esteem in which Bernie held him. Of course his name had been mentioned in the article in the Merewether newsletter where I had first seen the name of Jean-Paul Delamotte.

Sky Cassidy's poem, put together by Paul Kavanagh, had been translated into French by Ken Dutton and of course it had been a feature of the *Hunter Valley People* exhibition, an initiative of one of Jean-Paul Delamotte's special gifts to Australia, the *Association Culturelle Franco-Australienne*. I was able to tell Jean-Paul of the success of his interview on ABC Radio and how there had been many positive reactions to my reading of that poem (in English). Essentially I had seen how this particular project had not only had an impact around the world in 1988, it was again a newsworthy event 24 years later. I naturally told him of my fascination with Paul Wenz and how I had bought a copy of *L'Écharde*. Even after I had returned to Australia he asked me about the book and whether or not I had any trouble understanding it. I assured him that I hadn't and that it had led me to read more of his writing.

Monique was similarly very interested in us and our work and we spent a most enjoyable and entertaining few hours with them both.

2013 was always going to be an exciting and challenging year for me with the highlight obviously being the chance to be an international university exchange student at the University of La Rochelle. On 1 September that year, my final semester in my Diploma course commenced and even with plenty of time to get ready nothing could have really prepared me for all of the challenges that I was to face.

However, the experience turned out to be so extraordinary that I felt I just had to write a book about it and so *A Fortuitous Foray into France* was born.

In addition to studying French as a second language at the University of La Rochelle, we had the opportunity to study any of the many subjects available there. In my original Arts degree I had majored in English Literature and when I saw that a French Literature course was available I jumped at the chance. I had little doubt that undertaking such a challenge – studying with local Francophones and needing to read French literature as well as critical reviews – was possibly going to be beyond me. However, it proved to be a wonderful challenge.

We had two major novels to read for the course, *La Chartreuse de Parme* by Stendhal and *Les Faux-monnayeurs* by André Gide. There was that name again. The thought didn't escape me that here I was on a Kelver Hartley scholarship, studying André Gide in France. It provided more drive to complete this subject and to do as well as I possibly could. My notes from the first lecture on Gide, given by Monsieur Serge Linkès, suggested that he was '*un personnage étrange*' (a strange character), perhaps just the personality with whom Kelver Hartley could relate.

Despite having won a Nobel Prize for Literature, Gide's decision to reject Marcel Proust's first manuscript brought him some degree of notoriety. At the same time there were other coincidences still to come for me concerning Gide. Retired Queensland Judge Des Derrington once told me that he kept in touch with the French language by reading the Maigret novels of George Simenon. I followed his lead and became a Simenon fan. Imagine my surprise to go to La Rochelle and find that Simenon had lived in the La Rochelle area for several years during the Second World War. Gide published his works and the two became very close friends.

Then in searching for some information on Paul Wenz for this essay I was amazed to find that Wenz and Gide had gone to the same school and were also friends. Indeed Gide wrote a preface for the Zulma publication of *L'Écharde,* in which he said : '*Je contemple avec admiration ce colosse superbe.*' (Wenz was a very big man.)

Then a final irony – while Gide refused Proust's first manuscript for *la Nouvelle Revue Française* (which was later to become the publishing house Gallimard), Jean Paul Delamotte's first literary texts were published by Gallimard.

Little did I know what an extraordinary treasure trove of French literature was to be uncovered when I first spotted the newsletter on Merewether Beach, nor did I know the amazing people that I was to meet because of it.

**Notes:**
1. *Making Waves*, July 2012, <http://makingwaves.yolasire.com>.
2. Gerry Collins, *A Fortuous Foray into France*, Brolga Publishing, 2022.
3. See Kenneth Dutton (ed), *Kelver Hartley: A Memoir,* 2000, Boombana, Mount Nebo.

# 'A very special man ...'

## Alan Ventress

Jean-Paul was a very special man who did so much for Franco-Australian relations.

I first met Jean-Paul and his charming wife Monique when I was the Mitchell Librarian at the State Library of NSW between 1993-2001.

As you are aware Jean-Paul's primary interest in the Mitchell Library was the work of Paul Wenz. I particularly remember the fun we had together when Jean-Paul showed me a photo of Wenz sitting on a case of Krug champagne in the most desolate of Australian bush surrounds near Forbes in New South Wales, in the property Wenz had just purchased.

Jean-Paul was exceptionally keen to publicise the work of Wenz which was generally unknown or forgotten in Australia and he donated a number of his literary works in French and English to the Mitchell Library, State Library of NSW. One title I remember was *The Thorn in the Flesh*, though Wenz was more well known for his *Diary of a New Chum*.

Jean-Paul was the archetype cultured Frenchman who had a great love of Australia and its literature, especially around the time that Wenz flourished. He was a wonderful advocate for the Mitchell Library and I cherish the friendship we had.

I recall introducing him to the music of Josephine Baker which had somehow passed him by. Nevertheless, he thoroughly enjoyed her work and what she stood for.

**Note:** In *The Road to Nanima*, Jean-Paul notes (214), 14 November 2000:

> *Alan Ventress tellement gentil, ce matin, avec ses cadeaux (et je viens d'écouter le CD Joséphine Baker qui se termine, bien sûr, par 'J'ai deux amours ... "*

In the Shakespeare Room (NSW State Library) at Jean-Paul's *Reciprocity* speech as the Kelver Hartley Fellow, 1997 : (left) Ken Dutton, Monique, Kay Suters, Jean-Paul

# *Diary of a New Chum,* or The road to Boulogne-Billancourt

## William Noonan

When I left Sydney by plane that night it was too dark to see the country. After the broken sleep of two long flights I took the train, then the métro, then dragged my suitcases up the steps at an hour that was still far too early, impatient to have my first glimpse of Boulogne-Billancourt. I saw an avenue bordered by plane trees with a view of an ornate park in the distance, stretching up the hill from the other side of the river. Cars, buses and the occasional self-service bicycle rumbled past. Some headed out across the bridge, others joined the morning scrum at the roundabout like animals feeding. Nobody took any notice of me. The streetscape was familiar enough, though little was I to know that I was about to enter a corner of France unlike any I had ever encountered, to meet a man who would become my host, mentor, friend and much more for the next ten years. As I rang the bell marked '*gardien*' on that bleary, rainy September morning, I did not realise that something had happened.

Paris? Yes, I had seen it. I had admired it, passed through, changed stations, spent time enough in its bars and on friends' couches, though traffic, noise and tales of unscrupulous landlords had spoilt much of the illusion. So what was I doing here?

In early 2009, I found myself in my hometown of Sydney, thankfully not engaged to a woman of four hours' acquaintance in a fancy-dress French peasant's costume, but short on funds and future plans at the tail end of a much-delayed PhD project. I had spent extended periods in France before, but it seemed time to return to complete the library research I had not managed with the greatest efficiency during earlier visits. I also hoped to have an assistant lecturing job that would pay the rent for a year while giving me just enough holidays to finish writing my long-overdue thesis. That, and perhaps try to work out exactly what it was that had fascinated me about France since my teenage years. Discreet enquiries among friends and colleagues threw up a few leads and – despite misgivings at the plummy language exercises my future employers insisted I record on audio cassette, a medium forgotten for so long that it was starting to become fashionable again and much sooner than I expected – I soon found myself searching for accommodation not too far from central Paris.

The first, though not the only, acquaintance to mention the mysterious *Association littéraire franco-australienne* was Jessica, no-nonsense mentor and thoroughly Francophile fairy-godmother to a host of lost postgraduate students, who knew something of ALFA's activities through Newcastle's Ken Dutton. After sharing an anecdote about a young Frenchman who had applied for a language tutoring job at Newcastle with a recommendation from one Eugène Ionesco, Ken passed over a coloured slip of paper. It bore an italicised boldface quotation (Stendhal, perhaps or Banjo Patterson?), a line drawing of a small house and a large tree, and an email address whose *petitemaison* component suggested a link with the drawing and whose *@wanadoo.fr* domain somehow suggested both early adoption and sentimental attachment. I would learn soon enough that literary reciprocity was far too important a matter to bear the tyranny of the aerogramme or the nationalist clunkiness of a Minitel terminal, though could already see that a different kind of exceptionalism was at work here.

A certain J-P D answered my enquiry in an effusive prose style that carried no trace of the passive-aggressive *bien cordialement* that had by then become the default sign-off in French email exchanges. Jean-Paul Delamotte – his name finally revealed as an incidental aside in a later exchange – explained by means of an impeccable sequence of tenses that the studio that had hosted Australian artists in the past was, regrettably, not currently welcoming visitors. ALFA, however, would be very pleased to host me for a month in l*a petite maison*, a dwelling that offered Spartan but sufficient comfort, whose Japanese affinities would no doubt appreciate that shoes be removed indoors, and which was located at the bottom of a garden and in proximity to what seemed to be the unlikely combination of a woodshed, a Studiolo and a métro station. Further enquiry brought a bashful aside that financial, administrative and any other practical matters were best dealt with in person and preferably by the mysterious, but clearly beloved Monique. I was to pass on my fondest regards to Australia in general and Newcastle in particular.

I stood in front of no. 11 that morning, surely not the first young-ish Australian to do so, with very little idea of what to expect. The bell for '*gardien*' rang somewhere inside and the door opened, revealing a grey-haired gentleman with a slight figure, corduroys and a scarf or two and a beaming smile. Jean-Paul shut the door on the morning traffic and showed me in, past an ornate central staircase, a book-filled study with twinned writing desks and into a simply appointed kitchen. The coffee offered was just what my head needed, but it still took a few moments for my senses to adjust to an atmosphere of complete calm, in which my new host began to ask questions in a mixture of French and English as we looked out into a leafy garden.

Had I travelled well? How was Newcastle? How was Ken? Had I ever been to the cemetery in Forbes? Had I already made the acquaintance of that adopted citizen of Forbes, Paul Wenz? I'm not sure how I would have digested these questions had I arrived after a full night's sleep, but they were asked with such courtesy that it was easiest to follow along with a conversational logic that I would soon come to know very well. Coffee finished, Jean-Paul declared himself a terrible host – how much better Monique, on a rare excursion out of town, in fact to her father's funeral – managed these things – and led me from the warm calm of the kitchen and into the green and slightly dripping calm of the garden, down a Japanese-inspired path.

This was nothing like the Paris I had encountered in previous trips, lively enough but noisy, stressful and never especially solicitous of shy and tired new arrivals. The tree from the line drawing had gone, but *la petite maison* was otherwise very much as described: an old servants' cottage at the bottom of the garden, built above a garage and woodshed, with vines strung across to the sheer concrete wall of the modern apartment building next door. There was old-fashioned patterned wallpaper here, minimalist Japanese there. Cartoons, doodles and more serious artworks by previous occupants hung in frames on the walls. Books – many of them in old-fashioned cream cardboard covers and bearing the line drawing of house and tree – were shelved in every room. The garden was Monique's doing, the Japanese touches were the work of their daughter Guibourg, but the sense of space, calm and Australiana led me to feel I was about to move into an exquisitely detailed model of my new host's mind.

Clearly not used to being home alone for long, Jean-Paul kept me company during my first few days of jetlag and administration. Between the more mundane business of mobile phone contracts, contacting employers and lining up drinks with a few old friends, he showed me around the neighbourhood: bakery and supermarket, Musées Albert Kahn and Années Trente, a church with a family connection, a favourite diary-writing bench overlooking a duck-pond. As a postgraduate student with what felt like permanent writer's block, I couldn't help admiring someone approaching three times my age who wrote longhand and even retyped a diary for pleasure. If *la petite maison* was Jean-Paul in microcosm, Boulogne and its environs were his macrocosm, stretching from the Parc de Saint-Cloud, where he would stroll most afternoons to the Australian Embassy, just on the other side of the river in central Paris.

Monique and then Guibourg returned and I started work. My month's tenure in Boulogne evolved into an open-ended stay with the briefest of discussions while watering the plants one afternoon. Tea was taken in the basement Studiolo, embarrassing gaps in my knowledge of Australian art and literature were filled with great tact and I began to learn more of Jean-Paul and Monique's work to build cultural and literary links with Australia following their first long stint in Newcastle in the 1970s. Manners and mannerisms were more other-worldly than old-world: tea might be drunk from precious china cups or – for a real treat – from an almost empty honey-jar. Conversations would take nostalgic and sometimes unexpected directions; postcards were written, signed and stamped mid-meal to conjure up far-away friends and relatives. Visitors' books at both ends of the garden contained warm greetings, recipes for memorable lunch dishes and the names of the good, the great and sometimes the unexpected. Of the many photographic memories pinned to a cork board and shown to visitors – eucalypts, Sydney ferries, social and literary gatherings – the proudest was one of Gough Whitlam grumpily abandoning the number 72 bus stop for the metro entrance to return to his embassy after Sunday lunch.

Over time, I learned more about Jean-Paul and Monique's careers – and their romantic meeting – in the cinema industry before they decamped to Australia. I was treated to a short film directed by Jean-Paul and starring a young Jacques Perrin and to extracts from an eclectic and eccentrically catalogued library. Friends would come from the other side of Paris over to Boulogne for the joyful novelty of spending Sunday in a quiet garden: vast quantities of folding chairs would be unveiled, in memory of garden-parties of years past, and my friends would invariably be waylaid during the afternoon to be shown the cellar where ALFA's treasures were stored and to emerge with armfuls of slim, cream-bound books, published in homage to writers – few none of us had encountered during our compulsory Australian literature curriculum. Some would return time and time again to continue the conversation, others would stay on with me between other living arrangements and get to know Jean-Paul like I first had. Sometimes there were surprises in store: splicing an old audio cassette with sticky tape to hear the forgotten strains of *"Sayonara, Nakamura"* in the ABC's *Australia All Over* program was one thing; tea and biscuits (in china cups, this time) over the soundtrack to a 1970s film adaptation of Henry Miller's *Quiet Days in Clichy* – I was never sure how or why, though the cultivated yet distinctly Australian tones of Wayne Rodda in the opening sequence offered one clue – were quite another. Clichy, then as now, was a far cry from calm, bourgeois Boulogne, but I was coming to realise that the empire of literary reciprocity, that lay at least partly within its municipal borders and fully within my hosts' minds, had a longer and deeper history than I had realised.

Clues to this history often came out in mundane settings, not that the setting was ever entirely mundane. Bottles of sweet Cabernet d'Anjou would appear on the doorstep of the little house like mushrooms, unbidden but always touching, as if the same gracious host was welcoming a new guest time and time again. The provenance of an Aboriginal artwork (in the stairwell behind which we attached bits of wine-cork, to allow air to circulate and prevent mould) or a doodle ('... invites you to the opening of Mackie's Loo! Fancy dress, with hats!') would be revealed as an aside, while sweeping gravel off the garden path or sorting out the recycling. I had been welcomed from the beginning like a family member, though occasionally wondered, upon looking through the many entries in the visitor's book I had carefully moved to the top of the piano, where all these people were now. As the months and then the first couple of years passed by, I slowly came to realise that my own carefree and sometimes self-centred tenure had also marked a turning point for my hosts.

The PhD dissertation I somehow completed at the end of my first year in residence thanked Monique and Jean-Paul for offering surroundings combining the learned fun of Rabelais' Abbey of Theleme with the affectionate eccentricity of Laurence Sterne's Shandy Hall. This was intended as the warmest of compliments and I knew Jean-Paul well enough to be sure that he would take greater pleasure in being set in the company of classic literature than he would in being thanked directly for the long and arduous proofreading and citation-checking he had kindly undertaken. For all that, I have occasionally regretted writing an acknowledgement that focused more on my own hobby-horses than on his, though I'm not sure whether I am the only Francophile guest of *la petite maison* to have wondered whether I wasn't there under somewhat false pretences, having shown rather less interest in Australian art and literature than my host. Then again, showing more interest than he in such matters would have been difficult, as the publications of La Petite Maison neatly shelved behind the desk where I worked constantly reminded me.

Nostalgia takes many forms and I can remember many of the times I helped Jean-Paul back his little burgundy-coloured Renault out into the street. The main challenge was to squeeze past cars parked halfway over the cobbled driveway, though I did wonder whether the colour of the car had been chosen to match that of the narrowish iron gates or whether the gates themselves had been painted to minimise visible scratching. In Spring 2011, one of Jean-Paul's last expeditions by car took him to faraway l'Haÿ-les-Roses, on the way to Orly airport, to deliver the typescript of *La Route de Nanima* to the premises of a printer – the last of his kind, I was told – who was soon to retire from hand-setting type for the small print runs ordered by La Petite Maison. The book followed a short hagiography of Gough and Margaret Whitlam printed the previous year and was itself a fitting conclusion to the publishing activities of La Petite Maison: a compendium of diary extracts beginning in the 1970s and cataloguing Jean-Paul and Monique's pursuit of the French-Australian writer Paul Wenz and the literary and other acquaintances made on the way. It wasn't too long after this expedition that Jean-Paul returned to the driveway in Boulogne earlier than expected, one of the front corners of his car stove in by a truck that had cut a corner too sharply in traffic. Nobody was hurt, thankfully, yet Jean-Paul announced that from that day on, he would drive no more. His explanation, perhaps masking a fright he never spoke about, but proffered in a tone of almost joyful nostalgia: the accident had brought to mind a poem, '*Je n'aurai plus d'automobile*', which he had penned upon the sale of a Mini at the end of a long-ago sojourn in Australia.*

By September 2012, I had acquired a permanent lecturing job outside Paris, but also a French partner better versed in Australian literature and art than I, and we continued to spend most of our combined time in Boulogne. Friends – of our generation and of our hosts' – continued to visit and we had the privilege of meeting their granddaughter Eva as soon as she was old enough to be wheeled around the garden. Time was passing and we felt closer to the family than ever, but also that we were all slowly growing older. Jean-Paul had become, if anything, more sociable than usual since abandoning his car: afternoon expeditions to the Parc de Saint-Cloud would set out by bus and return, more often than not, by means of his beloved practice of urban hitchhiking, waving a neat binder showing his preferred destination into the afternoon traffic and, as often as not, inviting his surprised rescuer in for tea. Having become more accustomed than I had realised to life in Boulogne, with its family kindness and soothing calm, and as my own mostly expat friends began to settle down into a more adult existence, perhaps it was time to consider what exactly it was that drove Jean-Paul's nostalgia for Australia.

Pauline and I set off for Sydney over Christmas 2013, on our first trip together to Australia. Life was moving on: my sister was pregnant with our niece and my aging grandmother managed to join us for a beachside holiday. A post-Christmas road trip brought the time to visit friends and relatives, but also to carry out a commission from France: carry a copy of *La Route de Nanima* to the grazing property named in the title, a few minutes' drive outside Forbes, a town I had never visited. Armed with emailed directions, we located the property, drove up to the homestead, not meeting a soul, and left the book and a note on the veranda.

The Forbes municipal library (or Literary Institute, as its Art Deco façade proclaimed) was grander outside than inside, though Paul Wenz was accorded the space due to a local hero on the shelves near the front desk. Photos taken, our mission was complete, though the route back to Boulogne required a few steps, both physical and psychological.

We returned to France and to work and still saw plenty of Jean-Paul, Monique and their family. Work kept me away for longer and longer periods, but we still called Boulogne home and would still meet other friends, from Australia or from other corners of the world, at either end of a garden in which we held an impromptu party to celebrate our own civil union in 2015. The neat stacks of new books in the cellar behind the Studiolo had ceased to grow, but their memory stayed alive as visitors bore away enthusiastic gifts to read on the métro or at home. Jean-Paul, however, was getting older.

The big crisis came one summer as a stroke took him to hospital and the lethargy of a system running on a skeleton staff for the holiday period kept him there. I don't know how she did it, but Monique managed to bring him home after an extended stay and after alterations to the house that allowed him to stay in and near his beloved Studiolo. He was tired, had trouble swallowing and was sometimes in pain, but was home in the care of his beloved Monique with his family nearby. He still enjoyed visitors as much as he was able to find the energy. Days no longer spent writing were spent typing up old diaries and there were many times I crossed the garden fearing a medical emergency only to discover, to my great relief, that the internet connection was down or a file had somehow been misplaced. Time was passing and I could see only too well the effort Monique put in to make life as comfortable and as normal as possible for her beloved Jean-Paul. Tea was still taken, though visits were now shorter, and expeditions into the garden were rarer. My niece came to visit with her parents and made fast friends with Eva; Monique laughed long and loud at the bush-style fireplace made by scraping clear a circle of gravel from the courtyard, but we all wished that Jean-Paul had been able to come and see it for himself.

It was hard to know how else to be helpful without intruding, though our occasional visits to Australia provided one new opportunity, this time not to visit long-remembered places but to discuss a plan for the future: the return of Jean-Paul's literary archives to Sydney. Alex Byrne, thoroughly Francophile director of the State Library of New South Wales, welcomed me graciously on a sweaty afternoon two or three days before Christmas and explained that the plan was already, in principle, approved – the rest was a matter of logistics, and of working out how much material could be transported and catalogued. I liked his way of dealing, as Paul Wenz might have said, though my main job seemed to be to announce to the benefactor in person that the recipient was willing. Having heard more than one complaint from Jean-Paul over the years about the difficulty of donating books to public libraries, I knew that this at least would be good news.

Monique and Jean-Paul had done an excellent job over the years of dispelling any lingering sense of literary illegitimacy, especially once Pauline, who had written university papers on Australian art history and shared none of my resistance to an Australian literary canon I had been told I must cherish at school, came to live in Boulogne. Time was passing, however, and by the time we both found ourselves working in Dijon, three hundred kilometres away, it was clear that we could not remain indefinitely in a calm oasis we were already having trouble looking after properly. Autumn leaves piled up on the lawn, we were rarely there to chase the recycling truck that passed at our end of the garden and, most of all, we were less and less able to provide familiar companionship. A few years beforehand, any number of expatriate friends might have jumped at the chance, though most had now settled down elsewhere. Finally, a solution appeared from an unexpected quarter: my cousin from Melbourne, a professional opera singer, was moving to Paris to join her American partner who had just obtained a two-year residency. We had finally managed to convince some legitimate artists to take up residence, use the piano as something other than a sideboard, and give us another reason to return as often as possible.

The next time I had occasion to write to the State Library was in the autumn of 2019: the collections had arrived safely and been catalogued, and the equally Francophile John Vallance, whom I knew well from my schooldays as a thoroughly modern teacher of classical languages, had taken over as director. Jean-Paul was sadly not doing well and I was fairly sure that he didn't have much longer to live, though I like to think that he did appreciate the recognition of his contribution to Franco-Australian literary relations relayed from the other side of the world. I also had a sense of how much Monique had had to take on to look after him at home until his last moments and knew how much she deserved and needed a rest.

It was during a busy week at the start of the university year that we heard the sad news that Jean-Paul had passed away. Part of me wished I could have been there to say one last goodbye, though I suspect he would have preferred to do so on his own terms, warmly and calmly. It was almost exactly ten years since we first met, I reflected, as I cleared my diary to attend the funeral and organise train tickets to Boulogne, once more guests in *la petite maison*. The day was sad, as such events are, but a fitting way to remember a gracious host and old friend. I was asked to say a few words, among other friends, and could find nothing more fitting than a passage from Jean-Paul's French translation of Wenz' *Diary of a New Chum*. One or two of the friends who had been waylaid in the garden the best part of a decade beforehand attended the funeral. There seemed no more fitting way to get from church to cemetery than by taking the bus that ran the length of Boulogne and no more fitting place to be afterwards than Jean-Paul's beloved Studiolo.

I don't know what Jean-Paul would have made of the bushfires that covered much of Australia in late 2019 or the Covid crisis that broke out in early 2020, though I think he would have enjoyed the comedy of a final trip we made in his honour. My sister and her family were by now living in Orange, west of Sydney, and we spent Christmas there with my parents. On a hot Boxing Day, the others went to visit friends while Pauline and I borrowed a car and set off with little preparation on the hour or so's drive to Forbes, under a smoke-filled sky. The cemetery was easy enough to find, though it, like the rest of Forbes, was deserted. We had forgotten to bring water or hats and realised that we only knew that Paul Wenz was buried in the cemetery, not where. We didn't know what section to look in – Catholic, being French? Lutheran, with that Alsatian-sounding name? Jewish (or were we confusing him in the heat with another of Jean-Paul's stories, about finding the grave of banker and philanthropist Albert Kahn's brother, somewhere in Western Australia)? The one object we had not forgotten to bring was a smartphone and some confused Googling showed that Wenz had been buried 'with Anglican rites'. With only slightly more than half the cemetery to search now, we eventually came upon the grave of his wife Hettie Wenz, buried in 1959, but were too exhausted to do more. We returned to the car in defeat, sun now low in the sky, only to see an odd glint from the side of the gravestone as we drove past it on the way to the exit. One more internet search brought up a potted biography signed by none other than Jean-Paul Delamotte: Paul Wenz had been buried in the same grave as his wife. We returned and there was his name, etched not on the top but the side of the gravestone and almost obscured by grass. Unemployed at last? Crisis averted, we found an open service station for petrol and ice-cream, then headed back to join my sister for what seemed a fitting evening at a country pub. Back in Sydney a few days later, I was given a Mitchell Library reading room pass and requested a box of archives that I had surely seen before in the cellar in Boulogne, the contents of which included a hand-drawn treasure map of how to find Paul Wenz' grave. The next day, we boarded our flight back to France, little suspecting that our next trip to Australia would be unexpectedly delayed, but cheered by the feeling that our old friend would have enjoyed the story.

\* Jean-Paul Delamotte, « Adieu ! », *Vivre et revivre*, Petite Maison, 120-21.

**Note from Monique:** The name of the artist for work hung in the stairs of *la petite maison*, is **Dennis Nona** – Groupe linguiste Kal-lagaw-ya; **Title :** Waru Kazil (une nouvelle génération de petites tortues) 2005; origine – Ile de Badu (Détroit de Torres, Queensland).

# The making of a thesis – Memories of Jean-Paul Delamotte

## Helen Ledwidge

After receiving a Bachelor of Arts (Hons) and Diploma of Education from the University of Sydney, I taught for two years in state schools in New South Wales. I then spent the academic year 1966-67 as an English assistant at the Lycée Hélène Boucher in Paris. During this time I completed a *Diplôme de Littérature Française Contemporaine* at the Institut des Professeurs de Français à l'Etranger at 46, rue Saint-Jacques. At that time I aspired to study for the DUP (*Doctorat de l'Université de Paris*), but I was unable to stay on in Paris and I returned to Australia.

In 1987, my family and I returned to Paris where my husband had been posted to the Australian Embassy as Trade Commissioner. In 1988, Australia celebrated its Bicentenary and in 1989 France celebrated the Bicentenary of the French Revolution. These events caused me to reflect on Franco-Australian relations and the image that each country had of the other. At the same time I was hoping to settle on a topic for a doctoral thesis.

I had heard of the *Association Culturelle Franco-Australienne* and met its founder Jean-Paul Delamotte at an Embassy reception. He had just published a summary of his research on a forgotten Franco-Australian author Paul Wenz (1869-1939) and his enthusiasm for Wenz and his work was overwhelming. I read Jean-Paul's work '*A la recherche d'un écrivain perdu: Paul Wenz Français et Australien*' in *Le Lérot Rêveur*, no 46, December 1987. So began my study of Paul Wenz.

Thanks to Jean-Paul, I was able to read some of Paul Wenz's short stories in French which were reminiscent of the stories of pioneering Australians written by Barbara Bayton and Henry Lawson. I was also able to read Wenz's novel *L'Echarde*, which was later translated as *The Thorn in the Flesh*. I thought I had enough material for a thesis as there were three other novels – *Le Jardin des Coraux, L'Homme du Soleil*

*Couchant* and *Le Pays de Leurs Pères* – as well as numerous travel jottings and more short stories.

With Jean-Paul's encouragement I transcribed Wenz's correspondence with André Gide which is held at the Bibliothèque Jacques Doucet, Place du Panthéon. The collection comprises 17 letters from Paul Wenz and a carbon copy of a letter from André Gide to Wenz. The two were friends from their days at the Ecole Alsacienne. I visited the school, and through the archivist, Mme M Tramond, I obtained photos of the two students.

Jean-Paul introduced me to Denis Wenz and Claude Gonin, cousins and great-nephews of Paul Wenz. Mme Nicole Wenz was very supportive as was Denis, a writer himself. Claude Gonin became a great friend. He had fond memories of his '*Oncle Paul*' and provided information on Wenz family matters as well as photos. He also gave me the three Wenz novels mentioned above.

Things at the Sorbonne had changed. I returned to 46, rue St-Jacques which was now *l'UFR Didactique du Français Langue Etrangère de l'Université de la Sorbonne Nouvelle* (Paris III).

Professor Jean-Yves Tadié supervised my *Maîtrise de Lettres Modernes*. Professor Pierre-Edmond Robert directed my DEA (*Diplôme d'Etudes Approfondies*). He then directed my thesis under the *arrêté du 30 mars 1992*.

I eventually completed and submitted my thesis to the University of Paris and arrangements were made for me to defend my thesis on 7 October 1994. Jean-Paul at his expense paid for the following notice which appeared in *Le Monde* on 6 October 1994.

**Soutenances de thèses**

– Hélène Ledwidge, de Sydney (Australie), soutiendra, le vendredi 7 octobre, à 10h15, salle 33, 5, rue de l'Ecole-de-Médecine, pour l'obtention du doctorat (Sorbonne nouvelle, Paris III), sur le sujet « Paul Wenz (1869-1939) et l'image de l'Australie dans la littérature française ». Le jury comprendra Mme Nedeljkovic et MM Robert et Teyssandier.

Pour tout renseignement sur l'œuvre de Paul Wenz (ami d'André Gide et premier traducteur de Jack London) que Firmin Rose appelait « le romancier français de l'hémisphère Sud », s'adresser à l'Association culturelle franco-australienne, qui s'attache depuis plusieurs années à rééditer ses romans. Téléphone : 46-03-01-92.

Jean-Paul and Monique Delamotte, together with the three members of the Wenz family came to the Sorbonne to hear the defence of my thesis, called a *soutenance*, following which I was awarded the *Doctorat ès Lettres*. To celebrate my success, Jean-Paul took me and my supporters to lunch at the La Tourelle restaurant, 5 rue Hautefeuille. An unforgettable day.

Jean-Paul was an enthusiastic supporter of my endeavours. I was so touched at his mention of my thesis in his book *La Route de Nanima* (p 160). He added: (NB *La soutenance s'est bien passée et nous l'avons fêtée à la sortie dans ce charmant petit restaurant (la Tourelle) de la rue Hautefeuille* …).

Jean-Paul came to Australia as often as he could. We met up with him at Paddington in the flat he shared with the Suters' family. I particularly remember a memorable lunch at the Orient Hotel. He loved The Rocks area and old Sydney by the harbour.

Visits to Forbes and Nanima were always on the cards.

After Jean-Paul's death, Monique sent me a precious package of books by Jean-Paul recently published by ALFA (*Atelier Littéraire Franco-Australienne*) – La Petite Maison, 11 avenue de Lattre de Tassigny, 92100 Boulogne-Billancourt. One volume was *Douce Illusion* where Jean-Paul outlined the many obstacles in his path while attempting to bring 'the Master of Nanima' to the literary world. He valued 'reciprocity', but was often disillusioned by the reactions of others. I like to think he and I honestly shared any findings and found enjoyment in our mutual discoveries.

We exchanged emails up until his death. In his last email to me dated 17 January 2019, he spoke of still being involved in writing – mainly notes and transcriptions. He and Monique continued to host visitors from Australia to their home and to various studios. The

Delamottes' lovely ancestral home, formerly a merchant's house, was close to the river in Boulogne-Billancourt.

As his legacy, Jean-Paul sent the Archive of the Association Culturelle Franco-Australienne to the New South Wales State Library. This donation was celebrated with a reception on 26 November 2015 hosted by Dr Alex Byrne which I attended. Unfortunately, neither Jean-Paul nor Monique could be present.

Jean-Paul was a gentleman and a scholar. His kindness and generosity knew no bounds. His passing has left a void, as I have always regarded him not only as a mentor but as a friend. I cherish his description of me in his book *La Route de Nanima* (p 328), as '*Wenzienne accomplie et amie fidèle*'. A title of which I will always be proud.

Helen Ledwidge with Claude Gonin and Nicole and Denis Wenz before the *soutenance*.

Left: Jean-Paul and Helen after the award of the doctorate. Right: Monique and J-P.

# Travelling back in time …
## *à la rencontre de* Paul Wenz

## Solène Anglaret

There is no doubt about it, Paul Wenz was an avid traveller. If social media was around in his day, he might have been one of the many travel influencers we have today. His book *En époussetant la mappemonde*[1] gives a detailed account of the many countries he visited and the transport means he used. He seemed fascinated by both and keen to share his experience and knowledge with the world.

I vividly remember the day I found out about Paul. Mum had spoken to my grandma's sister, Nicole Wenz. She called me on a Monday morning to tell me about their conversation. Early Monday calls during my morning walks by the beach in Melbourne, Australia, were our new tradition. While the sun rose on my side of the world, it set back at my parents' place in Louviers, Normandy. Every time we spoke, there was and still is, so much to say. But hearing about this left me speechless. Nicole had said to Mum that I wasn't the first one in the family to publish a book while living Down Under. I had in fact just released my first book, a travel memoir called *Where to Next?*

Surprised and intrigued, I remember asking several questions. Who was this mysterious fellow author somewhere up our family tree? What did he write about and when? Where did he live? And, most importantly, what was he like? Growing up, I often felt as though I didn't belong, especially on that side of the family. From what I knew and could see, most of my relatives were rational thinkers, scientists, engineers and doctors. Everyone but me. For as long as I can remember, my mind has been filled with stories by day, which turn into vivid dreams and nightmares at night. I've always loved expressing them through speaking, writing and painting. That, and my heightened emotionality and hyperactivity, made me feel like the odd one out. Perhaps I wasn't the only one to be different after all.

Unfortunately, I quickly realised that Paul and I weren't actually blood related. Dear reader, I'd better warn you that this is a little tricky and that most people need to read or hear it two or three times to make sense of it somehow. Let me try to put it in the simplest way I can possibly master. Paul is my grandma's (Claudine) sister's (Nicole) husband's (Denis) dad's (René) uncle (Paul). Does that make sense? If not, perhaps the family tree pictured below will help.

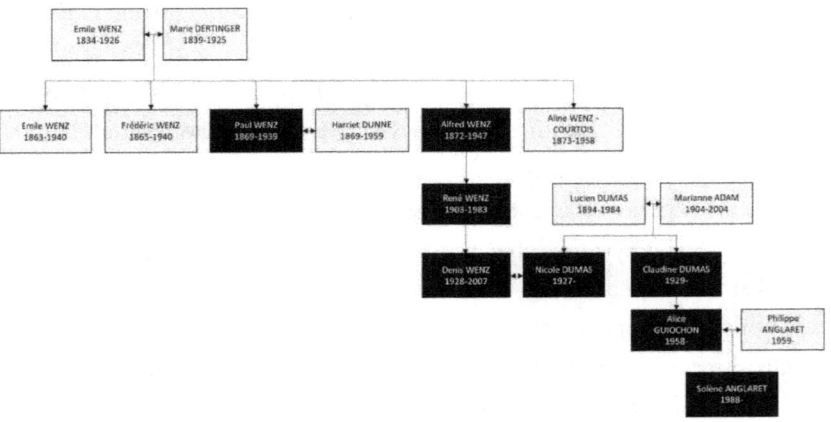

Paul and I are not only relatives by marriage rather than blood, on paper, we also have very little in common. Paul was a man. At 193cms, he was very tall, especially in those days. He lived between 1869 and 1939, so there is no way we could have crossed paths. In case you and I don't know each other yet, I am a woman. At 168cms, I'm of pretty average height. I was born in 1988 and was 30 when I discovered Paul's existence. It was shortly after, in April 2019, that I decided to follow his footsteps in the hope of finding out more about him and the life he led.

Somehow, I convinced Andy, my now husband, that driving more than seven hours each way from Melbourne to Forbes, through the Australian bush, would be a wonderful idea. There's no time like road-trip time! In many ways, it really was wonderful. That's, of course, if you forget about the loudest and dirtiest room we've ever slept in and the car problems we had on our way back. But aren't hiccups part of what makes an adventure truly unique and memorable? And both memorable and random it was.

Having made our way to Forbes, we met Dr Merrill Findlay, writer, scholar and change-maker. She knew so much about Paul, so much more than I did. She brought us to the gates of his estate, now owned by a different family. We took photos under the Wenz Lane sign. Can you believe it? Having a lane in your name, wow that's super cool! Maybe one day. I also paid my respect by leaning on his grave. Back at her house, Merrill showed us the many photos and books that she has collected over the years. One of the documents she shared with us, states that 'no Frenchman was more Australian; no Australian was more French than the Franco-Australian writer Paul Wenz'. From what I've discovered about him so far, that sentence makes total sense. Merrill was so welcoming and generous. She opened her home and her mind to us and I am beyond grateful to have been able to discover a bit more about my mysterious ancestor through her interest and meticulous gathering of information about his life.

After a few days filled with emotions and stories, we headed back south to Melbourne. I will always remember this road trip. When I close my eyes, I can picture and almost smell the dry, vast and barren countryside. Thanks to Paul, we got to see another side of Australia, one that many travellers and even locals don't visit. Along the way, we listened to music and spoke a lot. Upon reflection, this is something we don't do enough of, simply be in each other's presence, either in silence or bounded through both deep and futile conversations. We spend so much time in front of our screens. Don't get me wrong, travelling before smartphones was way more difficult. I remember the times we got lost with our paper maps and smile at the thought of stepping onto them to find the way, like the fictional character Joey in the American sitcom *Friends*. What do you think travelling at the end of the 19th century would have been like? I find it extremely difficult to imagine. I wonder how Paul coped during the many months at sea. Although sceptical about my chances of survival, I wish I could travel back in time to experience it. Taking place more than 100 years apart, our stories are marked by the societies around each of us and the notion and experience of time that underpins them. What took a few months on a boat then, only takes a few hours by plane now. The world has changed drastically. It keeps on changing. Somehow, it feels as though the clocks are turning faster, and faster, and faster.

I know that earlier I said that Paul and I didn't seem to have much in common. Well, my curiosity has led me to find out otherwise. Had we lived at the same era, I'd like to think that Paul and I could have been friends. For starters, we both love to travel, not as a hobby or just for holidays, but as a lifestyle. According to his diaries, Paul's travels took him all over the world. In 1890, at just 21 years of age, he moved to London, where I live now. He didn't enjoy the busy business vibes, so he moved to Algeria in 1891 where he lived for just over a year. In 1892, he left France for a business trip on behalf of the family's very successful wool business Wenz & Co. The journey lasted two years! His whole life was one of adventures. He crossed the equator more than fourteen times and kept changing his route between Australia and Europe, visiting Japan, China, Russia, Argentina, Chili, Bolivia, Ecuador, many of the Pacific and Caribbean Islands, Senegal, Mauritania, Niger, Ivory Coast and many more countries along the way. More than a century later, having worked in the travel industry for many years and seized the incredible opportunity to visit over 50 countries to date, I can profoundly relate to Paul's insatiable curiosity about our planet and our cultures.

To travel is to move.
To move is to breathe.

To breathe is to live.

For a large part of his life, Paul didn't travel alone. Having decided to move to Australia in 1897, he met his wife on the boat that led him to his new life. Her name was Harriet Dunne, though she went by the name of Hettie. She was the daughter of a wealthy Australian grazier. Coincidence? Perhaps. Or you might call it fate as Paul was moving to Australia with the idea of settling down as a grazier himself. So, once they arrived, he bought a large sheep and cattle station called Nanima, on the Lachlan River, between Forbes and Cowra in Central Western New South Wales. They got married in September 1898 and, as far as we know, *travelled* happily ever after.

A mere 124 years later, Andy and I tied the knot. Although we met at work, rather than out at sea, we've visited many cities and countries together. Our paths first crossed in a modern office in Hatfield, north of London, in the United Kingdom. Eventually, we moved in together. I'm pretty sure people around us thought we were settling down. Life had different plans. In 2015, I was offered a job in China and moved to Shanghai on my own for two years. The long-distance was tough, but it gave us the immense chance to meet in different places and explore Malaysia, Hong-Kong, Abu Dhabi and many places in China. After two years, surprising many (again!), we both decided to quit everything and move to Melbourne, Australia. He'd always dreamt of working there and, always keen for an adventure, I was happy to go anywhere with him. Little did I know back then that I was following the footsteps of one of my ancestors.

Paul and Hettie didn't have any children, which was unusual in those days and still is today, in the eyes of many. Unfortunately, as mentioned in the biography edited by Jean-Paul Delamotte in 1998,[2] they would have loved to and did try to expand their family but experienced several miscarriages. This tragedy meant that they led unconventional lives, away from the beaten path and what is traditionally expected. More than a century later, that's how I hope to live too. Back in 2007, at 18 years of age, I moved abroad for the first time, spending a year in Norway. I have lived overseas and travelled extensively ever since. Andy and I don't actually want to have children and, though it's more common now, it's still misunderstood and judged. For example, I was shocked when my hairdresser said: 'What? Why? That's such a shame. You'll regret it for the rest of your life.' She is far from being the only one who has asked or responded in such a way. There is so much that still needs to be done to debunk these attitudes, deeply anchored in our patriarchal societies. I wish I could travel back in time and meet Hettie. I wonder if she had friends and family to confide in about her miscarriages and heartbreak. I hope she did. Although I know little about her, she sounds like the kind of woman I admire and aspire to be. She must have had countless stories to tell.

But, for the most part, Paul was the one telling the stories. Allegedly, he started writing in Namina. That doesn't surprise me as, even today, the place is so vast, empty and quiet. I can only imagine what it would have been like in those days and without all the technology getting in the way of creativity. Did he write out of boredom or was becoming a writer his dream? If it were the latter, we would have something else in common. During our first year in Australia, I wrote all day every day and absolutely loved it!

Perhaps, given the opportunity, Paul would have loved to quit the family business and become a full-time writer like his school friend, the famous André Gide, or maybe he was happy with the way things were. Over the years, André and Paul stayed in touch and exchanged many letters. Did jealousy cross his mind or was he happy to occupy the niche of a French author in Australia? Hopefully, he was very proud of the latter, as he ought to be. Indeed, he left us with a wide range of short stories and novels, mostly in French and a few in English. He was a prolific and dedicated writer, an inspiration five generations on ... and beyond.

One of his novels, *Le Pays de leurs pères*,[3] made a particularly strong impression on me. It is the story of a boy of English heritage who grows up in Australia. The boy dreams of travelling to London to see and experience the city. When the First

World War breaks, the opportunity arises and he seizes it. Enlisting in the army, he travels by boat full of hope. Unfortunately, he arrives in Gallipoli instead of the UK. There he fights in a deadlybattle and, in a heart-breaking twist of events, loses his eyesight. His injury leads to him being transported to a hospital in London. He is consumed by sadness and despair as this is so far from what he had imagined. Having finally made it to the city of his dreams, he can't see it for himself. But all is not lost as he falls in love with the nurse who looks after him. After a while, he finds out that she loves him too. So, it is with her and through her eyes that he experiences the city he had hoped to reach and explore his whole life.

Although Paul and Hettie were alive during World War I, Paul was too old to be sent to battle, so this novel isn't based on something he would have experienced or witnessed first-hand. However, the war did have a significant impact on their lives. They happened to be in France in 1914 and endured the devastating bombing of Reims. They decided to stay on. In 1915, Paul became a liaison officer at the Franco-British military hospital. He was also in touch with the Australian press and sent descriptions of the events to newspapers in Sydney and Forbes. Hettie joined the war efforts too and worked for the Red Cross.

There is no escaping the war out there.
For the war is also in here.
Where is it hiding, the silver lining?

I wonder what messages Paul was intending to impart through *Le Pays de leurs pères*. Often, as writers, we don't just describe our characters, we inhabit them, or they inhabit us. In many ways, I would even say that they are us and we are them. So, rightly or wrongly, I interpret the story as highlighting the difference one might find between the expectations and the reality of a life on the road. The places we dream of might not be those we fall in love with and end up settling in. I'd like to think that he was telling us to be present and open every step of the way, instead of solely focusing on the destination and the image or fantasy we might have of it.

Like most of us, I've been guilty of romanticising certain places and prone to getting fixated on the way things should be rather than the way they simply are. India is one of these countries that I've put on a pedestal and can't wait to travel to. I've been close to making my way there several times. The latest was just before COVID-19 hit. I had secured a voluntary role at a women's shelter in Jodhpur and was about to start the visa process. But life decided otherwise and the pandemic stranded us all. So, India continues to feel like an unattainable dream. It's hard to express, but somewhere deep in my soul, I am drawn to the country and its culture. I know that there is something meaningful and powerful there for me to discover. It might simply be that I'm not ready to experience it yet. And it could be a very different journey than the one I've imagined and built up in my mind – not unlike the character in Paul's book.

Something else I found between the lines of Paul's novel is that life will give you ups and downs, success and challenges, happiness and despair, all at once. Even in the darkest clouds, whether we see it or not, a silver lining holds us. Like on a tightrope, I picture us walking along it without realising it. What does this mean in practice and in the context of travel? Let me give you an example. When the pandemic started, Andy and I were still living in Australia and I was working in the travel industry. Unfortunately, in October 2020, I lost my job. Isolated in Melbourne – one of the longest lockdown cities in the world – and so far away from our families, we made the very difficult decision to leave. This meant losing our visa and saying goodbye to living in Australia for good. It also meant packing everything we owned within six weeks and moving internationally while everyone else stayed at home. How many people do you think were on our 300-passenger flight from Melbourne to Doha where we stopped over? Exactly 16. And picture this, all the flight attendants dressed in full protective equipment. What was meant to be a flight seemed more like a hospital's operating room. It was surreal and, for hypersensitive me, quite traumatic.

You might be wondering … where was the silver lining then? Well, Brexit or EU-Exit was taking place. By entering the country before 1 January 2021, I was able to obtain the right to remain and work in the UK. Not only did I apply for a pre-settled status on 24 December 2020, but I also received the best possible gift on the same day: a settled status! The reasons behind being given a settled status directly will remain a mystery, but I chose to see it as a sign that we were where we were meant to be. Many moments like these can also be found in Paul's travel diaries. Only by looking backwards at his life and at our own, do we have the opportunity to connect the dots and make sense of our unique human experience.

I couldn't write about Paul without mentioning his fascination for the cultures and people around him. The account of his travels often mentions how surprised he was to find similarities with people that initially seemed so different to him. What I will say too is that language has considerably evolved and that some of the words he used would be unacceptable and considered racist today. As someone deeply involved in equity, diversity and inclusion, while I understand that the times were different, I condemn the words used. In the same way, I can only assume that, in five generations from now, a similar statement might be made about some of the words and expressions I have employed in this piece and others. I welcome this as an opportunity to continuously learn, unlearn and relearn in the name of kindness, respect and justice. Together, I believe that we can break down borders and bring the world closer together one adventure, one story, one conversation at a time.

I will never truly be able to travel back in time *à la rencontre de Paul*.

I will never be able to know what his life would have been like. I will never be able to experience the world in the way that he did.

I wish I could. There are so many questions I'd love to ask Paul and Hettie. I wonder if they know that I exist. I guess it depends on what you believe. Perhaps they can see me, see us. If they do, I hope that they recognise themselves in this piece. I am humbled at the thought of having walked in their footsteps somewhere between Forbes and Cowra, or elsewhere in the world. Who knows? I can only imagine what they would make of the world we live in today. Would they embrace or resent modern travel? They might find it comfortable and easy, or fast and superficial. What if it was all of that and none of it at the same time? Every day, we have the opportunity to both accept the way things are and do everything we can to make them better. Little by little, through our words and our actions, we have the ability to make a difference in the world around us. A small step in a meaningful and positive direction, is better than no step at all. And, soon enough, a step can turn into a jog, a run, until we collectively take-off.

In a daydream, I see Paul and Hettie on an airplane for the first-time holding hands. I picture them and think about how much they would have travelled if they could have flown and the joy they would have felt. This will stay a daydream. In 1938, Paul travelled to France for the last time. On his way back in June 1939, he caught what he thought was a cold and carried on with his life. Unfortunately, the cold turned out to be pneumonia and he passed away on 23 August at the age of 70. I hope all his wonderful and colourful travel memories flashed by as he took his last few breaths. May that happen to me too.

Despite all the circumstances and years that separate us and our lives, Paul and I are now connected. Some of our differences are blatantly obvious but, as it turns out, we also have a lot in common. We are both curious travellers and avid storytellers, in awe of the nature and of the world around us. We both chose to live life off the beaten path. And, most importantly, we were both immensely lucky to receive the greatest gift of all – love.

**Notes:**

1. Paul Wenz, *En époussetant la mappemonde*, collection of travel diaries and 2 short stories, 'En Nouvelle Calédonie' & 'Fausse alerte', La Petite Maison, 2009 (first published in 1905).
2. Jean-Paul Delamotte, *Paul WENZ 1869-1939, sa vie – son œuvre,* La Petite Maison, 1998,
3. Paul Wenz, *Le Pays de leurs pères,* Calmann-Lévy, Paris, 1919.

# The Forgotten Legacy of Hettie Wenz and her books

## Merrill Findlay

I first met Jean-Paul Delamotte more than twenty years ago in my local library. He was in Forbes on one of his regular pilgrimages to 'Wenz Country' and I was visiting my mother, a retired farmer, who had settled in Forbes after the death of my father. This chance encounter triggered my ongoing fascination with Paul and Hettie Wenz and their books that evolved, over the years, into a warm friendship with Jean-Paul.

At the time of our meeting, some 600 books were stacked, uncatalogued and unloved in the back room of the Forbes library. Most had once belonged to Paul and Hettie and their extended families. Jean-Paul believed they should be moved to a city institution where they could be properly conserved and made accessible to scholars. He even suggested, on one of his visits, that he buy the Collection himself. I was horrified. We locals had campaigned over many years to keep the books in Forbes in accordance with Hettie's will. They were part of our cultural heritage, as were the couple's grave in the Forbes cemetery, their homestead at the eastern rim of Forbes Shire, the miscellaneous non-literary Wenz artefacts in the Forbes Museum and private homes, the many Paul and Hettie stories in local folklore and Paul's literary output, most of it authored at Nanima Station. On this matter, we were intractably parochial! We'd even Australianised the family surname and thought pronouncing it with a German 'V' pretentious! Of course, we were, and are happy to share this legacy with city-based scholars and the rest of the world, but, from our perspective, the books must stay in Forbes. So no, dear Jean-Paul, you could not have them!

In 2004, I painstakingly catalogued the Collection and, after Forbes Shire Council passed a resolution to apply for funding for the conservation of the books, prepared a submission to the National

Library of Australia's Community Heritage Fund. The sum we received enabled Council to hire historian Stephen Gapps to undertake a Heritage Significance Assessment. As Gapps concluded in his report:

> There has been a deal of historiography on Paul Wenz, as he represents a rare figure in Australian literary traditions and in the story of Australian multiculturalism, particularly in regional Australia. Wenz's associations with other literary figures and important historical characters, such as Lawrence Hargraves, have been emphasized as part of his significance for Australian literary history, as well as Australian history in general. The fact that Wenz was based for thirty years on a rural property in mid-western NSW has always been slightly incongruous to such a well-read literary figure. However, this apparent incongruity is one of the key factors of the importance of Paul Wenz to Australian history.[1]

Jean-Paul and other Francophone scholars were primarily interested in Wenz as a French-Australian literary figure, a 'multicultural writer', and, more recently, a 'transnational' writer.[2] They have tended to dismiss Hettie (Harriet Annette) née Dunne and her achievements and have shown limited interest in the diverse non-literary endeavours the couple was part of, including their contributions to the pastoral, agricultural and dairy industries, and to communities along the Galari-Lachlan River. But, of course, until very recently, scholars have not had easy access to what we are now calling the 'Paul & Hettie Wenz Collection', in its new home at the Forbes Historical Museum.

As I've discovered, these volumes allow us to tell much richer, deeper, and more contextualised stories about the Wenzes' lives and legacies in ways that transcend traditional disciplinary boundaries, especially when they are augmented by personal letters, photographs and newspaper articles of the era via Trove. What I have found most intriguing are the hand-written inscriptions and annotations in the books mapping Paul and Hettie's lives and offering us glimpses into their minds and the experiences that shaped them. Hettie's inscriptions are of particular interest to me because they are allowing me to fill in some gaps in her life story: her journey from Netley, her family's vast pastoral station on the Barka-Darling River near Menindee in far-western New South Wales, to Linden, her parents John and Elizabeth Dunne's Italianate mansion in William Street, Prahran, in what is now the City of Stonnington, Melbourne; her teenage years at the exclusive ladies college, Oberwyl, in St Kilda; her first Grand Tour of Europe with her family in 1891; her second voyage in 1896 when she met Paul; the couple's marriage in St John's Anglican Church, East St Kilda; her life at Nanima; her journeys abroad with Paul, including their years in Europe before, during and after WWI and her last years at Nanima and the Pacific Hotel in Manly on the ocean beachfront.

Hettie's inscriptions have shown me, for example, that her primary family home was not Netley Station near Menindee, but Linden in Melbourne. The inscriptions have also told me that Hettie and her four surviving sisters – Sarah Jane ("Sahalie"), Mabel, Alice, and Lillian – completed their schooling at Oberwyl, a private-enterprise college established in 1878 by prominent Swiss-born artist, teacher and art patron Elise Pfund *née* Tschaggeny. Pfund and her husband James Pfund, the colony of Victoria's Surveyor General, purchased a Greco-Regency mansion, converted it into a boarding school and renamed it for Elise's hometown in the Swiss Alps. According to one of Elise Pfund's successors, Oberwyl meant 'Up at the top', a name worthy of the high hopes she held for her college and her students. The building is now a private home listed on the Victorian Heritage Register.

Oberwyl was one of many public and private schools established in Victoria after the 1872 Education Act made education compulsory for all children aged 6-15 years. It catered for girls from kindergarten to secondary level and offered a curriculum that included reading, writing, arithmetic, history, geography, mapping, nature study, scripture, French and possibly German. Classes in dancing, drama, drawing, elocution, singing, physical culture, needlework and 'charitable work' were also available.³ I have found no direct evidence that the Dunne girls attended Oberwyl while Elise Pfund was principal, however, although one of Hettie's books, *Daisy* by Susan Warner (1868), was awarded to 'H. Dunne' as a 'Prize for history, writing and arithmetic' in 1880. But was it from Oberwyl or some other school? Another of Hettie's books, *Mildred's Mistake: Still-life Study*, by F. Levien (1877) was 'Présenter à Mademoiselle Henrietta (*sic*) Dunne ... Pour le progrès dans la langue française, Françoise McDowell'. So far, I have found no evidence that this book was from Oberwyl either. *Mildred's Mistake* at least suggests that Hettie may have been a proficient French speaker by the time she met the Frenchman she would marry.

Madame Pfund sold Oberwyl in 1885 to French-born sisters Berthe Mouchette and Marie Lion after the death, the previous year, of Madame Mouchette's husband Nicolas, Chancelier and Acting Consul at the French Consulate, Melbourne.⁴

An inscription in a beautifully bound copy of *Canadian Pictures Drawn with Pen and Pencil* by the Marquis of Lorne states that this book was presented for 'general merit' on December 22, 1885. Hettie would have been sixteen at the time.

For privileged girls like Hettie Dunne, her sisters and their school friends, the 1880s in Melbourne was a time of great optimism and faith in the future: the economy was booming, new technologies were transforming everyday lives – telephones, cable cars, electric lights, hydraulic elevators, multi-storey buildings – and educated European women, such as Elise Pfund and Berthe Mouchette, were raising their aspirations way beyond the limits prescribed by their patriarchal colonial society. Circumstantial evidence suggests that both Pfund and Mouchette were also influenced by the then-emerging feminist ideals of the New Woman and passed them on, either directly or indirectly, to their students.

During these formative school years, Hettie experienced two public events that brought the rest of the world to Melbourne. The first was the Melbourne International Exhibition of 1880 held in the purpose-built Exhibition Building in Carlton Gardens. Hettie would have been eleven years old, but even at this age must have been aware that her city was hosting an event of international significance. She almost certainly saw the extravagant Exhibition Building rising from Carlton Gardens and heard her parents commenting on articles about the Exhibition in the local press – because there was no escaping the media coverage at the time. On the opening weekend, for example, all the city's newspapers and magazines published special Exhibition supplements: twelve pages in the *Age* and eight in both the *Argus* and *Leader*. Her parents would almost certainly have received invitations to concerts, balls, soirées and conferences timed to coincide with the Exhibition. Coincidentally, the Australian agents for Wenz & Co had opened offices in Melbourne, Sydney and Perth the previous year.[5]

Hettie and her family could have been amongst the thousands who attended the Exhibition opening on 1 October 1880 and were almost certainly amongst the 1.5 million visitors who passed through the doors of the venue over the following months to see the 32,000 exhibits from the 33 participating countries.[6] Melbourne journalist, banker and literary figure, Henry Gyles Turner, summed up the impact of the 1880 International Exhibition: 'much of the narrow provincialism of the colonists vanished …,' he wrote, 'and Collins Street began to take on a cosmopolitan aspect.'[7]

The books in the Forbes Collection suggest that Hettie internalised this 'cosmopolitan aspect' too and grew into it over the ensuing years.

In 1885, London celebrity journalist and 'social influencer', George Augustus Sala, coined the perfect epithet for this time and place: 'Marvellous Melbourne', – a term still used today.[8] As likely as not, however, the Dunne girls and their young friends took the marvels of these boom years for granted. How could they have imagined that all too soon, the boom would bust? But not yet. Because, in 1888, when Hettie was eighteen or nineteen, the world once again came to Marvellous Melbourne, this time to celebrate 'the Centenary of the birth of Australia'.

By now the city's population had reached nearly half a million, making it one of the largest conurbations in the British Empire. Attendances at the 1888 Exhibition well exceeded this number though. Between the grand opening on 1 August and the final day in March 1889, a total of 2,003,593 people passed through the doors, and not just for the agricultural, mining, and engineering displays. They also came for High Culture. The music program, for example, was curated and directed by English composer and conductor Sir Frederick Cowen and offered 211 orchestral concerts, 30 choral performances, and 22 concerts of popular music and opera excerpts all performed by Melbourne's new Centennial Orchestra, the precursor of today's Orchestra Victoria. A total of 467,299 people attended these events.

Hettie was still at Oberwyl at the time of the Centennial Exhibition. We know this from a copy of Bacon's *Essays* (1886) inscribed 'Hettie Dunne, Oberwyl, February 4, 1888'. But why was a Melbourne teenager reading the essays of a sixteenth/seventeenth-century philosopher, statesman, and jurist? Ah, if only the books could tell us more. Intriguingly, another of Hettie's books, *A New Method of Learning to Read, Write and Speak a Language in Six Months Adapted to the Italian,* by HG Ollendorff, revised by Charles Lapworth (1885), bears the same date as the Bacon *Essays,* but without any reference to Oberwyl. If nothing else, it tells us that Hettie had a passion for languages and was already anticipating a trip to Italy.

And there's more evidence of the Dunne girls' presence at Oberwyl in the late 1880s. An article on page 11 of the December 1890 issue of *Table Talk* magazine describes the school's annual Soiree Musicale et Dramatique. Hettie and her sister Mabel are listed as members of a violin sextet that performed "Variations" by the Romantic Prussian composer Friedrich Hermann. Mabel and another young pianist played Moritz Moszkowski's "Spanish Dance No 2" for four hands. And little sister Lillian was a 'mimosa' or wattle tree in the evening's feature event, a specially written play in French called *L'Australie-Allégorie.*

To me, *Table Talk*'s outline of *L'Australie-Allégorie* is spooky. It reveals the imperialist colonial imaginary Hettie and her sisters were imbibing at this time:

> Australia is asleep and has slept for one thousand years when one day, the Genie of the Black comes in great haste and awakes her, calling her to save her country, as strangers are invading her shores. Australia demands to see them before she judges them, and the Genie is sent to bring them to her. Then enter the Sailor, Squatter, Miner, and Farmer, each in turn telling her their purpose of coming to her lands.
>
> Australia is pleased with them, and turning to the Genie, rebukes him for not having taken better care of the beautiful land, and consents to give the new comers a trial. The representatives of some of Australia's products now enter singing and report themselves to their Queen, she in turn introducing them to their new masters, and the curtain falls on all joining in the National Hymn.

According to the *Table Talk* correspondent, 'The young performers acquitted themselves admirably, and the purity of their pronunciation was much admired.' At the end of the show, audience members demanded a repeat performance for charity, but on 'a larger stage'. By this time Oberwyl's reputation as an elite school was well-established. French composer and musicologist Oscar Comettant, who visited Australia as the French Government's representative on the 1888-89 Centennial Exhibition's judging panel and stayed on to write an account of his travels, awarded the school his highest praise:

> I do not think that anywhere in Europe there is an institution for young ladies that is better organised or more wisely directed ... Every year more stress was put upon the teaching of our language [French] ... our literature, our arts and our history ... the young Australians of St Kilda were formed in our habits of elegance without losing their native charm ... When I left Melbourne the institution had more than a hundred pupils and twenty-seven teachers.[10]

And then Hettie's school days were over. One of her books from this era, *John Halifax, Gentleman* by Dina M Mulock (1856) has several twigs of rosemary pressed between its much-annotated pages. The inscription reads 'Hettie Dunne 3/2/90 Linden'. What memories do these now-faded sprigs hold from that Summer of 1890? What was this smart young woman hoping for the rest of her life? Again, I wish the books could tell us more.

The following year, 1891, Hettie boarded the SS *Arcadia* with her family for a Grand Tour of Europe. The Collection includes many of the travel books she bought before and during the trip, as well as a volume acquired from the Officers' Library, *The Early Kings of Norway* (1875) by the Scottish essayist Thomas Carlyle. The inscription on the title page reads 'H. Dunne, R.M.S. *Arcardia*, 1891', but several stamps inside the book tell us that it came from the 'Officers Library, SS *Arcadia,* P&O S.N. Co.' (Peninsular and Oriental Steam Navigation Company). Did one of the ship's officers present Hettie with the Carlyle as a memento, or did she borrow it and forget to return it? And why Carlyle?

Other inscriptions inform us of the family's itinerary: Summer in London, Scotland, Norway, and Germany with *The Highlands of Scotland: Time & fare tables of approaches from all parts and steamer & coach routes in the district* (1890), Bennett's *Handbook For Travellers in Norway* (1890), and S. Baring-Gould's *Germany* (1890), for example. November in Venice, with John Ruskin's *The Stones of Venice I & II* (1890) and Mrs Oliphant's *The Makers of Venice: doges, conquerors, painters, and men of letters* (1889), which bears a stamp from Piazza San Marco. And Milan and Northern Italy in December, with Baedeker's *Italy: Handbook for travellers Pt 1, Northern Italy.*

By the time the Dunnes returned from Europe, Melbourne's boom years had ended. Over the next decade, the eastern Australian colonies would experience a banking crisis, economic depression, soaring unemployment, hunger, bankruptcies, class conflict, militant trade unionism, shearers' and maritime workers' strikes, ethnonationalism (white supremacism), feminism, socialism, social

Darwinism, forced relocation of First Nations communities, species extinction, rabbit plagues, drought, stock losses, land and water degradation, the Federation movement, over-exposure to Lawson and Patterson's poetry and prose ... and a measles epidemic. Tragically, it was measles that affected the Dunne family the most.

In 1893, the year the banks crashed, the measles virus killed 4% of Victoria's European population, a total of 659 people,[11] including Hettie's father. He died at Linden 'of bronco-pneumonia following measles' in September of that year leaving an estate valued at £34,360 in real estate and personal assets.[12] He bequeathed Linden and an annuity to his wife Elizabeth, a lump sum of £20,000 to his son Walter, with 'the rest divided equally amongst his other children'.[13] Two books in the Collection give us a glimpse into the mind of this man: Volumes I and II of Field-Marshal Count Helmuth von Moltke's *The Franco-German War of 1870-71*, translated by Clara Bell and Henry W. Fischer (1891), inscribed: 'John Dunne 3/10/91 Linden'. Another book, *Wilson's Tales of the Borders and of Scotland*, is inscribed: 'Hettie Dunne from Father October 13th 1887, Adelaide'.

John Dunne had been running Netley Station, often in absentia, since the death of his brother Joe in a horse accident in 1874, and the station was still formally owned by Joe Dunne's Estate.[14] The brothers had acquired Netley about 1857 after it had been abandoned for some years because of the Barkandji resistance to the invasion and colonisation of their Country.

The Dunne brothers must have felt secure by 1862, however, because, in that year, Joe married Adelaide woman Harriet Sullivan at Netley.[15] Six years later, in 1868 Hettie's father married Elizabeth Fitzgibbon, also from Adelaide, at the station.[16] Their first child, Harriet Annette, was born the following year and probably named for Joe's wife.

Joe and John Dunne had big dreams for their pastoral spread. By 1871 they had expanded its borders to encompass almost a million acres (404,700 hectares) of rangelands from the western bank of the Barka-Darling River to the South Australian border. In good seasons, the station shore over 100,000 merinos and sent hundreds of bales of wool downstream on barges towed by paddle steamers. If the Barka was low, the wool left the station by Afghan camel train. The Dunnes also ran cattle and horses and produced irrigation lucerne as fodder for their stud stock. Like other remote station operations, Netley would have been dependent on the labour of Barkindji people who stayed in the area to retain their cultural links with Country. By the early twentieth century, Netley was home to a multicultural community of some 200 people, with a store, a pub, a blacksmith's shop, a cemetery, irrigated orchards and vegetable gardens, and, eventually, a school.

Hettie retained her connections to Netley, as several books attest. *A First Latin course: Principia Latina Pt 1* (1883), for example, is inscribed on a back page: 'H&S Dunne, Netley' (the 'S' would be sister Sarah Jane). This suggests that Hettie and her older siblings might have spent their early years at Netley and attended the school across the river on Tolarno Station, or been taught by a governess, or were boarders at Oberwyl. Paul Wenz also spent time at Netley and drew on his experiences there for at least one of his novels.

The Dunne family sold Netley in 1948 to Weinteriga Pastoral Company,[17] after most of Weinteriga Station had been resumed for closer settlement. This famous station had been 'taken up' in 1852 by explorer John McKinley who sold it the following year to the Commissioner of Lands, George M Perry, and his brother AT Perry.[18]

George Perry was appointed police magistrate at Menindee and, with two troopers, probably members of the feared NSW Native Police, successfully repressed the Barkindji resistance and secured their traditional homelands for the Dunnes and other pastoralists. Barkindji leaders never gave up their struggle for their Country though.

In 1986, more than 130 years after George Perry and his brother occupied Weinteriga Station and 'pacified' the resistance, the Western Regional Land Council purchased what remained of the old station on behalf of the Wilcannia Local Aboriginal Land Council that also represents the Menindee mob. Weinteriga is now run by Barkindji people for the benefit of Barkindji people. A decade later, in 1997, Barkindji traditional owners submitted a claim through Wilcannia Local

Land Council for a vast swathe of their Country, including Netley Station and the towns of Broken Hill, Menindee, Wilcannia, Pooncarie and Dareton. Eighteen years later, in 2015, the court finally ruled in their favour in the largest native title case in the state's history. At last, the Barkindji's rights, as traditional owners, were acknowledged.[19] But it was the Barkindji people who paid the price of John and Elizabeth Dunne's privileged lifestyle: the family mansion in Prahran, the school fees for Oberwyl, the Grand Tour of Europe and Hettie's books.

Even though we can't know what Hettie and Paul would have thought about the Barkindji people land claims, we do know that they were very aware of the way the colonial system of land theft worked. Paul referred to it briefly in *Their Fathers' Land: For King and Empire*: 'We intend to kill Aborigines only as a last resort', a fictional fortune seeker confides to his journal. 'There are too many Whites who shoot them as if they were game.'[20]

**Notes:**

1. S Gapps, Assessment of Significance of the Wenz Collection of Books, Forbes Shire Council, 2005.
2. M Jacklin, 'The Transnational Turn in Australian Literary Studies', *Arts Papers,* January 2009, 1-14.
3. H Halliday, Oberwyl (extant), 35 Burnett Street, St Kilda, St Kilda Historical Society, 2022; 'Oberwyl – It "Means Up At The Top"', *Herald* (Melbourne), 1926, 10; J Brown, 'Grand St Kilda house Oberwyl for sale, offering insight to Melbourne's history', *Domain,* 23 February 2016; R Peterson, 'Oberwyl (Formerly Etloe Hall), …', *A Place of Sensuous Resort Buildings of St Kilda and Their People*, St Kilda Historical Society, 2005; 'Oberwyl, *Heritage Register: Victorian Heritage Database Report*, 2016.
4. J Drury, 'Nicolas Emile Mouchette (1838-1884 )Acting Consul de France', *Explorations,* no 20, June 1996, 13-15.
5. M Blackman, 'Wenz, Paul (1869-1939), *The French-Australian Dictionary of Biography,* 2019.
6. T Leader, 'The Melbourne International Exhibition', *Melbourne Leader*, Supplement, 1889, 1-8.
7. A Sanders, 'Less Than Six Degrees of Separation', lecture 18 May 2011, National Portrait Gallery, Australia, cited in A Hope, 'Emma Minnie Boyd. Art and Opportunity in Marvellous Melbourne', <australianarthistory.com>.
8. 'He came, he saw, he marvelled', *Age,* 10 January 2004, <theage.com.au>.
9. Royle, '"Preparing to Exhibit:'
10. O Comettant, *In the Land of Kangaroos and Gold Mines* (trans by Judith Armstrong), Rigby, Adelaide, 1980, 158.
11. PJ Dowling, '"A Great Deal of Sickness" Introduced diseases among the Aboriginal People of colonial Southeast Australia 1988-1900', PhD thesis, Australian National University, 1997.
12. Family Notices, *Herald* (Melbourne), 11 Sept 1893, 2.
13. 'Wills and Estates, *Argus,* 3 Nov 1893, 3.
14. Death of Mr J Pile. Cuthero and Netley Stations, *Barrier Miner* (Broken Hill), 1924, 3.
15. Notice in *South Australian Advertiser,* 7 June 1862, 2.
16. South Australian Register, Sat 20 Jun 1868, 7.
17. 'Netley Sold', *Chronicle* (Adelaide), 23 March 1948, 11.
18. B Arnold, 'Bindara Station: History', http://bindarastation.com/ 2021.
19. J Breen & G Coote, 'Largest native title claim in NSW acknowledges Barkandji people in state's far west', *ABC News*, Sydney, 16 June 2015.
20. Paul Wenz, *Their Fathers' Land: For King and Empire* (introduced & translated by Marie Ramsland), ETT Imprint, Exile Bay, 2018, 27.

# "Le Thé"
# Denis Wenz[1]

Nicole Wenz explique l'origine de cette nouvelle écrite par son mari :

> L'Australienne qui nous a raconté l'essentiel de la nouvelle « le thé » s'appelait madame Bon (ou Boni ?). Elle habitait Roubaix, comme nous, en 1962, parce que son mari était alors chargé de cours (d'archéologie, je crois) à l'université de Lille. Il était français et ... avait écrit des livres ...
> Comme nous avons connu et reçu beaucoup d'Australiens, je ne sais plus avec lesquels nous sommes allés dans cet émouvant cimetière de Villers-Bretonneux et là Denis a dit : « il faut absolument que j'écrive cette nouvelle » ... Il n'avait pas gardé de brouillon et je ne peux pas vous donner de date exacte ...
> (Denis Wenz 1928-2007)

### Le Thé
### (un clin d'œil à P. W.)

Young Tim était resté en France, ni à Paris, ni sur la côte d'Azur, mais quelque part entre Villers-Bretonneux et Corbie (Somme). Sa tombe ne portait pas 'connu de Dieu', bien qu'il le fût certainement. Une inscription indiquait aux hommes son nom, celui de son unité et le chiffre 1917, année de sa mort.

It avait eu peu d'amis en France, occupé qu'il était à faire la guerre. Ses parents, Old Tim et Mary, avaient pourtant reçu l'adresse d'un couple âgé qui avait logé Young Tim chez eux pendant plusieurs périodes de repos à l'arrière. Monsieur et Madame Quesnoy habitaient un village dont le nom se terminait en 'court', pas bien loin de la tombe où Young Tim prenait son dernier repos. Dans ses lettres, Young Tim les appelait Victor et Louise.

A l'autre bout du monde, du côté de Cowra en Nouvelle-Galles du-Sud, Old Tim et Mary étaient des propriétaires d'une grande ferme à moutons. Eux, leur régisseur et le personnel faisaient tourner l'exploitation : entretient des clôtures, tonte des bêtes, vente des agneaux. Ils pensaient à Tim en se levant le matin et tout au long de la journée, en particulier à l'heure du 'high tea'. Lors de la préparation rituelle de cette boisson – la théière portée vers la bouilloire, jamais l'inverse – , il leur semblait que Young Tim allait revenir des 'paddocks' pour s'attabler avec eux. Ils ne parlaient presque jamais de lui. Quand ils le faisaient, c'était tout uniment, presque avec une feinte indifférence. La peine est une rivière souterraine dans ces contrées, et le travail du deuil laisse peu de traces sur ces visages cuivrés par le soleil.

Il n'y eut cette année-là ni sécheresse mémorable, ni inondation catastrophique. L'agnelage fut bon. Si peu de temps après la guerre, le monde avait faim de laine. Les balles à forte odeur partirent à bon prix dans les aboiements du 'Wool Exchange'. Old Tim et Mary décidèrent de s'offrir un voyage 'home' puisque, comme tout le monde, ils appelaient 'chez nous' les îles où ils n'avaient jamais mis les pieds.

Une fois en Angleterre, le dangereux voyage que Young Tim avait fait vers la France (et, en sens inverse, tant de ses copains blessés, d'infirmiers, d'infirmières et d'accompagnateurs) était devenu chose facile. Ils louèrent une voiture avec chauffeur et bientôt le clocher du village de Victor et Louise se mit à paraître et disparaître à chaque pli du terrain, comme les clochers de cette région en ont l'habitude.

Accueil chaleureux. L'anglais un peu hésitant du chauffeur permettait suffisamment la conversation. L'extérieur de la maison en briques n'annonçait pas la propreté méticuleuse de l'intérieur. Le jardin ressemblait à la page d'un livre de 'leçons de choses' qui aurait montré les légumes français sous leurs meilleures couleurs. Un fourneau à charbon ronflait dans la pièce principale.

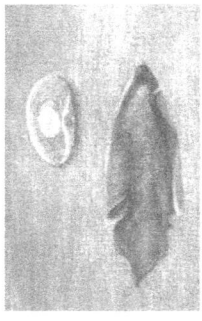

Tout bonnement et sans bruit, le souvenir de Young Tim était venu prendre sa place : la patère derrière la porte, où pendait son chapeau 'digger', le seau à pâtée qu'il portait volontiers aux bêtes, les manches retroussées pour aider à la vaisselle. On singea même gentiment son français rudimentaire.

Sachant que les 'Anglais' aiment cette potion magiquement excentrique, Louise avait acheté du thé. Elle l'avait préparé à la façon de son café/chicorée habituel et le pot était resté de longues heures sur le coin de la 'cuisinière'. Ce que peut être le résultat de cette méthode, je ne l'ai jamais su d'expérience. Il paraît que la couleur, l'amertume, la force de ce liquide peuvent faire reculer les plus courageux. Old Tim et Mary ont échangé un coup d'œil. Puis, comme ce thé avait aussi le goût de l'apaisement et de l'amitié, lentement – gorgée après gorgée, comme un nectar – ils l'ont bu. [2]

**Notes:**
1. Paul Wenz, *Their Fathers' Land: For King and Empire* (intro & trans by Marie Ramsland), ETT Imprint, 2018, 169-72; email from Nicole Wenz to Marie Ramsland, 27 September 2017.
2. Artwork, *A Quiet Presence* by Lee Zaunders, 2022 (acrylic paint on archival canvas paper).

# *Chaleureuses rencontres*

# Kevin Tang

'*Contentons-nous de dire que le théâtre, comme la Vie, est un songe, sans trop nous soucier du mensonge*', Bernard Grasset

I met Jean-Paul and Monique Delamotte in Newcastle in the 1990s during their many trips to Australia. At the time I was studying French seriously as an undergraduate as well as Latin and English literature in the Bachelor of Arts. It was a matter of local story-telling that I knew that Jean-Paul and Monique together with their Novocastrian daughter Guibourg had lived in Perkins Street Newcastle for some time in the 1970s. At the time, I wanted to study French intensely to go to France to study there. I eventually completed an Honours thesis on nineteenth-century author and poet Gérard de Nerval, a subject which I had gathered information and researched over several years. I was assisted greatly by my teachers at the time to acquire a certain amount of cultural baggage and advanced cultural understanding chiefly by Professor KR Dutton, Dr Marie Ramsland and the Marie-Laure Vuaille. To those people and to Jean-Paul Delamotte, I will always be indebted for their vision and expertise. The Delamottes had commenced their extraordinary exchange with Australian culture and literary life – that which they coined *réciprocité culturelle*.

Jean-Paul was an author in his own right in France having been published by Editions Gallimard and Plon in the 1960s when it counted and he also had his own private publishing house La Petite Maison named fondly after the small house in their back garden in Paris. Jean-Paul and Monique Delamotte offered me, over time, an ineffable access to the subtleties of French culture both literary and social. Jean-Paul was effectively a Cultural Ambassador for France and Australia for decades. I was part of the numerous Australians who were invited, welcomed warmly and entertained in their home in Paris – a vision into their world of *Réciprocité Culturelle*. Australia and its literary culture became a labour of love and devotion to Jean-Paul who spent decades forging relations between Australia and France.

In 1998 I was awarded a Hartley Scholarship to study in France under the auspices of the Kelver Hartley Foundation. My knowledge of the French language and culture were still quite academic at that time. Although I had met many French people in Newcastle and Sydney, the Hartley scholarship would give me the chance to experience the reality of the French language, to rely upon it like I would English in Australia. This cannot be underestimated as my primary goal. My language reality in French would be in France and it was vindicated there. My language reality in Australia was in the languages I spoke here. This was a cross-cultural phenomenon, which I would gradually understand as my connection to France deepened.

That year with Helen Thursby, Barbara Carruthers and Kathleen Chapman, we took the gift of the Foundation left by Professor of French Kelver Hayward Hartley (1909-1988). At the time it was one of the most generous travelling scholarships in the English-speaking world. We arrived in Paris in June of that year with what seemed to be months before any formal course of instruction was to commence; it wasn't even close to *le 15 août* – the traditional end of the French Summer holidays when schools and institutions reopened. We set about immersing ourselves in every aspect of French culture by wandering around Paris and meeting our contacts. The original circuit for Hartleians included Paris, Vichy, Nevers and Besançon. These were traditional courses taught at tertiary level with other students from Europe and around the world. The courses and teachers were of an extremely high quality and followed an old format with little interaction. I was free to study and immerse myself in France and its language, literature and culture. It was a great time in my life. I would make great life-long friends in Vichy, Besançon and Paris. Importantly, it was one of the great trips of a lifetime.

Hartleians took courses in French language and literature of various periods, phonetics, history and culture at institutions connected to the University of Clermont-Ferrand and the University of Franche-

Comté. We would acquire a certain way of speaking French having been exposed for a long period to the *débit de parole,* the way the French speak French, eg tempo, expression, vocabulary and syntax – such things can only be acquired by time and exposure to people and by reading and writing. Over time these aspects of the teaching and learning of French language have fallen by the wayside. I had been taught by teachers who valued a certain cultural literacy and sensitivity. I would also be able to gain an insight into French academic thought and structure. This was the original scholarship envisioned and implemented not only by Hartley, but by the *Centre pour l'éducation, et de documentation et du rayonnement du Français* (CPEDERF) and admirably administered by Annie and David Bancroft in Nevers in the Nievre in Central France.

***

As I recall, it was already a hot summer in Paris in June of that year. This was pre-Brexit France with the Franc and many old-fashioned institutions alive and well. We had flown via Hong Kong to Paris where we stayed for a few days. At the time I was quite familiar with Hong Kong. Soon after arriving in Paris, we made contact with Jean-Paul and Monique Delamotte.

They lived on the western edge of Paris. A short metro ride from where we were based. We were staying in the rue de Fourcy in The Marais in the *3ème arrondissement.* It was so fortunate to be there *en plein* Marais among the well-known streets – rue des Rosiers, rue des Blancs Manteaux, rue de Turenne and rue Saint-Antoine. We walked over the river to Metro Cardinal Lemoine in the heart of the Latin Quarter where we took the metro line 10 to the terminus stop Boulogne – Pont de Saint Cloud. We took the exit ramp out of the station marked *numéros impairs* – odd numbers for Ave de Lattre de Tassigny – to number 11. Like so many guests of Jean-Paul and Monique, I came to know the trajectory to their home in Paris so well as I went there on countless other occasions over time. Each time, there was a curious feeling of nostalgia for Australia – its people and events.

Monique and Jean-Paul received us warmly into their home

through the large double doors at street level into le *hall* or the entry where we walked into the house from street level up a rather grand flight of marble stairs.

It was a *hôtel particulier* in the proper sense. For at least two decades it had been an informal cultural embassy for Australians in Paris especially for Gough and Margaret Whitlam and various other Ambassadors, such was Jean-Paul's intimacy with the Australian Embassy in the rue Jean Reay at the *Palais Seidler* just near the Eiffel Tower. We settled in the *piano nobile* – the level that best captures the house and its 'feeling'; in French one would say the rooms had a more noble feel to them – height and proportions. We sat in the book-lined drawing room first with the large partners desk to one side by the window. It was high up and insulated from the street level and the general hustle and bustle. We spoke socially about different things, about our time so far in Paris. We had been to Versailles in the days before and there were a whole host of other places which we would visit: the Musées Rodin, Jacquemart-André, Nissim de Camondo, Picasso (the old museum), Cognacq-Jay, Orsay and many more. We spoke about Place des Vosges, the Tuilleries and the Luxembourg Gardens. We spoke about going to Rueil-Malmaison where Napoleon's house with Josephine was located – Le Châeau de Malmaison.

We were then ushered into the Dining room and we were served a formal dinner. The menu was: *en entrée Terrine de lièvre, en plat principal Pot au Feu* and *en dessert* was a selection of fruit and cheese. I also recall that night Jean-Paul and Monique's daughter Guibourg joined us for dinner. The conversation was about current affairs and it was enjoyable – we had just been in Australia a matter of weeks before, which Jean-Paul loved. Jean-Paul was fascinated by my background and I related to him how my family had come to live in Australia from Hong Kong in the last years of the Menzies era. Then Jean-Paul and Monique reminisced about their days in Newcastle.

We sat in the dining room with a painting by Paul Emile Chabas – a friend of Jean-Paul's family – that hung over the sideboard on one wall; it was an ethereal painting of a lady gazing over a pond with what seemed to be Wisteria blooms. The dining table at which we were sitting was where renowned Australian artist Lloyd Rees sat some years ago with Monique in the 1980s before he died. Rees was a great friend of the Delamottes. Notably, at that same dining table, the Delamottes received the Whitlams, Peter and Chantal Curtis, Peter Weir, Colleen McCullough, Geoffrey Dutton, Morris West, Patrick White, Nancy Keesing, Frank Moorhouse, David Malouf, Tim Winton, together with scores of other Australian academic, political and literary identities and figures. Also in their company were Kay and architect Brian Suters from Newcastle and Australians, academic Ross Steele and publisher Tom Thompson. Jean-Paul's hospitality was legendary over the years. Indeed, his table had also been graced by many identities in France: Jacques Chirac, Eugene Ionesco, Dominique Aury (Jean Paulhan's muse), Madame Milhaud (widow of Darius Milhaud of *Les Six* with Francis Poulenc), Lucette Destouches (Celine's widow) and many others.

As was the custom, Jean-Paul and Monique discussed and advised us as how best to follow our research interests and, whilst we were in France, to make more contacts, eg university academics and, perhaps, some authors. There were museums and libraries to visit, places of signal cultural importance. I was fascinated by a painting in the Louvre collection – *L'Embarquement pour Cythère* by Antoine Watteau. I would ultimately discuss it for a certain purpose in my Honours thesis. Jean-Paul noted that I should go to see it and also to study it *de près*. Monique had an encyclopaedic knowledge of the small private museums of Paris. Their knowledge and *savoir-faire* were invaluable. Jean-Paul advocated writing to or seeking to meet people in person or to bear witness to some phenomenon. That was his way of making connections under the rubric of *réciprocité*. This was a notion particular to Jean-Paul that is – it was an idea of social exchange of Australian culture with French culture, and ideas and perspectives were traded. He championed Australian Literature in France on the notion of *réciprocité*.

After dinner, we were invited to send a short communication by fax to Australia – a handwritten letter. The fax machine was in Monique's bookbinding studio to the left of the stairs leading up to the house. It was a wonderful idea and we each wrote a couple of short letters to our close friends and relatives. We were encouraged to stay in touch and we were invited to inscribe the *Livre d'Or* for the *Association Culturelle Franco-Australienne* (ACFA). Before we left Jean-Paul and Monique that night, we were each given some precious editions of books by La Petite Maison, Jean-Paul's private literary house, each book carefully inscribed personally to mark the occasion of the visit to Boulogne. They were in egg-shell coloured volumes much like those published by Gallimard (in France, the sign of the most serious literature) and contained pages of Australian literature, translations and poems. I was given, as gifts, over the years almost the whole production of La Petite Maison on every visit I made to Jean-Paul.

Later that year about a week before Christmas, I went back to the Delamottes. I had arranged to spend Christmas in London with some old friends. I stayed at the Studio Noël for a few days before taking the Eurostar between the Gare du Nord and Waterloo Station, which was where the Eurostar used to come into London before St Pancras Station.

In 2000, I met Jean-Paul quite by surprise one afternoon at Edgecliff Station in Sydney. Sydney had hosted the Olympics that year and Jean-Paul had left the trip to Australia until later than usual.

I saw Jean-Paul walking down the hill towards me from Ocean Street Edgecliff. It was not a cold day but Jean-Paul, who was *frileux* at the best of times, was dressed for cold weather. In the blazing hot summer in the Antipodes, a Frenchman was dressed for winter. Jean-Paul had an aversion to cold weather. I recall in the heat of the Sydney summer that year, Jean-Paul walked towards me astonished – with a beige wool scarf around his neck – and I note that each time I saw him he was dressed similarly. I recalled that Australia was *le pays du soleil brulant*. I immediately thought of Dorothea McKellar's Poem, "I love a sunburnt country…".

That day, I was on the way to see Nicholas Pounder the book-seller in Double Bay. Having had this chance encounter with Jean-Paul, we spent a short time catching up and speaking French in a café in the Edgecliff Centre. We always spoke French with a few words of English to heighten the Australian topics we covered. Jean-Paul recounted what he had done that morning: on the trip so far, he had seen the Whitlams; there was a mention of Simon Leys – known as Pierre Rykmans the Orientalist who wrote on the shipwreck of the *Batavia* – and also our mutual acquaintance Jean Chesneaux the old Sorbonne Professor of Orientalism who was also a China expert. He had been in Australia recently. There was a collection of other names who had assisted Jean-Paul in his *réciprocité* strategy including The Hon. John Spender QC and Carla Zampatti. On all of their visits to Australia, the Delamottes were on tight timetables and they would have a break in Singapore on the way back to Paris always staying at the Goodwood Park Hotel.

I must have travelled to Paris some twenty times since the Hartley Scholarship year, including the period when I was living in London.

I recall in November 2000, Jean-Paul arranged to meet me in the Quadrangle at the University of Sydney after having had lunch with Ross Steele and Angus Martin. I had commenced reading for a Law degree and was living at St Paul's College within the University of Sydney. I was asked to assist Jean-Paul in the Fisher Library to see if all of his books were noted in the catalogue collection. I recall we spent some time doing this. Jean-Paul noted that he would send any missing titles to the library on his return to Paris.

Afterwards, I took Jean-Paul for a walking tour of St Paul's College. He was curious about its history dating from the1850s. I recall walking through the college Library and showing him early editions of *The Pauline*, the college magazine, a couple of them containing photographs of Ken Dutton as the Senior Tutor in the years when the Reverend APB (Peter) Bennie (1915-202) was the Warden (1963-1985). Jean-Paul was enchanted. We then walked around the dark wooded corridors and saw some photographs of each year, also showing Ken Dutton in the late 1960s and early 1970s. We went upstairs to see the Blacket Room no 15 – which

The Hon. EG Whitlam QC occupied as a student in college. There was also a famous portrait by Clifton Pugh in the dining hall. This encounter was memorialised in Jean-Paul's book entitled *La Route de Nanima.*\*

\*\*\*

On my last occasion in Paris in 2019 in April (before the Covid 19 Pandemic and the day after the great fire of Notre Dame), I went again to the familiar house where *Atelier Littéraire Franco-Australien* (ALFA) resided, 11 ave de Lattre de Tassigny – named after one of the Maréchaux de France who fought in Indochina. The Delamottes' home in Paris had a mythical identity as an alternative cultural centre for Australians to gather, meet and socialise – thousands of Australians had come through its doors over the 40 years that Jean-Paul had deployed his notion of *réciprocité culturelle*. It was a labour of devotion and a powerful antidote to the tyranny of distance between France and the Antipodes.

I have a vivid recollection of Monique receiving me at the door, fine in stature almost bird-like. She related how devastated she felt at the great fire which had destroyed Notre Dame the day before. Notre Dame was one of the cradles of French culture and she lamented that she would never go into the same building again in this lifetime. It was the very place where the first Kings of France were coronated on the Ile de la Cité. As it happened, just the day before, I left the Hôtel Lutetia in the *6ème arrondissement*, with the unfolding disaster in the centre of Paris as a backdrop. I saw the eerie green and grey column of smoke rise above the city.

That day, Jean-Paul was in his dressing gown and slippers – *à la vieille France*. Under the house there was a book room, study which was used informally for Jean-Paul's recreation. He was reading. His eyes lit up as I walked into the room. Monique and I sat *au chevet* … it was a small, single Empire sleigh bed and Jean-Paul sat up in the bed with his knees slightly bent – in the manner of Proust almost. It was a Proustian moment. We had tea and cakes at the bedside laughing and chatting about Australian memories and events. The whole conversation was infused with memories of

Australia as we sipped on orange tea with *friandises* served by Monique. We spoke about Australia and life and the many books and photographs which surrounded him. The walls were lined with Australian works. It was a literary life which he had led, a writerly life, *romanesque* in every sense of the word, full of cultural references and his beloved notion of *réciprocité*. The Delamottes' house had become an informal Australian embassy (1970s – 2000s) and a place of some social importance for Australia – *un lieu insolite*.

In the study downstairs, Jean-Paul was surrounded by photos and memorabilia of years of *cinéma français* at MGM when he knew and mixed with the old stars of French cinema – the photographs in black and white from the 1960s and 1970s depicted: Yves Montand, Simone Signoret, Jean-Paul Belmondo and others glowering out of the frames. We spoke about Australia and all of our mutual friends and what they were doing. He inscribed another small volume from Editions La Petite Maison as a gift for me, as he had done on so many other occasions together with a photo card of Nanima, the homestead near Forbes where Paul Wenz, the early French author (originally from Reims)/grazier had lived. It was a magical moment. Australia was everywhere in that room.

That day was the last time I saw Jean-Paul Delamotte. He and Monique had stopped travelling to Australia in about 2010. It was 2019. How time flies. I left the house that day with a great sense of nostalgia, as always. I walked into the evening light. I thought to myself: Newcastle / Sydney / Paris – what a trajectory. *Belles retrouvailles … Réciprocité culturelle.*

I kept in continuous contact with the Delamottes, for a period of some 25 years as I travelled regularly to France. As it happens, I still do. At times I followed up on friends and acquaintances with whom Jean-Paul had put me in touch. In many ways I am proof of *la réciprocité culturelle* which was so dear to Jean-Paul Delamotte. *La réciprocité culturelle* engendered by Jean-Paul was a project of epic proportions which he single-handedly undertook to promote and spread for some 40 years between France and the Antipodes. It was a continuous flow of visitors, information, scholars and news. Jean-Paul Delamotte devoted every waking hour to his pursuit of réciprocité culturelle between France and Australia.

*C'était ce charme, cette richesse de culture, de humanisme et de dynamisme qui permettent de comprendre l'attrait qu'exerce l'Australie sur Jean-Paul Delamotte.*

*Vive la Réciprocité Culturelle!*


\* Jean-Paul Delamotte, *La Route de Nanima*, La Petite Maison, 2011, 217.
'*Kevin, qui a une personnalité hors du commun, avec une grande gentillesse, m'avait apporté une coupure annonçant la vente d'une autre Nanima (près de Wellington).*'

**NOTE** from Monique: '[Kevin] is a remarkable Kelver Hartley student, *fidèle en amitié.*'

# Kelver Hartley and Marguerite Yourcenar
# A Tale of Absence and Presence

## Sandi Warren

Kelver Hartley asserted his presence in my life in 2001 in the most profound way when I became the fortunate beneficiary of a Kelver Hartley Scholarship which enabled selected students at the University of Newcastle the opportunity to travel to France and undertake a course of French language and cultural studies generously funded by the Kelver Hartley Bequest Foundation. I had begun my studies of the French language in high school in the late 1960s and though there had been somewhat of a hiatus between then and recommencing my tertiary experience in Newcastle thirty years later, the passion I felt for this magnificent language was undimmed and I quickly reacquainted myself with its demands for perfection. As my studies progressed, I became enthralled by vignettes from the life of Kelver Hartley, the Foundation Professor of French at the University of Newcastle who pursued an impoverished existence in retirement in order that he might provide students with the opportunity to enrich their French experience by completing a course of study in that country, culminating in examinations and the submission of a *projet* on a topic which had particularly enticed us during our experience.

Upon my return to Australia, I felt confident that I had respected the memory of this extraordinary man and had honoured the intentions of his bequest. I was not to know then that those studies would form the genesis for a re-acquaintance years later with the Professor's spectre. Whilst convalescing from a broken leg, I was given a copy of *Mémoires d'Hadrien* – a novel by the acclaimed French writer, Marguerite Yourcenar – and, having become inextricably intrigued by her writing style, I sought to investigate the driving forces which motivated the passion underlying her literary corpus. Again, I approached the Hartley Bequest Program for assistance necessitated by international research, both at Harvard University where Mme Yourcenar's archives are held uniquely in the Houghton Library, followed by six weeks in Clermont-Ferrand, in Central France where the SIEY (Sociéte Internationale d'Etudes Yourcenariennes) is based. Extensive hours in the Houghton Library provided me with the exquisite gift of touching the pages on which she had written and corrected drafts of her many novels, poems and opinion pieces for which she was renowned and revealed for me the depths of her emotions generated by both the absence and presence of her parents as they informed her life's writings. I was also afforded the unique opportunity of a private tour of her home on Mount Desert Island, Maine, which is now a museum to her life and writing and is comprehensively curated by Dr Joan E. Howard, author of Invention of a Life, her pains-taking translation of *L'Invention d'une vie*, Josyane Savigneau's biography of Mme Yourcenar. More recently, in 2018, Dr Howard completed her account based on the powerful relation between Mme Yourcenar and Grace Frick, entitled *We Met in Paris, Grace Frick and her Life with Marguerite Yourcenar*. The two women kindled their relationship in Paris just prior to the outbreak of WWII and became life partners firstly in New York and later purchasing their Maine home where they would sit on opposite sides of a partners' desk, one writing in French and the other translating to English. It is the firm view of Dr Howard that Grace Frick was the "power behind the throne" in this often-contested relationship.

The subsequent six weeks spent at the University of Clermont Auvergne in Clermont-Ferrand provided me with access to their collection of journal articles examining the literary corpus of Mme Yourcenar together with the opportunity to attend a Colloquium convened by the SIEY on her writing, at which many international Yourcenarian experts presented papers. This research would later inform my Doctoral Thesis entitled *Marguerite Yourcenar: a Quest for Ataraxia; a locus amœnus hindered by absence and presence*, submitted in 2013. The great man, Kelver Hartley, who led such an impoverished life in order to enable his vision, was ironically the catalyst for the richness of my academic achievements, funding an incomparable pathway to unimagined opportunity. His enigmatic persona and the privations of his life have ensured that his enduring gifts enable a presence in the life of others created, by his very absence.

So, while the impact of the absent Professor Hartley is undeniable, who was Marguerite Yourcenar, whose diminutive stature belied the power of her intelligence and the forthright expression of her opinions which forged her impression into the passions of the twentieth century? Her birth in Brussels in 1903 was followed ten days later by the death of her mother from puerperal fever, which subsequently led to an unconventional life for the young Marguerite with her often errant playboy father Michel and, in his absence, her very strict and uncompromising grandmother Noémi. Michel's erudition and passion for history underpinned his persona and heavily influenced the œuvre of his daughter whose education was entirely in his hands. Yourcenar's corpus was initiated in her teens with two collections of poetry, the foundations of which lay in Greek myth, a reflection of Michel's influence. Subsequent collaboration with her father created an anagram of her birthname – Marguerite Cleenewerck de Crayencour - a pseudonym which allowed the writer's rebirth as Marguerite Yourcenar, in which guise she would create an extensive corpus, truncated by her death in 1987. Her novels are replete with the atmosphere of pervading death and darkness suffused with the motifs of antithesis: birth and death, absence and presence, past and present.

Maternal absence has been traditionally and emphatically suggested in the plethora of articles submitted as the "motor of Yourcenar's fiction" and the major catalyst for the spectres which pervade the Yourcenarian corpus. The portrait of the ideal mother, absent from the author's own life, is variously portrayed in her texts and juxtaposed dramatically by her pale counterparts who play shadowy roles to their male protagonist. Yet, it is my contention that paternal presence and/or absence as the motivating force for her writing has been a serious omission in related scholarship. Undeniably, the process of compiling the erudite opus of *Mémoires d'Hadrien* intensified her recall of Michel into proximate modernity, her identification of Michel with Emperor Hadrian being widely accepted. Discovery by father and daughter of a statue of the emperor whilst together in wartime London and later in the Villa Adriana near Rome would forever entwine the two most important males in the author's memory. Examination of the life of the author and its influence on her self-reflexive style of penmanship, evidence of which insistently underlies her texts but was vehemently denied by Mme Yourcenar, reveal the literary struggles for liberation of her memories – her subliminal quest for *ataraxia* (that state of tranquillity, free from emotional disturbance or torment wrought by memory or loss) which would ultimately be attainable only by her death; a death which terminated the life of the elusive identity once created by father and daughter, the motives of which, together with the haunting implications of the relationship between them, remain unexplained.

Yet, the connection between Hartley and Yourcenar will, for me, remain inextricable and profound – a tale of both absence and presence – an undeniable exemplification of *réciprocité*, where the Professor's dreams of instilling enduring French passion in the recipients of his bequest have resulted in my burgeoning quest for the emotional stimuli underlying a French writer's literary canon.

# Postgraduate Reminiscences
## Travis Watters

During the day, the irregular little square in front of Saint-Médard is home to a lively fruit and vegetable market, its stalls aligned in rows under pointed tent roofs. To the north the square narrows, funnelling me up the cobbled ascent of Rue Mouffetard. I pick my way past patisseries and cheese shops, organic grocers and wine merchants, dodging the wicker baskets of neatly arranged bottles encroaching on this ancient thoroughfare of the Latin Quarter. Above the shops and restaurants, I catch glimpses of beamed ceilings and book-lined walls through tall, narrow windows underscored by bright boxes of late geraniums. I am on my way to the Sorbonne for the very first time. Over the coming year I will walk this street almost every day, under the leaden drizzle of autumn, through the dark mornings of winter and into the exhilarating brightness of spring.

Having reached the top of the ambitiously named Montagne Sainte-Geneviève, I turn left into Rue Clovis, passing a chattering group of students waiting outside the great double doors of the prestigious Lycée Henri-IV. The gothic bell tower, a vestige of the medieval abbey that once stood here, is today overshadowed by the vast dome of the Panthéon, the resting place of the great and the good of France. I cross the square in front of the Bibliothèque Sainte-Geneviève, passing behind the Faculté de Droit, to emerge onto the Rue Saint-Jacques. Descending from here in a straight line towards the Seine, this street was once the north-south axis of Roman Lutetia. The modern street is dominated by the pale stone mass of the Sorbonne, its slender, oblong chimneys and domed observatory rising above the university's steeply pitched roof.

Crossing the road I reach into my bag for a folded sheet, the faint carbon-paper imprint of a hand-completed form that had arrived in my Australian letterbox three months earlier, granting me permission to enrol in a *Maîtrise* focusing on Romance Linguistics. I present this to the brightly uniformed man guarding a door midway down the building and am admitted into the sombre interior of my new academic world. The idiosyncrasies of this building will slowly become familiar to me, but for now the system of lettered staircases by which offices, library and lecture theatres are organised appears bafflingly arcane. And so I penetrate deeper into the building, choosing a corridor at random, following stairs upwards and around, turning back in the direction from which I believe I have just come, only to find myself in an unfamiliar courtyard. Gathering my courage, I approach a lady who stands smoking in the corner and ask for help. She exhales, nodding wordlessly, points to a door on the far side of the courtyard and smiles. I thank her, enter the building again through the indicated door and promptly find myself facing the office I need, the elusive *escalier* G curling up to the right.

I am in Paris as a Postgraduate Scholar on the Hartley Bequest Program. Three years earlier, as a student of French at the University of Newcastle, I had spent part of my Honours year in France on the undergraduate program funded by the same bequest. Moving between Vichy, Paris and Besançon, I had put my French to the test, researched and written my Honours thesis and fallen deeper in love with the country and culture. Now, I was a postgraduate research student at the same institution at which Kelver Hartley himself had studied. His bequest, I was gratefully aware, had again presented me with an incomparable opportunity. 'It's extremely rare to have an Australian student here,' the secretary had informed me as she stamped my enrolment papers, an observation my research supervisor would later echo.

I was under the guidance of Professor Jean-Pierre Chambon, a linguist whose passion for Gallo-Romance languages was evident and infectious. During our weekly meetings, he would at times present me with medieval manuscripts written in Occitan or Franco-Provençal, patiently encouraging me to slow down, focus and trace the calligraphic swirls of the script with my eyes until individual letters and abbreviations began to stand out. At other times he would take me to L'Écritoire, his favoured café on Place de la Sorbonne, where a collection of his colleagues and PhD students would be crowded around a table, arguing over etymology or enthusiastically debating toponymy. My research, examining the treatment of hereditary words in French lexicography, was only broadly related to their discussions, but sitting at that table facing the fountains that animated the square, with the pillared façade and dome of the Sorbonne chapel rising tall to the right, I felt gratitude for the privileged window I had been given into this world.

Classes at this most traditional of institutions were equally memorable. Gone were the whiteboards, data projectors and breeze block lecture theatres of my former places of study, replaced by the curved wooden benches, painted ceilings and muralled walls of the grand *amphithéâtres*, or the cramped, over-heated classrooms tucked up high under the roof, accessible only to the initiated and by the careful navigation of three separate staircases. Here I took notes on linguistic typology, compiled glossaries in Sardinian and translated hagiographic texts from old Franco-Provençal into French. The language that had been the focus of my study in Newcastle was now the vehicle for my learning and research.

Visits to the university library, at first intimidating, were always a source of inspiration. The stairs, curving up from the ground floor, deposited me in a vast wood-panelled reading room, the tall windows opposite giving onto the paved expanse of the *Cour d'Honneur* and ornate stone façade of the chapel. Shaded reading lamps bathed the long wooden desks in an academic glow, while the sightless busts of venerable scholars gazed down from their pedestals, inspiring a reverential hush. To access a book here was an appropriately laborious affair. Two ancient computer terminals gave begrudging access to information on the library's holdings, but if these were in use or on strike, a visit to the paper catalogue was required, the well-thumbed index cards housed in deep, narrow wooden drawers. From here a *cote* could be retrieved and copied onto a dedicated slip of paper, carried to a little window at the far end of of the room and handed to a waiting assistant. Following a short absence, the assistant would reappear either to whisper the good news that the desired book would be delivered to the reading room within half an hour, or to shake her head regretfully and inform me that my request could not be fulfilled. After my first thwarted attempt to access a specific book, I made sure always to carry a sheaf of journal articles in my bag so a trip to the library would never be wasted.

My first interaction with Paris was as a wide-eyed tourist in my second year of university. With my parents I dutifully visited the canonical sights, too overwhelmed by the size of the city and too unsure of my French to venture far beyond the tourist trail. I next visited Paris as part of the undergraduate program of the Hartley Bequest – one of four lucky students sharing a room in the Marais and the experience of a lifetime. Now, on this third occasion, Paris was my temporary home. I had a little apartment with creaking herringbone floors, a bank account and electricity bills in my name that arrived at my Left Bank address. The city was now both familiar and different. Places that held memories of family holidays and undergraduate adventures stood mere streets away from scenes of everyday life: the low-ceilinged office where I took out a health insurance policy, the narrow-fronted supermarket that opened out unexpectedly to spread over two full floors, and the condensation-obscured laundromat whose detergent perfumed half the *quartier*. To me there were now two parallel Parises.

I soon became adept at student life in the French capital, walking wherever possible, as much for the joy of moving through the city's fabled streets as for the accumulated savings, and taking my main meal at the *Resto U* student cafeteria with others aiming to stretch their budgets. Here, less than €2.50 would buy 3 courses and access to a rotating roll call of French culinary staples: *carottes râpées* in vinegar and mustard, *poulet rôti* with broccoli sautéed in garlic and little white bowls of *île flottante,* all supported by the ubiquitous baguette and generous portions of cheese. On weekends, with the university cafeteria closed, I reverted to my Anglo-Saxon roots, the multiple courses of a Gallic lunch replaced by a humble sandwich.

So comfortable was I in this rhythm of student life that spring took me by surprise. I had spent the winter engrossed in my studies, meeting with my supervisor in cafés when the inevitable strikes closed the Sorbonne and its library for weeks at a time. Suddenly I no longer walked up Rue Mouffetard in the dark, umbrella at the ready; suddenly my heavy winter coat became a burden, slung over my arm as I emerged into the spring sun and daffodils of Place de la Contrescarpe. But with the heady air of renewal came assessments, the deadline for submission of my thesis and the reality that my time in Paris was now quickly drawing to an end.

Before my thoughts could turn to packing and to what life might look like upon my return to Australia, however, a final *rendez-vous* with an unavoidable aspect of French academic life awaited me, one which I had long dreaded: the oral exam. The mystery surrounding this institution was as deep and unfathomable to me as the terror it inspired. I was therefore fretfully nervous as I knocked on Professor Lemaréchal's office door, where a small group of fellow students had gathered to wait, seemingly far less fearful than I. At the end of my assessment, a 30-minute ordeal during which I was quizzed on a broad range of issues in linguistic typology and asked to support my positions with examples, the professor put down his pen, folded his hands and looked up at me. '*Vous n'avez rien dit de faux,*' he declared with a smile. Unsure whether to take this as a compliment or consolation, I was nevertheless elated: I had completed the final requirement of my degree.

As I walked home from the Sorbonne for the very last time that day, retracing my steps along the path that was now so familiar to me, my mind wandered back over the events of the year. I had learnt a lot, both about my academic field and about myself, and had made friends with people I am still close to almost 15 years later. Harder to describe, however, was the feeling that Paris, that this part of the Latin Quarter populated by students and tourists, was now a part of me. And it is here that I still stay whenever I have the opportunity of returning to Paris, walking the familiar old streets, sitting on the *terrasse* of L'Écritoire and reliving an extraordinary year.

# In French, in English

## Marion Halligan

I have just read my two stories about Kelver Hartley, for the first time in more than a decade.* They made me tearful. For the sadness of his last years – I won't say for his whole life, he made choices and may have been happy with them. I don't want to be patronising.

But the stories are about my life too and my tears were for that also. Time passing and the sorrow of things. *Les neiges d'antan*, Doctor Hartley taught us, where are they now. I mourned the good student of French that I never was.

And yet ... I wish all those relatives and neighbours who thought that studying French was the most time-wasting and irrelevant activity they could barely conceive of were still around, to see how important it has been in my life. My French is a marvellous skill which I am proud of, though, alas, were I to write it down it would gather even more red-gilt picture frames than those proses of fifty years ago.

I have just spent two months in France, getting by very nicely. Choosing cheeses of the desired ripeness, asking the butcher for the cuts of meat I wanted – the only trick here is not to inquire the price first; like whatever brand of fashion, if you have to ask the price you can't afford it. Buying a monthly metro and bus ticket, a *carte orange*. Ringing up the Musée Rodin to ask had I left my wallet there. Dining with friends who reckon they are learning English to talk to their daughter-in-law but show little signs of it. Reading out the guidebooks while my partner drives, translating as I go.

And I have discovered where my strength lies. I still stick to the present tense, or occasionally the perfect. I still stumble, realising I have got myself into a syntactical situation I have no idea how to get out of. But there is one thing I am very good at.

Paris friends invite us to visit them at their house in Normandy. I get us on the train, changing at Lisieux. They meet us at Deauville. They are actually English, but have lived in France for thirty or forty years. Teaching at one of the Paris universities. They are bilingual, talking between themselves in whichever language comes to them in any situation. When our hostess talks to her husband about his driving it is always in French. So is her gardening. I ask her names of flowers, trees, she only knows them in French.

They drive us along the coast to Cabourg. We take tea at the grand hotel, which has a magnificent sweeping wedding-cake front to the town, and another front giving on to the promenade above the beach. We are here because this is Proust's Balbec, as posters and placards all over the place remind us. After tea we walk along the promenade, which has a number of signs, like lecterns, with quotations from Proust's novels. Proust is a writer we never read with Doctor Hartley, probably too late for him. I have read some of the novels but in English; I thought that was enough of a task. But these quotations: I begin reading them out, translating as I go, then stop, embarrassed, remembering I am with people much more proficient than I in Proust's French. But they motion me to go on, and I realise they read the French as French, do not think of it in terms of their other language. So I go on translating, and make a good fist of it, somehow I know how to get Proust's words into English. What am I saying? That finally, it is English that I am good at?

I'd like to be bilingual. I'd like to be able to construct beautiful French sentences. I'm old enough and wise enough to know that the first will never happen, and the second is unlikely. But what I can do is turn French into English, with ease and facility.

I wonder what Kelver would think of that? He knew I wrote much better essays in French than the weekly prose exercises, and he valued this talent. I know he'd deplore my lack of skills still in the writing and speaking of French – getting by was never a value of his – after all the time I have spent in France. But maybe he would appreciate this funny ability of mine to turn French speedily and smoothly into good if sometimes approximate English. And I am sure he would be pleased that France and things French have always been a huge part of my cultural baggage. I owe at least the beginnings of my rampant Francophilia to him.

Several years ago I was travelling in France with my grown-up children. We were staying in St Flour, in the high old town by the medieval cathedral. We'd eaten a marvellous dinner of aligot and other local goodies, and gone to bed early. We hadn't been asleep for very long when we were woken by the banging of nails and the whining of saws. Somebody was embarked on serious building projects downstairs. I pulled the bedclothes over my ears and prepared to go back to sleep. Not so my children. They were enraged. They couldn't possibly sleep through this. You can't make this sort of noise at night in a French town!

My son James went to school in France when he was eight, the age where language is seriously taught. He knows French grammar (and English) and his vocabulary was developed at later schools in France and French schools in Canberra. He rang up reception; she was asleep, she complained. Lucky you, said James, we're not. She couldn't do anything. She gave him the number of the police.

Instead, he went downstairs, bare-chested, barefooted, wearing only his boxer shorts. It was hot. A bunch of men were building a bar in the café next door, they wanted it finished by morning. James berated them, in fluid vernacular French, with just enough accent to make them wonder how on earth he could speak so well and not be a native. He told them it was not French to do this, that it was against the law, and if they didn't stop he would call the police. What on earth were they thinking of, he scolded.

They stopped. Next morning, when I paid the bill, the foyer was full of grumpy French people. They hadn't been able to sleep a wink for all the building noise. Not one of them had thought to go down and tell it to stop. I was very proud of my son. That's what children are for: to speak the French you can't.

At the launch of *A Toast to Dr Appleton*, *chez les* Ramsland, 2007: Dale Newman, Marion Halligan, Marie Ramsland & Carole Mandicourt

**Note:**
* Marion Halligan, *A Toast to Professor Appleton* (French translations by Carole Mandicourt; illustrated by Dale Newman), Boombana Publications, Mt Nebo, 2007, 87-90. Reproduced with permission (7 Feb 2023). The book features two short stories about Halligan's French lecturer Kelver Hartley at Newcastle University: 'Salut, Dr Appleton' and 'Vale Professor Appleton'.

# A French Village

### By Frédéric Krivine, Philippe Triboit, Emmanuel Daucé

# Suzanne Evans

*A French Village* is one of the most compelling TV series I have ever watched. I became so immersed in the drama that I felt that I had stepped back in time to share with the inhabitants of the fictional village of Villeneuve their day-to-day struggles during the German occupation of 1940 to 1945. These were ordinary people living through extraordinary times and I became one of them. My heart went out to the resistance fighters who showed unbelievable courage in their efforts to maintain their ideals, despite the pain and suffering it caused them and their loved ones. I felt the gut-wrenching sadness as I watched the inhumane treatment of Jewish men, women and children, housed in appalling conditions as they are unknowingly awaiting deportation in make-shift accommodation at the local school. I felt sheer anger for the immoral actions of the collaborators and those that sought to profit from the occupation. And I wondered what choice I would have made if confronted with the same day-to-day horrors that faced the villagers. My answer often shocked and saddened me as I realised I could never be as courageous as the village doctor, Daniel Larcher (Robin Renucci), the resistance fighter Albert (Laurent Bateau), Marie Germain (Nade Dieu) or Rita (Axelle Maricq), the Jewish mother of a tiny baby.

    The seventh and final season of the series, which jumps back and forth in time between 1946, 1975 and 2001, is equally compelling. My tears again flowed as I watched those villagers that I had come to know as they struggled with the scars of war that would remain for ever part of their lives. *A French Village* left me with a deep understanding of the deep inhumanity of war and also with a deep feeling of loss for each of the characters whose lives ended far too soon or who remained forever changed by the horrors that they had endured.

## *Un village français*

*Un village français* est l'une des séries télévisées les plus captivantes que j'aie jamais regardée. J'ai été tellement absorbée par ce drame que j'ai eu l'impression que j'étais remontée dans le temps pour partager la lutte quotidienne des habitants du village fictif de Villeneuve pendant les années d'occupation allemande de 1940 à 1945. C'étaient des gens ordinaires qui vivaient des temps extraordinaires et je suis devenue l'une d'entre eux. Mon cœur s'est serré pour les combattants du maquis qui ont fait preuve d'un courage incroyable dans leurs efforts pour maintenir leurs idéaux, malgré la douleur et la souffrance que cela a créé pour eux et pour leurs proches. j'ai ressenti une tristesse déchirante en regardant le traitement inhumain des hommes, des femmes et des enfants juifs logés dans des conditions épouvantables alors qu'ils attendaient, sans le savoir, les déportations vers les camps de la mort. J'ai éprouvé une franche colère contre les actions immorales des collaborateurs et de ceux qui ont cherché à profiter de l'Occupation. Et à plusieurs reprises je me suis demandé quel choix j'aurais fait si j'avais été confrontée aux mêmes horreurs quotidiennes que les villageois ont affrontées. Ma réponse m'a souvent choquée et attristée lorsque je me suis rendu compte que je n'aurais jamais pu être aussi courageuse que le médecin du village, Daniel Larcher, le combattant du maquis, Marie Germaine ou Rita, la mère juive du petit garçon, David.

La septième et dernière saison de la série, composée de cinq épisodes où les évènements sautent dans le temps entre 1946, 1975 et 2001, est tout aussi émouvante. Les larmes coulaient de nouveau tandis que je regardais les villageois, que j'avais appris à connaître si bien, faire face aux cicatrices mentales laissées par la guerre, des cicatrices qui resteraient pour toujours dans la vie de chacun des survivants. *Un village français* m'a permis de mieux comprendre l'inhumanité de la guerre et m'a laissé un profond sentiment de perte pour chacun des villageois dont la vie s'est terminée bien trop tôt ou qui sont restés à jamais changés pas les horreurs qu'ils avaient endurées.

# *Un village français* : a Personal Take
# Gay Bookallil

As a Francophile, I enjoy watching French films, which are usually of a high quality and which also help me keep in touch with the French language. During the recent Covid pandemic, with more time on my hands, I was encouraged to watch the television series *Un village français*. This drama, originally screened on France 3 over seven seasons, covers the German occupation during WWII of a fictional French village, Villeneuve. The series appealed particularly to me. Firstly, because I love history and historically-based drama, but also for sentimental reasons. The region of the Franche-Comté, more particularly the Jura, in eastern France was chosen for the location of Villeneuve. I had spent four months studying in Besançon the capital of the Franche-Comté and during my time there and on subsequent visits, I have toured much of the area.

Historically, *Un village français* does not deal with well-known grand events of WWII but rather with the lives, challenges and choices of ordinary citizens, in their various capacities, under German occupation. On display is the full gamut of responses, from direct retaliation, through resistance, avoidance, reluctant cooperation to full collaboration. For some, the arrival of the German army is seen as a commercial or a political opportunity, while others attempt to hold the community together through limited dealings with the enemy authority. Many just carry on quietly, hoping to ensure their own and their families' survival. All this speaks to us of the deprivation, fear, suffering, courage or self-interest of people in wartime and poses for us the question: 'How could people have endured such long and difficult years of enemy occupation?'

Colette, my landlady in Besançon, was seven years old when the occupying army arrived in the small town further east in which she grew up and where her father was the local butcher. Their shop was taken over by the invaders although, from what I understand, the family continued to live there. According to Colette, the Germans were kind to her but, even so, they were not welcome. This is borne out by the fact that her elder two brothers joined the Resistance. She had a booklet describing the undertakings of that small local band of activists. As with many such groups, lives were lost. In the booklet is described an incident towards the end of the war where members were awaiting an arms drop from an Allied plane. It seems the group was betrayed, with the resulting tragic loss of life or capture. Another story told me was that of an industrialist in the Besançon area who employed young men to help them avoid deportation and forced labour in Germany under the *Service du travail obligatoire (STO)* scheme. Many of these young men helped boost the ranks of the Resistance.

Also, while in Besançon, I visited *Le Musée de la Résistance et de la Déportation* that brought home the reality of war, its suffering and cruelty. I found it very moving, particularly the plight of the local Jewish community; so much so that, more recently, I took my granddaughter to see it. On watching *Un village français*, I remembered the photos of frightened children and their discarded belongings in that museum.

Other experiences include visits to a French friend who lived in Baunes-les-Dames in the Franche-Comté. She had chanced upon a small cemetery of US soldiers from WWII, which she spent several years researching. As she told me, she thought that the men buried there, who had come to France's aid, should not be forgotten. Then, ten years later, I joined a French group in the Jura on a week of *randonnées en raquettes*. One of our outings, which went as far as the Swiss border, gave me insight into why that part of France was a favourite escape route. Its isolation and the ease of access to the frontier were ideal although, certainly during the war, evasion was dangerous because of patrolling German forces. In the television series, there were a number of incidences where people attempted to escape across the border into Switzerland, usually with the assistance of sympathetic locals. Some succeeded but others failed, with tragic consequences.

Although *Un village français* is fictional, it appears to have relied on historical realities. Mostly, one season of ten or more episodes covers one year of the War and, as time goes on, the viewer notices the changes in both living conditions and attitudes as the inhabitants of Villeneuve adapt to their straitened circumstances and to the cruelties around them. Life continues. The final season, covering post-war recovery and retribution, is interesting. Not all cruel and self-serving characters receive their comeuppance. Some continue to thrive as they had thrived during the war. Other well-intentioned citizens, such as the mayor who tried, through minimal cooperation, to help the villagers have the bare necessities, are vilified. This, even though they had risked far more than the majority who had kept a low profile. But it all reflects real life. Another example is the local Communist leader. He, although cowardly and incompetent in opposing the Germans during the occupation, is rewarded politically, his more capable comrades having either lost their lives or their illusions. At the other end of the political divide is a wealthy, blatantly anti-Semite woman who has collaborated, often enthusiastically, with the Germans but avoids reprisals through shrewdness and influence.

I have mentioned only a few of the wealth of characters and incidents in this well-acted human story. The teachers, shop-keepers, farmers, workers, police, militia, officials, housewives and even children all have their own challenges and choices to make. And, just as the French represent a wide range of humanity, so too, among the Germans, there is goodness and evil, leaders and followers. With such a compelling series, I found it impossible not to become emotionally involved in the fate of the various individuals. For *Un village français* seemed all very real to me, not something happening in an unknown country nor to unknowable people – a most satisfying and rewarding viewing experience.

### Un village français : une perspective personnelle

En 2002, j'ai passé six mois en France pour mes études. Ce séjour et les visites ultérieures ont produit en moi un profond attachement à tout ce qui est français. Alors, quand, pendant le confinement provoqué par la Covid, une amie m'a suggéré de regarder la série télévisée *Un village français*, j'ai accepté avec enthousiasme. Cela m'a beaucoup plu, d'autant plus que j'adore l'histoire, y compris les œuvres de fiction historiques, à condition qu'elles soient bien faites et réalistes.

Une fois plongée dans le récit, je me suis vite rendu compte qu'il y avait pour moi une autre dimension, un côté sentimental et personnel. En effet, l'action d'*Un Village français* est centrée sur le village fictif de Villeneuve, situé dans le Jura en Franche-Comté. Or, c'est à Besançon, capitale de cette région, que j'ai suivi mes études. Les amitiés que j'y ai nouées, ainsi que mes visites, à l'époque et plus tard, ont contribué à mon appréciation de l'histoire locale.

Sur le plan historique, *Un Village français* ne traite pas de grands événements connus de la Seconde Guerre mondiale. Il s'intéresse plutôt à la vie, aux défis et aux choix des citoyens ordinaires, dans leurs diverses fonctions, sous l'occupation allemande. La gamme complète de réponses est présentée, des représailles directes à la collaboration totale, en passant par la résistance et l'évitement. Pour certains Français, l'arrivée des Allemands est considérée comme une opportunité commerciale ou politique, tandis que d'autres tentent de maintenir l'unité de la communauté en limitant leurs relations avec les autorités ennemies. La plupart gardent un profil bas, en espérant assurer leur propre survie et celle de leur famille. Partout, comme dans tous les pays en guerre, il y a le dénuement, la peur et la souffrance mais, en même temps, le courage ou l'intérêt personnel.

Je voudrais revenir sur les rencontres et les événements qui ont influencé mes réactions à la série. Colette, ma logeuse à Besançon, avait sept ans lors de l'arrivée de l'armée d'occupation dans un village plus à l'est, où elle a grandi et où son père était boucher. La boucherie a été réquisitionnée par l'ennemi, bien que, d'après ce que j'ai compris, la famille ait continué à y résider. Selon Colette, les Allemands étaient gentils avec elle, mais ils n'étaient quand même pas les bienvenus. En témoigne le fait que ses deux frères aînés se sont engagés dans la Résistance. Dans ma chambre, j'ai trouvé une brochure détaillant les exploits de ce petit groupe de résistants. Comme pour beaucoup de membres de ces groupes, il y a eu des morts tragiques.

    La brochure décrit un incident survenu vers la fin de la guerre au cours duquel les résistants attendaient un largage d'armes livrées par un avion allié. Il semble que le groupe ait été trahi, ce qui a entraîné la mort ou la capture de ces hommes. Ailleurs, j'ai entendu parler d'un industriel de la région qui avait employé des jeunes hommes qui, autrement, auraient été envoyés en Allemagne dans le cadre du *Service du travail obligatoire* (STO). Beaucoup de ces jeunes ont contribué à renforcer les rangs de la Résistance.

    Pendant mon séjour à Besançon, j'ai visité le *Musée de la Résistance et de la Déportation,* ce qui m'a sensibilisée aux réalités de la guerre, aux souffrances qu'elle a causées et à sa cruauté. J'ai trouvé l'exposition tellement émouvante, surtout le destin cruel de la communauté juive, que dix-sept ans plus tard, j'y ai emmené ma petite-fille. En regardant *Un village français*, je me suis rappelé les photos des enfants effrayés et leurs effets personnels confisqués.

    D'autres expériences incluent des visites chez une amie française qui vivait à Baume-les-Dames en Franche-Comté. Elle était tombée par hasard sur un petit cimetière de soldats américains, sur lequel elle a passé plusieurs années à faire des recherches. Comme elle me l'a dit, elle croyait que ceux qui y étaient enterrés étaient venus aider la France et, donc, ne devaient pas être oubliés. Puis, dix ans plus tard, j'ai fait une randonnée en raquettes dans le Jura. Une sortie, qui nous a conduits jusqu'à la frontière suisse, m'a permis de comprendre pourquoi ce coin de la France était un lieu d'évasion privilégié. Son isolement et sa facilité d'accès à la frontière suisse, un pays neutre, étaient idéaux, bien que, certainement pendant la guerre, il ait été dangereux de tenter de s'échapper à cause des patrouilles allemandes. Dans la séries, il y a plusieurs incidents où des personnes ont essayé de passer la frontière, généralement avec l'aide d'habitants sympathisants. Certaines tentatives ont réussi mais d'autres ont échoué, avec des conséquences dramatiques.

    Quoiqu'*Un village français* soit une fiction, la série semble s'appuyer sur des réalités historiques. Généralement, une saison d'une dizaine d'épisodes couvre une année de guerre. Au fil du temps, le spectateur constate la détérioration de la qualité de vie ainsi que l'évolution du comportement des villageois, au fur et à mesure que ceux-ci s'adaptent à leurs privations et aux cruautés qu'ils doivent subir. Pourtant, la vie continue et, un jour, la guerre prend fin. La dernière saison, qui traite de l'après-guerre, est révélatrice. Quelques-uns des personnages cruels, égoïstes et calculateurs ne reçoivent pas de juste punition. Ils continuent à prospérer comme ils ont prospéré pendant la guerre. D'autres citoyens bien intentionnés, comme le maire qui a essayé, par une collaboration nécessaire mais minimale, d'aider les habitants, sont dénoncés ; et ceci, bien qu'ils aient risqué beaucoup plus que la plupart de leurs concitoyens. Bien sûr, tout ceci reflète la vie réelle.

Un autre exemple d'injustice apparente est le cas du chef de la cellule communiste de Villeneuve. Celui-ci, bien que lâche et incompétent pendant la lutte contre l'ennemi, a été promu à un rôle plus important, car ses camarades plus courageux et capables ont perdu la vie ou leurs illusions. A l'autre extrémité de l'échiquier politique se trouve une femme riche et ouvertement antisémite qui, après avoir collaboré volontairement avec les Allemands, évite les représailles grâce à sa ruse et à ses amis influents.

Je n'ai mentionné que quelques-uns des nombreux personnages et incidents de cette histoire humaine bien interprétée. Les enseignants, les commerçants, les agriculteurs, les ouvriers, la police, la milice, les fonctionnaires, les femmes au foyer et même les enfants ont tous leurs propres défis et leurs décisions à prendre. De même que les rôles français représentent un large éventail d'humanité, de même, chez les Allemands, il y a de bonnes et de mauvaises personnes, ceux qui mènent et ceux qui suivent. Avec une série aussi fascinante, il m'a été impossible de ne pas m'impliquer émotionnellement dans le destin des différents personnages. En effet, *Un village français* m'a semblé réel et non pas quelque chose qui se passait dans un pays inconnu avec des personnes inconnues. Cela a été pour moi une expérience visuelle des plus satisfaisantes et gratifiantes.

# Réminiscences et souvenirs affectueux
## Emmanuelle Souillac

C'est à la fois un honneur et un plaisir d'avoir été invitée à contribuer à l'hommage à Jean-Paul Delamotte. Franco-australienne depuis l'âge de neuf ans, j'ai grandi de toute évidence dans la réciprocité culturelle. Mon père, Henri Souillac, était arrivé en Australie en 1957, comme professeur de littérature française à l'université d'Adélaïde. En 1963, il est devenu le premier Conseiller culturel de France à Canberra. Enfant, je rencontrais à la maison les étudiants de mon père, dont Colin Nettelbeck, devenu plus tard l'ami de Jean-Paul et Monique lorsque Jean-Paul enseignait à La Trobe University.

Avant de les rencontrer tous deux, j'avais pleinement vécu de merveilleux moments d'échanges culturels grâce aux tournées australiennes et aux visites du mime Marceau, du Grand Ballet Classique de France de Claude Giraud et son épouse, la danseuse étoile Liane Daydé, de la compagnie des Tréteaux de Paris dirigée par Jean de Rigaud, du flûtiste Jean-Pierre Rampal, du quatuor à cordes Parrenin, de l'écrivain Michel Butor, autant d'événements parmi bien d'autres admirablement accueillis par le public australien.

Au cours de mes études à l'Université d'Adélaïde, j'avais étudié la littérature australienne, enseignée pour la première fois par les professeurs Brian Elliott et Adrian Mitchell et je rêvais de la faire connaître en France dans les milieux universitaires.

Alors, à mon retour en Europe, lorsque mon père m'a conseillée de rencontrer Jean-Paul et Monique, je me suis retrouvée dans l'harmonie et la continuité de ce que j'avais vécu en Australie. Je suis donc devenue membre de l'Association Culturelle Franco-Australienne dès 1988. Mon mari, mes enfants et moi étions merveilleusement accueillis dans la maison de Boulogne : j'ai retrouvé en Jean-Paul la même passion pour les littératures française et australienne et leur réciprocité que j'avais pu partager en Australie auprès de mon père et de mes professeurs (Jim Cornell, Elliott Forsyth, Brian Elliott, Adrian Mitchell).

Les précieuses soirées de Boulogne où j'ai rencontré Frank Moorhouse, un des auteurs étudiés lors de mes études, et puis Tim Winton, Peter Carey, Rodney Hall, John Marsden, de jeunes auteurs à l'époque que Jean-Paul avait conviés aux « *Belles étrangères* » de 1990 à l'initiative du Centre national du Livre au centre Georges Pompidou. Jean-Paul, lui-même écrivain, avait à cœur de faire connaître sur la scène française les jeunes auteurs australiens et, en somme, mon rêve était réalisé. Ce n'était qu'auprès d'eux que je pouvais partager mon intérêt pour la littérature australienne.

A la lecture de *Sans hâte : cette nuit*, publié chez Plon en 1967, j'ai découvert Jean-Paul écrivain dont le style me fait irrésistiblement penser, dans ma culture anglophone, à Joyce et à Virginia Woolf, dans un Paris des années soixante où l'on se promène au fil des monologues intérieurs.

Je me suis délectée en lisant *Amours de rencontre,* non seulement par son style admirable, mais aussi son humour. Au fil des pages, je retrouvais tous ceux que j'avais connus dans l'Australie des années soixante et soixante-dix, ravie de découvrir un réseau d'amitiés partagées à Melbourne. S'y trouvent toutes les problématiques qui ont émaillé mes passions, mes études et mes rencontres comme le dit Jean-Paul dans *Amours de rencontre 2*, dans « … [la littérature australienne] tout n'y est pas rose, loin de là. D'abord les Aborigènes posent bien entendu (avec une énergie nouvelle) le problème de leur propre mode d'expression, qui se trouve à présent confronté à l'écriture ainsi qu'à une langue étrangère mais prodigieusement porteuse.[2]». J'ai pris conscience de cette « richesse spirituelle » lors de mes études en lisant les mythes et légendes aborigènes traduites par le poète australien Roland Robinson.

Jean-Paul mentionne Jacques et Betty Villeminot, « maîtres en l'art de voyager et d'écrire », que j'avais rencontrés en Australie et en France. Ils ont aussi fortement contribué à la connaissance de l'Australie dans leurs conférences de *Connaissance du monde*.

L'ambiance chaleureuse a favorisé des amitiés. Je suis restée en contact avec Kirsten Jeffcoat, photographe du « bush » australien, Anne Sauvêtre, traductrice d'œuvres australiennes et Christine Michel, professeure de français et spécialiste de poésie australienne.

Il y avait une connivence et une compréhension mutuelle entre personnes ayant connu et aimé l'Australie profonde. C'est chez Monique et Jean-Paul que je les rencontrais. C'est comme cela qu'un soir, lors d'un dîner, je fis la connaissance de Michèle Decoust assise à côté de moi, qui me fit l'honneur de m'offrir son livre *L'Inversion des saisons*, puisque nous avions en commun l'amour du « bush ».[2]

Des projets ont aussi été nourris par ces rencontres.

Jean-Paul et Monique furent invités en 1992 à l'ambassade d'Australie au vernissage de l'exposition « Rêveries d'enfants ». C'était un projet de peintures d'enfants inspirées par les motifs aborigènes choisis par Pamela Croft, une artiste aborigène en résidence à la cité internationale des arts que j'avais rencontrée et fais venir à Gagny où nous avions pu mener cette collaboration avec le Conservatoire. A la grande joie de Jean-Paul, l'ambassadeur, tel un « station owner », siffla très fort dans ses doigts afin d'attirer l'attention de la cinquantaine de très jeunes artistes présents, très excités devant le buffet et d'obtenir le silence pour faire son « speech » de compliments. L'ambassadeur obtint que cette exposition fasse le tour des Alliances Françaises d'Australie.

Pendant plusieurs années en plein Paris, quai des Grands Augustins, Elaine Lewis a tenu une librairie australienne dans Paris intra-muros. J'avais rencontré Elaine chez Jean-Paul et Monique, très présents dans ce projet. Tout comme Jean-Paul j'avais connu et soutenu en 1992 la première librairie purement australienne, « Cannibal Pierce », installée à Saint Denis. C'est dans cette librairie que j'avais acheté des documents anciens pour ma maîtrise.

Lors d'une des soirées merveilleuses chez Jean-Paul et Monique, comme je m'étais liée d'amitié avec Christine Michel, elle me présenta Michel Fabre, professeur de littérature anglaise à l'université de Paris III et spécialiste de littérature australienne. Quel ne fut pas mon bonheur, alors que nous discutions de mon sujet de maîtrise, quand il me proposa de diriger mes travaux. Voilà un exemple de rencontre magique qui pouvait se produire chez Jean-Paul et Monique.

La musique n'était pas en reste et ils avaient organisé un concert de musique de chambre … en quelle année déjà ?

Je ne me priverai pas d'évoquer mes deux filles encore petites jouant avec les poupées barbies de Guibourg au rez-de-jardin lors d'une soirée festive chez Jean-Paul, ni même un après-midi ensoleillé dans le jardin, une coupe de champagne à la main, pendant que Monique expliquait, devant la glycine en fleur, que les mêmes oiseaux revenaient d'une année sur l'autre.

Ces moments poétiques et pleins de charme, talents de Jean-Paul et Monique, ont ponctué les années de l'Association.

Mes souvenirs seraient incomplets, si je n'évoquais pas le soin particulier apporté à l'objet 'livre' par la maison d'édition La Petite Maison : les qualités des pages non-coupées (papier de Charente !), sa trame, sans oublier la ravissante petite gravure imprimée à l'arrière du livre représentant le jardin de Jean-Paul et Monique et la glycine. C'est un plaisir de toucher ce papier, de tourner les pages faisant de la lecture une expérience.

Ce témoignage est modeste, mais il a l'ambition de raviver les souvenirs précieux d'un passé choyé et encore proche.

**Notes:**
1. Jean-Paul Delamotte, *Amours de rencontre (2)*, La Petite Maison, Boulogne, 1993, 46-54.
2. Michèle Decoust, *L'Inversion des saisons. Une passion australienne*, Robert Laffont, Paris, 1987.

**Note** from Monique : The design on the back of La Petite Maison publications is based on this original sketch by Brian Suters. La petite maison was originally a coach house before the main house was built in 1880. We have no precise records. It was renovated and opened to Australian visitors, inaugurated on 26 April 1984 by Margaret Whitlam and her friends Claire Nicolls and Dorothy Macpherson. The first guest was Michael Thornhill; then Michael Connon, Nance Irvine ... and on and on until, '*c'est fermée le vingt neuf aout 1991*', signed Margaret Whitlam. Last visitor was Frank who wrote in the *Livre d'Or*: 'By hook or by crook I'll be last in this book'. The Ici-*Aussie* Studio was ready to take over – and Guibourg moves in *la petite maison*.

**IN ESSENCE** (G Collins) : In addition to knowing Jean-Paul very well, Emmanuelle lived a parallel life in Australia enabling her to understand more fully than most what it was that attracted Jean-Paul to our nation and its literature. The daughter of a French diplomat, she had gone to school and university in Australia where she studied and became attracted to Australian literature. Her contribution stands out because, like Jean-Paul, she returned to France but didn't leave Australia completely. It remained in her heart and she was able to feed the hunger for more by being a regular visitor to the Delamotte household. Here again is an observation of Australian culture through French eyes – it's a fascinating read.

# Jean-Paul ou la « douce obstination »
## Jean-Pierre Langellier

Un mot revenait sous la plume de Jean-Paul Delamotte : « douceur ». Ce mot semblait l'accompagner dans ses écrits autant que dans sa vie. Les hôtes de passage qui eurent la chance d'être un jour accueillis dans le chaleureux hôtel particulier familial de Boulogne, dont Monique entretient seule, désormais, la flamme spirituelle, se souviennent de cette douceur qui émanait de Jean-Paul : son regard attentif, sa parole bienveillante, son écoute respectueuse.

Cette douceur, Jean-Paul l'a logée au cœur de sa démarche, au service de son objectif, maintes fois et fièrement proclamé : la réciprocité culturelle franco-australienne. Dès lors, cette douceur devenait l'arme d'un noble combat. Un combat sans naïveté, lucide, tenace, l'incitant à défendre ses convictions avec la fermeté nécessaire. Cette « douce obstination », Jean-Paul pouvait la déployer avec l'énergie et la foi « de ceux qui aiment ce qu'ils font et tâchent de le faire de leur mieux ». Il s'apparentait alors aux personnages chers à la romancière Elizabeth Jolley, qui, rappelait-il, « disent les choses douces avec un peu de cruauté, les choses cruelles avec un peu de douceur ... »

La douceur de Jean-Paul, si assidue qu'elle fût, échouait pourtant à convaincre certains décideurs trop indifférents. Qu'importe ! Il resta fidèle toute sa vie à cette « douce illusion » – titre d'un de ses livres – qui imprégnait aussi bien son amitié de jeunesse avec le futur président français, Jacques Chirac, que son aventure culturelle franco-australienne : « Ce qui compte », confiait-il, « ce n'est pas tant l'illusion que la douceur. Et la douceur d'avoir œuvré, si peu, si maladroitement que ce soit, pour une cause aussi valable me suffit amplement. J'en suis même comblé. »

Jean-Paul était un grand modeste qui « n'aimait pas du tout dire "je" : « C'est mon défaut principal ». Il s'en moquait – « J'ai échappé à l'importance », observait-il en citant un personnage de Stendhal : « L'importance ! Monsieur, n'est-ce rien ? Le respect des sots … » Faisant sienne l'opinion d'un autre auteur français, Crébillon fils : « De toutes les vertus, celle qui dans le monde m'a toujours paru réussir le moins à celui qui la pratique, c'est la modestie. » Jean-Paul déplorait avoir subi les conséquences de son « manque d'importance » revendiqué.

Un surcroît d'outrecuidance de sa part aurait-il pu profiter à ses démarches franco-australiennes ? Jean-Paul semble l'avoir cru. Au point d'émettre quelques regrets, et même, un jour de trop grande humilité, de battre sa coulpe : « Je m'accuse ! Car j'aurais dû, en dépit des obstacles […] forcer le barrage ! » Lorsque guettait la lassitude, il s'interrogeait : Pourquoi se donner tant de mal ? Ne vaudrait-il pas mieux « arrêter les frais » ? Mais il chassait vite ses doutes : « Ma faculté d'espoir est littéralement désespérante. », à l'exemple d'un Victor Hugo qui s'exclamait : « J'ai besoin de beaucoup espérer ! ».

Alors, tant pis si ses nombreuses missives adressées à Bernard Pivot, grand manitou d'une prestigieuse émission télévisée littéraire, restaient sans réponse ! Jean-Paul poursuivait son chemin franco-australien, « sans illusions, ni découragement ». En conservant intacts, son souci de l'indépendance, et son goût pour la liberté, « cette conquête de l'esprit ». En se grisant même parfois d'un souffle d'optimisme : « Et si la beauté était contagieuse ? L'intelligence, pas la bêtise ? L'amour plutôt que la haine ? Le désir et non la froideur ? »

« Dieu que j'aime l'Australie ! » Ce cri du cœur jailli de la poitrine d'un « *aussiephile* enthousiaste », on l'entend souvent dans les écrits de Jean-Paul. Dès ses premiers pas d'éphémère *new chum* en compagnie de Monique, « l'unique », il s'était épris de « ce grand lascar de pays chaud et chaleureux », « ce bon vieux pays neuf des antipodes », « cette Extrême-Europe » dont il regrettait que son « isolement involontairement splendide » l'ait soustrait jadis à l'admiration de Châteaubriand et de Victor Hugo.

Amant de l'Australie, Jean-Paul ne cessera de vanter les qualités de son peuple – dynamisme, créativité, ténacité, générosité – mêlées d'une « sorte de fatalisme » et de « cette modestie rédhibitoire » qu'il avait diagnostiquée en lui-même. Sur les plages de Sydney, comme dans le confort ouaté de *l'Indian Pacific*, dans le silence des riches bibliothèques universitaires comme en plein *bush*, Jean-Paul se sentait *at home*.

La myopie du regard des Français sur l'Australie, trop souvent réduite à « ses kangourous et ses moutons », l'irritait d'autant plus qu'il voyait en elle « le pays le mieux à même de relayer ce qui a fait le charme de la France ». Pour mieux faire connaître à Paris la littérature et le cinéma australiens qu'il aimait, les auteurs et cinéastes qu'il admirait, Jean-Paul s'échinait à combattre les préjugés de ses compatriotes, à ouvrir des brèches salutaires dans le mur des indifférences, à nouer enfin ce dialogue « entre sourds », tant de fois dénoncé et déploré. Pour persuader les tièdes et les sceptiques – diplomates, fonctionnaires, journalistes, éditeurs, distributeurs de films – Jean-Paul avait besoin de constituer un « *lobby aussie* ».

Ainsi naquit en 1980, l'Association culturelle Franco-Australienne (ACFA). Puis, en 1995, son fils légitime, l'Atelier Littéraire Franco-Australien (ALFA). Tous deux logés, à Boulogne, sous l'enseigne bienfaitrice de *La Petite Maison*. L'association, l'atelier et la maison d'édition, Jean-Paul les tenait à bout de bras avec l'aide indéfectible de Monique. N'avait-il pas proclamé : « Je n'y peux rien, j'ai la religion du couple. « C'est beaucoup, deux ? – *Of course* ... »

« Amoureux de l'ubiquité », Jean-Paul était un voyageur heureux, toujours prêt à s'émerveiller des gens et des choses. Comme son double, Clovis, le passager de *L'Indien-Pacifique*, il ne pouvait se séparer de « son carnet à spirale et/ou de son magnétophone ». Monique veille aujourd'hui sur ces dizaines de carnets mis en ordre avec soin dans le grand bureau où Jean-Paul collectionnait ses souvenirs depuis son premier périple, une traversée des Etats-Unis à l'âge de dix-huit ans.

Car, si le cinéma, - « mon second métier, devenu une seconde nature » - lui permit de gagner sa vie, Jean-Paul était avant tout un écrivain, et se vivait comme tel. Dans *L'Indien-Pacifique*, il s'amusait à donner du métier d'écrivain, une trentaine de définitions réjouissantes.

Retenons-en trois, qui lui conviennent : « Je suis un rêveur qui tire des plans sur la comète » ; « Un artisan qui fignole de son mieux l'ouvrage quotidien » ; « Un professeur qui sait qu'il ne sait rien ». C'était un exercice de style, à la manière d'un Raymond Queneau ou d'un Georges Pérec.

Comme eux, Jean-Paul savourait les espiègleries du vocabulaire, les glissements de sens, les badinages intellectuels, les *footnotes* fantaisistes. Tout l'Eros du langage. Grand amateur de champagne, il jouait avec les mots comme avec les bulles d'une belle cuvée. Pour retrouver son souvenir, ouvrons donc un livre de Jean-Paul, avec, nous aussi, une coupe à la main!

**IN ESSENCE** (G Collins): Jean-Pierre Langellier, with all the skill of an experience journalist from *Le Monde*, grabs the reader's attention from the beginning of his contribution, using Delamotte's perfect paradox in the heading of his piece. Anyone who met Jean-Paul would be instantly charmed by his 'sweet' nature. Many though were able to observe and indeed benefit from his dogged determination to achieve the many great ideas constantly streaming through his extraordinary brain. Langellier respected his wordplays and admired this '*aussiephile enthousiaste*' and his enthusiasm for this '*vieux pays neuf*'. This is a highlight for any French speaker or French student.

# *Hommage à Jean-Paul Delamotte : éditeur, traducteur, romancier, homme de lettres*

## Hélène Savoie Colombani

Lorsqu'on apprend le décès de quelqu'un que l'on a connu et apprécié, on subit d'abord un choc, suivi d'une vague de souvenirs proches ou lointains, qui affluent spontanément à la mémoire ou que l'on doit parfois rappeler et convoquer, s'ils se sont un peu perdus au fil du temps. Quels sont ceux que l'on va privilégier ? Les traits de caractère, les qualités, voire des défauts du défunt, certaines anecdotes, ses réflexions, ou bien ses œuvres et ses réalisations professionnelles ?

Tout d'abord, j'ai gardé un souvenir émouvant du couple uni que formaient Jean-Paul et sa souriante épouse Monique, ainsi que de leur jeune fille Guibourg. Tous les deux avaient ce charme un peu désuet de la bonne société française, celle qu'on ne voit plus à présent que dans les films du passé ; j'ai en mémoire leur discrétion, leur courtoisie et ce langage châtié que l'on n'entend plus guère en France.

Nos relations furent d'abord d'ordre professionnel, et circonscrites à mes séjours australiens ou parisiens pour y organiser des salons littéraires en tant que chargée de mission pour le livre et la lecture.[2] Je l'invitais à y participer avec d'autres éditeurs. Les collections de « La Petite Maison » furent donc présentes aux expositions que j'organisai à Sydney[3] dans le superbe hall de l'Alliance Française, puis à l'Université de Sydney, en partenariat avec l'Ambassade de France en Australie, les Alliances Françaises d'Australie, les Universités de Sydney, du NSW, et de Newcastle, les ambassades de divers états francophones (le Canada, le Luxembourg, la Belgique, le Liban, l'île Maurice …), et l'Association des Auteurs Australiens (ASA). Les personnalités invitées et un nombreux public participèrent à ces semaines, d'autant plus appréciées que les nombreux francophones d'Australie ne disposaient d'aucune librairie française.

Nous avions plaisir à partager cette passion du livre qui nous animait.

Nos rencontres eurent lieu au « Salon du livre de Paris ». Avec Monique, Jean-Paul assistait aux diverses activités littéraires que nous y avions programmées. Vivant en France, il ne pouvait se rendre à nos « Semaines du livre » australiennes, mais il nous apporta son chaleureux soutien.[4] Il y consacra un article élogieux dans la revue *France-Australie*. Il était cité dans les milieux intellectuels australiens pour sa connaissance du milieu universitaire et sa maîtrise de la langue anglaise qu'il mettait au service de ses traductions.

Fidèles aux Semaines du livre de Sydney, des universitaires et écrivains australiens étaient nos amis communs : le Dr Marie Ramsland, dont le travail et les traductions de grands écrivains français sont admirables, le Professeur John Ramsland, grand historien de l'Australie, et les professeurs Ross Steele, Angus Martin, ou Maurice Blackman, spécialistes de la littérature française, pour ne citer qu'eux.

Certaines stars des Lettres australiennes comme David Malouf, de notoriété internationale, nous honoraient de leur présence. Les amitiés qui se lièrent alors se prolongèrent bien longtemps après que les Semaines du livre eurent pris fin, elles ne furent d'ailleurs pas remplacées, au grand regret des amoureux de la Littérature franco-australienne dont Jean-Paul était un ardent défenseur, qui déploraient l'absence d'une librairie ou de la presse française dans ce pôle multiculturel qu'est Sydney.

Les Semaines du livre étaient fréquentées par les Australiens francophiles à qui la Mission pour le Livre présentait les œuvres des auteurs classiques du Pacifique.[5] Des poètes et romanciers contemporains accompagnaient les exposants.

Jean-Paul et moi-même avions une même motivation : faire connaître les littératures d'Australie et du Pacifique, lui, par ses traductions et ses publications ; pour ma part, j'avais à cœur de développer un réseau d'échanges culturels autour du livre et de faire la promotion des auteurs francophones du Pacifique dont les écrits sont intrinsèquement mêlés dès l'origine à l'histoire de l'Australie, aux aléas de la colonisation pénale puis libre, aux douloureux épisodes de la guerre du Pacifique qu'ils ont subie, ou à leurs échanges de bon- ou parfois de moins bon- voisinage.

Henri Rochefort, grande figure de la Commune de Paris, expédié au bagne calédonien, s'enfuit avec la complicité des loges australiennes. Ses écrits, qui furent également édités par « La Petite Maison », portent témoignage de cette spectaculaire évasion. Les œuvres de Paul Wenz, un Français installé en Australie à la fin du 19ème siècle, furent redécouvertes grâce aux rééditions de Jean-Paul. Moins connues du public australien, les mémoires de la communarde Louise Michel témoignant du bagne calédonien où elle fut exilée plus de dix ans et des traditions orales kanak, furent révélées au public australien par des éditions françaises et des conférences.

Cependant, malgré ce succès et cette affluence, à l'instar de Jean-Paul qui ne reçut que des encouragements sans réelle reconnaissance officielle pour ses activités éditoriales, la Mission pour le Livre rencontra au fil du temps de multiples obstacles durant ces Salons, et ces événements culturels renouvelés en dérangèrent certains.
Il semble que partout, les notions de culture ou de littérature, que Jean-Paul et moi considérions comme des facteurs de rapprochement des peuples aux antipodes de l'Europe – surtout quand ils ont une origine coloniale et une histoire aussi proches – soient jalousement maintenues dans l'ombre.

Nous en avons fait l'expérience dans nos domaines respectifs, mais nous ne retiendrons que les aspects positifs de ces tentatives d'ouverture, dont le plus évident fut l'amitié et les échanges des intellectuels et des écrivains des deux pays, et les souvenirs chaleureux que nous en conservons : ainsi le très réservé David Malouf, prix Femina étranger et prix Baudelaire, que j'eus l'honneur d'accueillir grâce à José Borghino, qui était alors directeur de l'Australian Society of Authors,[6] fut notre invité d'honneur et inaugura la semaine du Livre par une conférence, avant de rencontrer le large public de ses admirateurs.

J'avais, au cours du repas qui suivit avec David Malouf et José, demandé à l'écrivain s'il comptait faire paraître un texte inédit chez un éditeur français.[7] Il n'avait pas confirmé ni infirmé, mais j'eus la surprise de recevoir dans les mois qui suivirent un petit recueil joliment traduit en français et publié par Jean-Paul, intitulé *En fin de contes*,[8] qui contenait quelques nouvelles inspirées de l'Antiquité grecque et des exploits héroïques d'Achille et d'Hector, ou des ruses de guerre d'Ulysse qualifié d'anti héros. Malouf s'y livre à une exégèse pleine d'humour des mythes de l'Iliade.

La judicieuse initiative de Jean-Paul fut d'y joindre une interview de l'écrivain par Janet Hawley, journaliste du *Sydney Morning Herald magazine* (paru le 27 mars 1993), où la finesse d'analyse le dispute à l'intelligence. Le discret Malouf – chose exceptionnelle – se confie sur son œuvre et sur lui-même, d'où le titre de l'article : « *L'imagination incarnée* ». Je citerai cet aveu de l'écrivain : « *Comme si la première qualité de l'écrivain – et peut-on espérer en fin de compte – du lecteur, n'était pas* l'imagination ».

Voici une profession de foi qui ne peut qu'emporter notre adhésion.[9]

David Malouf y dénonce aussi les tendances actuelles du monde littéraire qui consistent à n'écrire que sur soi, ce que l'on est, ou sur une expérience strictement personnelle : « *Ce qui est dévalorisé dans tout cela, ce n'est pas seulement la dimension globale des choses que nous pourrions nous efforcer de comprendre, mais le pouvoir de l'imagination* ». La faculté imaginante est à la source de toute création, et il ne fait pas de doute que l'avis des grands savants, physiciens ou mathématiciens rejoint aussi ce postulat.

Rendons justice à Jean-Paul Delamotte qui a contribué par ses traductions et ses éditions à faire connaître en France les œuvres d'écrivains australiens comme Frank Moorhouse, David Malouf, Patrick White ou Katharine Prichard, et à révéler aux lecteurs français la beauté et l'originalité de la littérature du grand continent austral,[10] qui, il faut le dire, fut longtemps ignorée des cénacles parisiens.

**IN ESSENCE** (G Collins) : In choosing to come to Australia, Jean-Paul found himself close to parts of his native country, the French Pacific region. As he was striving to make Australian literature more recognisable to French readers, Hélène Savoie Colombani was attempting to do the same thing for French literature of the South Pacific. It was inevitable that their lives would cross. Hélène's observations of the Delamotte family and their legendary home in Paris as well as Jean-Paul's support of her efforts to support the French literary world of the Pacific added to the growing recognition of French literature in our part of the world. She highlights Jean-Paul's significant exposure to Australian authors such as Frank Moorhouse and David Malouf as well as his publishing significant French writing, including Henri Rochefort and Paul Wenz. She also highlights the work of two significant people behind this publication: Dr Marie Ramsland and Emeritus Professor John Ramsland.

**Notes:**

1. Lors d'un dîner dans le cadre de leur « petite maison » de Boulogne, en compagnie d'une de leurs amies de l'Ambassade d'Australie à Paris, en 2005..
2. Auprès du Haut-Commissaire de la République en Nouvelle-Calédonie.
3. Les « *Semaines du Livre Français d'Océanie* » eurent lieu à Sydney ou à Paris de 1996 à 2006.
4. Aux Semaines du livre organisées à Sydney, Laurent De Gaulle, alors Conseiller culturel à l'Ambassade de France en Australie, apporta un concours efficace et précieux. Cette manifestation fut inaugurée par l'Ambassadeur de France en Australie et par le Président du Congrès de la Nouvelle-Calédonie.
5. Les écrivains Jean Mariotti, Paul Bloc, Georges Baudoux ou les travaux des ethnologues, Leenhardt, Guiart, des pères maristes Dubois ou Lambert, dont les travaux sont les références pour la connaissance des îles françaises d'Océanie.
6. La Société des Auteurs Australiens (ASA).
7. Seuls les grands romans de Malouf ont été traduits et publiés chez Albin Michel, à l'exception de son œuvre poétique et de ses premiers livres.
8. David Malouf, *En fin de contes, nouvelles,* éditions La Petite Maison, 1999.
9. Ma thèse d'Etat sur l'Imaginaire et les mythes kanak, et mes travaux de recherche sur l'origine et le symbolisme de la création littéraire ( cf. mon mémoire sur la création romanesque de Jean Giono), y souscrivent totalement.
10. « *La littérature australienne n'est pas secondaire, elle ne se présente pas comme un épiphénomène, un surgeon exotique des lettres anglaises. Elle est vaste, riche, singulière dans sa diversité même. David Malouf s'y dessine un domaine très personnel...* » Claude-Michel Cluny, 1995

# Life Enhancer & the Art of Reciprocity

## Margie Bryant

It has been my great fortune to have known Jean-Paul since 1994. It is impossible to recall him without Monique by his side. The complimentary way in which they embraced and enhanced my life and work is one of the greatest gifts in my life.

We met through an SBS colleague of mine and dear friend to the Delamottes, David White.

I was producing *The Book Show* at the time and we clicked over a love of Literature. I was fascinated to discuss the translations Jean-Paul had undertaken bringing Australian Literature to a French audience.

In the years following, I got to know Guibourg too and was warmly embraced by the whole family.

Socially, the Delamottes were elegant, eclectic, warm and curious, so generously sharing many of their friends, like Brian and Kay Suters with whom I've been included in so many wonderful occasions in Newcastle, Sydney and Paris.

It was because of Jean-Paul on the occasion of my being awarded a Churchill Scholarship that I included Paris in my program. I confessed to him that I could speak but a handful of words in French. Undeterred, he offered to be my translator.

I still feel the embarrassment at my total lack of French despite Jean-Paul and Monique's patient efforts to encourage me to learn! The three months at the studio in rue d'Aguesseau hold many colourful memories despite some personal challenges I experienced. I would not have endured without Monique's care and wisdom. True friendship is sealed in the tough times and, during this time, Monique's gift for love and friendship overflowed.

It was a thrill for me to be able to reciprocate in a small way in my professional arena when Guibourg came to the ABC to intern with me whilst I was the Executive Producer of the Millennium Broadcast *2000 Today*. I think John-Paul and Monique would have approved if Guibourg chose a career in film and TV given how significant a part of their lives was spent with MGM. They were always so proud of all her achievements.

I love stories Monique shared with me about her time at MGM and particularly the anecdote about Jean-Paul's assertion that Monique put the M in MGM.

He recognised early on in their relationship Monique's incredible ability to make everything right in the world. Her charm, problem solving and powers of persuasion always got the best possible outcomes.

I have sometimes felt that much of my work which has mostly been telling stories about great creative Australians has been influenced by the Delamottes.

To have French friends, who have paid so much attention to Australian culture, has enabled me to overcome a kind of cultural cringe I'm ashamed of having felt. The Delamottes' knowledge of and support for Australian artists of all kinds is legendary and their enthusiasm contagious.

I was so saddened by Jean-Paul's passing, but fortunate to have been in London at the time and able to see Jean-Paul shortly following his passing, to say goodbye and express the love I feel for him.

On my recent trip to Paris in November 2022, Jean-Paul's spirit was very present for me. A highlight of the trip was taking Monique to a concert performance by Simone Young at the Grande Salle Pierre Boulez at the Cité de la Musique, Paris, followed by supper with Simone and her husband Greg Condon. Like me, Simone and Greg were fortunate enough to spend time in the beautiful home of the Delamottes whilst Simone was on her Churchill Scholarship. My reason for being in Paris was for the making of a documentary about Simone Young. Jean-Paul was so missed. I would have loved to speak with him about my current documentary, yet another Australian artist so supported by the Delamottes.

A love for Australia, passion for learning, elegance and charm are very much alive in Jean-Paul and Monique's daughter Guibourg and granddaughter Eva.

I've had this little fantasy for some time: Guibourg for French Ambassador to Australia.

Together the Delamotte family have turned reciprocity into a powerful vision for scholarship and friendship and, as someone on the receiving end of theirs, I am **eternally grateful.**

Jean-Paul – gone but never ever forgotten.

> April 28th 1995
>
> My month in Paris has been exceptional in so many ways and I couldn't have lasted a week without the friendship and generosity of the Delamottes.
>
> I was so fortunate to have both John and Tony visit during this time and thank you so much for your kindness towards them also.
>
> There would be no better place in Paris for any Churchill fellow to be than at the Cussio so I will be advertising the association.
>
> I feel my work in Paris has been very constructive, again impossible without your assistance – here's to French Australian co-productions!
>
> Aside from professional & cultural experiences facilitated by your generosity Jean-Paul and Monique, you have given me so much more than simply what you have done, your real gift has been what you are.
>
> All my gratitude & best wishes.
>
> Margot Bryant
> (Serendipity Productions
> 107 Mill Hill Rd.
> Bondi Junction N.S.W. Australia
> FAX S.B.S c/o Geoff Barnes
> 61-2-438 1590

From *Livres d'Or*

# A series of Magic Moments
## Virginia Wallace-Crabbe

On 17 March 2018, Jean-Paul and Monique received the following letter:

Dear Jean-Paul and Monique, it would be difficult to convey to you both the richness of pleasure Virginia and I get from receiving a communication from you. While Virginia maintains an outgoing personality her lesser half (that's me) retreats daily from the real world beyond our front gate. And I will only turn 80 this year while you, Jean-Paul, happen to be 86. Wow! My almost 80 years reward me with memories predominant among which are those relating to you both and to the real France you introduced us to … Here's an aside concerning introduction … Only a couple of nights ago I was describing to a Braidwood somebody the time you two were visiting Canberra and we caught up with you having drinks in Manuka during which Monique went out into the street to enjoy a cigarette. Me, Robin, I followed her, lit up and stood out there talking to her while an aged man in shabby clothes approached. He looked so neglected. But by the time he was beside where we were standing I was able to hold out my hand and say 'Hello Joe' because I realised I knew him. Of course now, so many years later, his face might ring a bell for me but no name would follow.

Back to the next thing, and suddenly and as if from nowhere his name had turned up in my oh-so-limited brain. Straight away Joe Gullet spoke to Monique in French explaining that when young he had attended the Sorbonne etc and so on. Monique responded brilliantly. It was a kind of magic moment.

For Virginia and myself Monique and Jean-Paul, you two have created a whole series of magic moments that have glittered and gleamed in our memories ever since. Absolutely unforgotten. And so to get your email a few days ago was a wonderful gift for us both. Have a great today, a lovely tomorrow and a long time after that.

Oh yes, and I have included here a drawing I finished of the dog, Sophie, in our studio and gardening area.   Warmest wishes, Robin and Virginia

Yes indeed … all the already mentioned warmest wishes from the unmet to you two, Sophie

It all began when Robin obtained two grants in 1984 – one from the Australian Literature Board and the other from the Arts Council. This allowed him to travel overseas, make contacts and enrich his skills for nearly a year: a month in Venice, then six months as artist-in-residence in the Power Studio, rue de l'Hôtel de Ville, in the *Cité Internationale des Arts* in Paris. Here, we spent a lot of time street-wandering and gallery-visiting and when Robin was working I would take off with my cameras and do street photography, mainly for my own interest as I have always loved that aspect of black-and-white photography. (Almost gone now with the advent of digital !)

In July 1985, I was contacted by someone at Australian Consolidated Press to cover the Paris Fashion Parades for their now defunct publication *Mode* magazine. Terrified at the prospect, I felt I should accept and, with help from a photographer friend in London, I found the right Parisian contacts in the photographic world who helped me overcome a few technical problems. So for two weeks, night and day, I stood beside the catwalk with mainly dozens of men (there was only one other female!) and took thousands of photos. Selected ones  were published in *Mode Magazine Australia* soon after and the National Gallery of Australia bought 29  transparencies for their fashion department.

Our time in Paris was followed by two months 'free' accommodation in the beautiful resort town of Villefranche-sur-Mer, near Nice. It was here that Robin wrote a few travel articles for the *Age* (Melbourne) and I supplied relevant photographs. Using the pseudonym Robert Wallace, Robin also wrote his first crime novel

*To Catch a Forger*. It was published in London in 1988 by Victor Gollancz. Others were to follow and became known as the Essington Holt series: *An Axe to Grind; Paint Out; Finger Play; The Forger* and *Payday*.

Jean-Paul wrote a short biography of Robin when he chose to translate an extract of twenty pages from Robin's autobiography *A Man's Childhood* (Ch 7, ETT Imprint, 1997), "In the Shade of Young Maidens", published in *La Nouvelle Revue Française*, 2003, 213:

> À l'ombre des jeunes filles …
>
> […] j'ai été invité au bord de la mer – un autre endroit autour de la Baie de Port Phillip – sous le toit des Harwood. Ça se passait en 1952, je crois : le grand succès, cette année-là, c'était la chanson du film High Noon, avec Grace Kelly ; peut-être bien que Singing in the Rain, avec Gene Kelly, était sorti à peu près en même temps. Merveilleuse année. J'avais quatorze ans. Oh, et la Reine Elizabeth II accédait au trône d'Angleterre.
>
> Je me retrouvais dans une maison, seul avec Diane Harwood et sa camarade de classe.

We met the Delamottes while we were in the Cité. According to Monique's cahiers, we enjoyed dinners and lunches with them on several occasions in 1985 from May to October. One unforgettable occasion was recorded in a series of photographs taken on 18 August. They depict Gough and Margaret Whitlam waiting with Jean-Paul and Monique for Bus 72. It never came.

We returned to France in 1986 and 1987 and were accommodated in *la petite maison: 1 août – 4 septembre; 10-18 janvier* and *18-25 novembre.* On each occasion we enjoyed the company of other visitors and guests, notable writers, painters, publishers and academics.

**From JP's Journal**  (p 4,549)
Mercredi 25 juin 1986 : Brian nous a conduits à Newcastle par une splendide journée. Dîner chez Brian & Kay. Appelé Robin et Virginia à **Braidwood** ...
Lundi 7 juillet 1986 : Braidwood chez Robin et Virginia. Il fait froid, mais on est très bien. Près du poêle, je traduis [*For the Term of his Natural Life*] tandis que R, V, M & G sont allés voir les chevaux.  Fait 250 pages. Restent 170 pages. "*I am on the home run*" selon Virginia.
Jeudi 10 juillet :  Nous sommes invités chez John Rowland (avec Robin et Virginia); Alec Bolton qui fait de si jolis livres était là. Champagne. Après déjeuner, regardé le poème de J R que je traduis, avec lui (*Paris-Canberra*).
 Vendredi 11 juillet : Nous avons été heureux, traités en amis par R et V, très proches d'eux.
Lundi 4 août (p 4,583) :  Robin et Virginia sont à Boulogne et ...
11  janvier 1987 : Dîner hier soir ici avec Robin, Virginie, Keith Goesch, Alan Wearne, Beatrice Lewis , Serge & Ilse.
13 janvier 1987 :  Rencontre Jean-Pierre Capron (artiste peintre, vieil ami), Claude GONIN (neveu de Paul WENZ) et Robin et Virginia.

**NOTE** from Monique : We never lost the contact over the years and Virginia sends every year wombat calendars to Eva.

*Braidwood Times* (18 April 2018), 'Celebrating 60 years exhibiting', Elspeth Kernebone:

'Every time Robin Wallace-Crabbe moved, he burnt all his artwork'. Retrospective.

**Waiting for Bus 72** : 18 August 1985 – a visual narrative (6 images taken by Virginia inside the house)

**Note** from Monique: The photos of GOUGH & MARGARET were taken on 18th August 1985

    *Au menu : 2 melons,*
*3 concombres à la crème*
*Boeuf mode en gelée, haricots verts en salade*
*2 Poulets froids pochés, mayonnaise fines herbes, salade Plateau de fromage Crème au caramel, biscuits*
*2 tartes aux fruits (prunes, abricots, pêches, groseilles)*

# 'A staunch promoter of cultural reciprocity'

# Michael Costigan*

Promoting international interest in Australian creative writing became one of the aims of the Australia Literature Board when, for its first decade (1973-83), this writer administered the Board's programs as its founding Director.

From that period, Jean-Paul Delamotte and his devoted wife, muse and practical organiser, Monique Delamotte, have been our country's leading allies in advancing literary and cultural relations with France.

At a ceremony celebrating 'a fulfilled life devoted to literature, friendship an love' in the Eglise Sainte Thérèse, Boulogne, on 27 September 2019, the Australian Ambassador Brendan Berne paid tribute to Jean-Paul's action for Australian culture. Others there and elsewhere referred to him as 'a staunch promoter of cultural reciprocity' and 'a publicist and champion of Australian literature' who also made 'an immense contribution to Australian culture'.

The priest at the funeral service spoke of literature as a form of religion, because it established a link between people.

The Delamotte couple's shared passion for Australia dates from soon after their arrival in 1974 to take up tutoring under Professor Ken Dutton in the University of Newcastle's French Department. Both had worked in different areas in the cinema industry in France, but had decided to migrate when adverse workplace circumstances required them to seek employment elsewhere.

In the period 1974-76, Delamotte, an irrepressible writer himself, found that his interest in Australian literature grew and intensified. Familiar up to then with few Australian writers other than Patrick White and Morris West, he was much impressed with a new wave of fiction, poetry and drama writers, some of them emerging with government support and encouragement.

He also became fascinated by the story and work of the French-Australian grazier, station owner and fiction writer Paul Wenz (1869-1939), who had produced Australian-themed works in French and had them published in France. Jean-Paul and Monique made friendships with a number of living Australian writers too. One was Frank Moorhouse, whose work Jean-Paul much admired.

When family health problems at home meant that the couple and their young daughter needed to return to Paris in 1977, they took with them an unquenchable desire to spread their new-found knowledge of Australian culture.

To help this, they were already planning to launch their own organisation – the Association Culturelle Franco-Australienne (ACFA). Long before returning, they had made themselves known to the Australia Council and especially the Literature Board. I was to learn more about the new Association and its multiple activities on visits to France on the Board's behalf in 1979 and 1983.

Since first meeting the Delamotte family in mid-1975, we Costigans have enjoyed a cherished friendship with them. It has been nourished by annual returns to the land – where she was born – by Guibourg and her young daughter Eva.

Although needing to remain in France, where soon after returning they moved into the spacious and delightful old house in Boulogne-Billancourt inherited from Jean-Paul's parents, Guibourg's parents continued to pay frequent visits (at least twenty) to Australia until her father's health began to decline several years ago. In both countries they found ways of making their Association's work even more fruitful, through contacts, publicity, lobbying, networking, conferences and other means.

At home they were tireless and generous in welcoming the visits of hundreds of Australian authors, publishers, film-makers, artists, musicians, politicians and diplomats to what became in fact an Australian cultural centre. They also often helped visitors with low cost accommodation in small studios set aside for that purpose. When appropriate they provided opportunities for travellers to meet their

French counterparts.

Another important initiative was to adapt the small coach house at the foot of their country garden as the base of the modest publishing house they established and named Editions La Petite Maison. Over the years, they have published there numerous copies in translation of the work of many well-known and new Australian authors, as well as a few of Jean-Paul's own books.

Jean-Paul was born in Boulogne on 21 October 1931. He remembered life in France during the Second World War with his father away on active service, but he preferred to speak little about it. At 20 he himself went on compulsory service in Algeria. He later had three years in the USA, at Amherst College and Harvard, where he graduated, followed by time completing a doctorate in politics at the Sorbonne in Paris.

Among Australian leaders who admired and supported the Delamottes were Gough and Margaret Whitlam, together with the Ambassador and poet John Rowland. In her role as Honorary President of their Association, Margaret Whitlam was present when in 1992 Governor-General Bill Hayden conferred Membership of the Order of Australia on Jean-Paul.

Patience was one of Jean-Paul Delamotte's conspicuous qualities. It combined with his extraordinary erudition and what his friend Brian Suters labelled as his lovable 'Gaelic idiosyncrasies'. He thought of himself as primarily a writer, but one who accepted with equanimity the fact that a good deal of his prolific writing, including novels, short stories, non-fiction, [poems] and huge[eight]-thousand page diary, did not achieve publication or adequate recognition while he lived. He was content with the belief that its time would come and that, through it, he will live on.

\* Michael Costigan, 'Jean-Paul Delamotte 1931-2019', sent to the *Sydney Morning Herald* Obituaries editor with a few amendments added later (permission to use sent by email).

# Australian 'Cultural Attaché' in Boulogne
## Peter Collins

In the seven years I spent as NSW Minister for the Arts (1988-1995), French influence and inspiration played a significant role in how I perceived my job and its broad creative opportunities. More than any other country, the French knew how to do the Arts. Jean-Paul Delamotte was central to that process.

I had studied French through high school at Waverley College. Alliance Française and one of my best friends, Herve-Pierre Lorand, was the son of the then French Consul. The Humanities were regarded as second-rate subjects in those days at Waverley, so I did not get to study history until I got to the University of Sydney where I loved Modern and Early Modern History and developed a lifelong fascination with Napoleon.

Some of my fellow Johnsmen at St John's College where I was a student 1967-8 thought this went a bit overboard when I displayed a large *Tricolore* in my room! Not deterred, my interest in modern French history moved on to embrace the French defeat in Indochina, which gave context to the Vietnam War controversy then raging on Australian campuses, starting with Sydney University. I was by then a commissioned officer in the Sydney University Regiment and equally active in student politics – often a minority of one.

In 1980, I made my first attempts to enter politics and met another contributor to this volume, Associate Professor Ross Steele, who was then very involved in the Liberal Party in the Eastern Suburbs of Sydney. Ross was an invaluable confidant and gave good advice; he was always a strong supporter. I won preselection for Willoughby and was elected to the NSW Parliament in 1981 – the only Liberal seat won back in the renewed Wranslide of popular Labor Premier Neville Wran.

Opposition numbers were so depleted in 1981 that nearly every player got a prize. I entered Parliament as a Shadow Minister and asked to be appointed Shadow Minister for the Arts. But there is no Minister for the Arts, my Parliamentary Leader said. There will be, I replied – and so it was. Premier Wran made himself Minister for the Arts in 1984.

Fast forward to 1988: Wran had retired in 1986, the same year I became Deputy Leader of the Liberal Party, and – in Australia's Bicentennial year – we were elected into government where I took the portfolios of Health and the Arts. One of my early and most important appointments was to establish an Arts Advisory Council with Gary Simpson as Chair and Ross Steele as Deputy. Ross had been a good sounding board on the Arts policy which I took to the election.

I also learnt than Ross's father had taught mine at a tiny bush school called Manifold in the Northern Rivers district of NSW. Ross had plenty to teach me in my new role and it was he who introduced me to Jean-Paul Delamotte, so appropriate too given his senior role in French studies at the University of Sydney.

Our Bicentennial Year in 1988 saw the world come to Sydney. In no other year, before or since, have so many world leaders, heads-of-state and prime ministers come to call on Australia. When I dined with French Defence Minister André Giraud on board the helicopter carrier *Jeanne d'Arc* in Botany Bay, I urged him to send warships befitting France's Pacific history to our Naval Review scheduled for Sydney Harbour that year. Giraud sent the famous cruiser *Colbert* rather than the usual frigate or corvette. The cooler relationship resulting from French Nuclear tests in the Pacific was warming up; it was a time for renewing friendships.

In 1989 my second year as Minister for the Arts, I visited France for what became my cultural epiphany, the French Bicentennial. Ross gave Jean-Paul the brief and what came out of it for me was the realisation of so much of what Jean-Paul dedicated his life to: enriching the cultural life of Australia and deepening cultural reciprocity between Australia and France.

What follows is just part of the journey that followed through the contacts and commitment of Jean-Paul.

I was the sole representative of the NSW Government (or any other State government) in Paris to attend the astonishing spectacle passing through Place de la Concorde on the evening before Bastille Day and the impressive Militaire Parade there on Bastille Day itself. I was also invited to the opening of the new Bastille Opera House attended by World Leaders: Bush arrived by Presidential motorcade; Mitterand flew into the square by helicopter! It was his show. Somehow I got to be part of this – and Jean-Paul made it look so easy.

The people driving these extraordinary events were the French Minister for Culture in the Mitterand government and the Artistic Director of the Bicentenaire parade, Jean-Paul Goude.

It may surprise you to read that one of my role models is Jack Lang. No, not the one that Paul Keating extolled. I mean the Minister for Culture Jack Lang who served as Mitterand's cultural czar from 1981 through to 1993. He showed that you do not need to be a national leader to leave a lasting legacy. A tireless creative force who embraced the widest possible spectrum of the Arts – not just for the high-end elite. And, annoyingly to his Ministerial colleagues, a constant media presence.

I wanted to meet Jack Lang, Minister of Culture, and did in 1994 in Paris at the Hotel Meurice – it was a most enjoyable discussion. He took an encyclopaedic approach to the Arts; Fashion and design of course, but rock, punk, cartoons, circus, graffiti. The Arts are about pushing the boundaries. He did not rule things in, or out. His job was to encourage, to be a catalyst, to excel, to be noticed.

Apart from driving Le Parc de la Villette, housing Europe's largest science museum which I visited, it was Lang who completed the spectacular conversion of the Gare d'Orsay railway station beside the Seine into the Musee d'Orsay museum of nineteenth-century art which Ross Steele and I also visited; who initiated the Bastille Opera House; and – perhaps most memorably – doubled the exhibition space in the Louvre when he added IM Pei's iconic glass pyramid.

Lang had commissioned Jean-Paul Goude to set the world

standard for major public events in the Bicentennial Parade. Again, thanks to Jean-Paul Delamotte, I met with Goude well after his Bastille triumph with praise still ringing. On the night of the Tianamin Square uprising and suppression, no one will forget the thousand drummers led by bicycles with the long banner WE WILL NOT FORGET; then the world, it seemed, marching past. A full-scale Russian locomotive followed by Cossack dancers and choir. An American football field with players and grandstand crowd. Unmatched moving spectacle.

Goude himself was relaxed and really downplayed his artistic mastery. (Think COCO Vanessa Paradis. Grace Jones. Cutting edge ad campaigns.) After 1989, I guess he really didn't have to explain what he was capable of. When Minister Lang got him before President Mitterand in the run-up to the Parade, the President took in the rather formal (and nervous!) Goude presentation, then smiled. 'If you succeed in only half your projects, it will be fine'. And it certainly was.

I was fortunate to visit the Delamotte home at Avenue de Lattre de Tassigny on more than one occasion so close to the Bois de Boulogne for dinner there with Jean-Paul, Monique and their exceptionally bright daughter Guibourg. My first visit was 3 October 1992. Their beautiful home has been a cultural exchange for visiting Australians since their return to Paris from Newcastle decades ago. Attached to the main residence was a guest cottage for artists and writers including our late friend Frank Moorhouse. Always welcome.

Monique and Jean-Paul have welcomed so many, including Gough and Margaret Whitlam, with a familiarity that makes you feel it could be Lang Road, Centennial Park. A sort of ambassadorial residence, with Jean-Paul rightly decorated by the Australian government for his relentless promotion of their second homeland which – with a twist of La Perouse's fate – could have been French.

Werrington House, where I live today with my wife Jennine, is built on land granted by Governor Phillip Gidley King to his daughter in 1806. The same King who was directed by Captain Arthur Phillip to meet with La Perouse, then in Botany Bay, on 2 February 1788, ostensibly to seek advice about Norfolk Island, but really to see what the French were up to and whether they might make any claim. On the next day, King and party farewelled La Perouse – the last Europeans to see the French explorer alive. The site for Werrington House was chosen by Governor King.

In 1994, I had a special request to make of Jean-Paul: to put together a very select Arts lunch to be held at the Australian Embassy in Paris. It was a tall order. I wanted to meet renowned film director Roman Polanski and his French actress wife Emmanuelle Seigner. To my delight, Polanski accepted, but his wife was working on a film. At Jean-Paul's suggestion, I enthusiastically added Daniel Toscan du Plantier to the list – he was Director General of the leading film company, Gaumont Films.

So, on 18 July 1994, I went into the book store next to the Hotel Meurice and purchased *Polanski* by John Parker hoping that he might inscribe it for me. At the Australian Embassy next to the Eiffel Tower, we assembled for lunch and Polanski was last to arrive. He and I talked about the film industry and I told him that I was pushing for the establishment of film studios in Sydney, likely to be at a repurposed Sydney Showground close to the city. He was very supportive and keen to know more about our potential in film.

When I asked him to inscribe the Parker book, he hesitated. He hadn't read the book published the previous year, but understood that parts of it were unacceptable. 'I am happy to sign something else for you though!' And the menu sufficed perfectly. A treasured possession. Sadly though, we have not seen this cinematic genius in Australia, much less to work here.

Toscan du Plantier was also fascinating with his knowledge and experience in rebuilding cinema in France and he too was interested in the revival of our stop/start film industry. Australian talent was beginning to receive recognition, but there was a long way to go before we could claim a continuous feed of films which might find overseas markets. Like Polanski, who still faces historic US charges going back half a century, du Plantier would later be embroiled in legal controversy himself after his wife Sophie was murdered in Ireland in December 1996.

Life through the Delamotte lens was never dull. He was a set of hands always ready to help, and demanded nothing in return. He lived in Australia and found 'the Paris end of Newcastle' up on The Hill atop a city which just keeps getting better. I guess he foresaw that too.

Maybe somewhere there will be room for one of those new blue Heritage plaques to recognise Jean-Paul and Monique and their visionary partnership ambitiously styled the Association Culturelle Franco-Australienne.

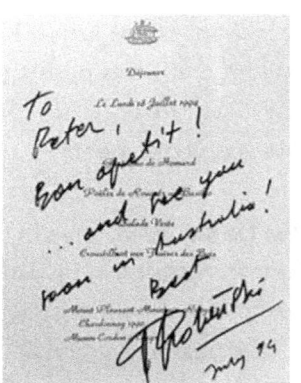

**Note** from Monique: Turning the pages of DANCESHOTS – given to me on this occasion – is a beautiful book exhibiting great talents and it was 30 years ago! I had great pleasure in recollecting the lovely time we shared with the Sydney Dance Company at our home on the 23rd March 1992.

With Peter & Dominque Collins, July 1994.

# Franco-Australian cultural exchange in mirror image: the papers of JP Delamotte and the ACFA

## Alex Byrne

Unfortunately I never had the opportunity to meet Jean-Paul and Monique Delamotte. But it is an honour to be asked to contribute to this book celebrating their achievements for both professional and personal reasons.

My love for France began as a seven-year-old Australian struggling to sleep on a *polochon* on my first brief visit to Nice. A few years later I spent school holidays with my parents in Paris and was fascinated to see the OAS slogans on railway bridges and culverts, '*L'Algérie est française et le restera*' (*Organisation Armée Secrète,* Secret Armed Organisation and 'Algeria is French and will remain so'). At the local biweekly markets, I saw the evacuated '*pieds-noirs*' trying to build new lives in the metropole selling clothes and trinkets. I didn't understand the horrors of the Algerian war of independence at that time, but it has since informed my understanding of colonialism broadly and the marks and scars it has left on Australia in particular.

Reading French literature and enjoying music and film stayed with me. Despite the distance from Australia, I was able to visit occasionally with my wife and children. But it was much later that I was able to engage with France in a professional capacity.

In 1997 I was charged with developing a new initiative on freedom of expression and free access to information (FAIFE) for the International Federation of Library Associations and Institutions (IFLA) and later elected president of that world body for libraries, librarians and information specialists. Those roles took me to Paris for meetings with colleagues and consultations at UNESCO especially during the heady years of the World Summit on the Information Society. We advanced the causes of human rights and the defence and promotion of culture in partnership with other civil society organisations including French colleagues.

An invitation to teach at a university in Lyon followed. It was a great experience, especially for eating at that city's famous *bouchons*, and the opportunity enabled me to research French library buildings.

When I was appointed as the New South Wales State Librarian in 2011, I celebrated the Library's extensive collections on the history and cultures of Australia. One of my first initiatives was to begin a mass digitisation program to make the materials more widely available and to aid their preservation. The collection is rivalled only by that of the National Library of Australia and features many treasures including the originals of some of the earliest maps and journals of the European exploration of Australia.

Among other priorities, I sought to promote and strengthen the State Library's collections relating to France including the records of the great French navigators. A highlight was the acquisition of the journal of Rose de Freycinet who accompanied her husband Louis to Sydney. She described her romantic story, including sailing disguised as a man, and the later shipwreck. Her journal demonstrated that a published version had been bowdlerised, apparently because of family sensitivities about Louis. Its promotion celebrated her achievement as the second European woman to circumnavigate the world. Her remarks on Sydney society in early colonial days are fascinating.[1]

Rose and Louis were not the first French navigators to visit Sydney. Also recorded in the Library's collections, Jean François de Galaup comte de Lapérouse arrived in Botany Bay less than a week after the First Fleet and could be said to have initiated Franco-Australian relations. He was received cordially but carefully by the British naval officers who arranged the conveyance of his last letters home before his disappearance in the Pacific.[2]

That early wariness set the tone for Franco-Australian relations. Over the following decades Australian attitudes to France and the French became little more than colonialist caricatures, generally moulded by English prejudices. The achievements of intrepid French explorers and scientists were overshadowed by anti-Napoleonic antagonism and British superciliousness. In the popular mind, France became a mélange of the cancan, couture, cuisine and champagne. After the First World War, nationalistic pride was stoked annually by repeating that *'N'oublions jamais l'Australie'* had been painted in the classrooms at Villers-Bretonneux. By the second half of the twentieth century, Australia and France were largely ignorant of each other but generally cordial.

Jean-Paul and Monique Delamotte came to Australia as tertiary teachers, but found much to inspire and inform them in the cultural ferment that followed the election of Gough Whitlam's Labor Government. When they arrived in Newcastle in 1974, prosperous but inhibited Australia was a place of creation, recently released from the inhibitions of 23 years of conservative rule. Teaching initially at the University of Newcastle and subsequently La Trobe University, Jean-Paul and Monique got to know and were welcomed into the burgeoning literary and film worlds. Jean-Paul loved the new Australian films, reviewing several for publications in France.[3]

The Delamottes maintained their strong interest in Australia following their return to France in 1977 and committed themselves to deepening cultural relations. They established the Association Culturelle Franco-Australienne (ACFA) in 1980 to foster cultural exchanges between the nations. A publishing house, La Petite Maison, was founded in 1983 to promote Australian literature in France. And they provided a studio, also called *La petite maison*, to host Australian visitors who shared their broad cultural interests.

As the New South Wales State Librarian I was privileged to accept the records of the Association Culturelle Franco-Australienne. Generously donated by the Delamottes, who also transferred the copyright to the State Library of NSW, the collection comprises some four metres of textual material, photographs and ephemera.[4] It includes correspondence with a host of Australian writers, academics, researchers and journalists. They include Nancy Cato, Donald Horne, Colleen McCullough, Phillip Adams, Alan Brissenden and Frank Moorhouse. Margaret and Gough Whitlam were strong supporters of the Association and frequent visitors to Jean-Paul and Monique. The collection also includes material relating to Paul Wenz, a French writer who improbably lived near Forbes in New South Wales from 1898 to 1939. Publication of his works in English and bringing him to the attention of Australian readers was a passionate project of Jean-Paul.

The papers form a treasure trove for researchers interested in the evolution of Australian cultural production since the mid-1970s. The Delamottes' deep and abiding interest in Australian writers, film makers and artists and the warmth of their hospitality are evident in the letters and other records. The influence they had on their guests is reflected in the friendships that were formed and in the works that were produced. Their commitment helped to foster a truly independent Australian cultural life, discarding the 'ties of Empire' that had shackled it to British models and expectations. And, of course, it deepened the relationship between Australia and France.

The warmth and strength of that relationship has been demonstrated in the heartfelt reactions of Australians to traumatic events in France including the outrages perpetrated in Nice, at the Bataclan and on *Charlie Hebdo*. For the last, I expressed our solidarity with France and its principles in an aquatint edition *Je suis Charlie* (see illustration), one of which I sent to Jean-Paul and Monique.

Thankfully the relationship between our nations also survived Prime Minister Scott Morrison's abrupt and inept cancellation of a contract for French submarines in favour of an Anglosphere alliance. President Macron's abrupt 'I know' in response to a journalist asking whether Morrison lied could have presaged a long-lasting antagonism But, fortunately, the election of a more considered Prime Minister and the underlying respect and friendship between France and Australia have allowed our nations to move on. The Delamottes' dedicated fostering of that relationship has contributed to our enduring *amitié*.

Jean-Paul and Monique Delamotte's shared passion for Australia has been mirrored in my lifelong attachment to France and French culture. That attachment has enriched my life but, except for some professional engagement, has mostly been a personal matter.

The Delamottes' four decades long support for Franco-Australian cultural exchange has been much more substantial, enriching the lives of many Australians, especially French friends and colleagues, and deepening cultural relations between our two nations. I am proud to have played a part in bringing their papers home to Sydney.

**Notes**:

1. Freycinet, Rose de (c1820). *Journal particulier de Rose pour Caroline (September 1817-October 1820)*. State Library of New South Wales SAFE / MLMSS 9158 vol 1. https://www2.sl.nsw.gov.au/archive/curio/exhibit/1260/indexc833.htlm

2 Robert J King, 'What brought Lapérouse to Botany Bay?', *Journal of the Royal Australian Historical Society*, vol 85, pt 2, 1999, 140-7.

3 Tom Thompson, (2020). 'Jean-Paul Delamotte (1931–2019)', *The French Australian Review*, no 67, Australian Summer 2019-2020, 67-74. https://www.isfar.org.au/wp-content/uploads/2020/02/67_JEAN-PAUL-DELAMOTTE-OBITUARY.pdf

4 State Library of NSW (nd), Archive of the Association Culturelle Franco-Australienne, 1975-2015. MLMSS 9740. <https://archival.sl.nsw.gov.au/Details/archive,110375609.

*Je suis Charlie* – Alex Byrne, aquatint, 2015.

# Pour rendre hommage ...

## Ilona Kiss

*Pour moi, le livre-objet forme un pont entre les belles traditions du livre classique et le monde de l'art contemporain. C'est un moyen de concrétiser une abstraction par l'art.*
*Le livre-objet parle une langue visible. C'est ma langue, c'est mon histoire, c'est mon voyage sur notre planète.*

**Versicules 2** mini-poèmes (4), 2011, technique mixte sur fond aquarelle
**Versicules** : *à l'instar des poètes japonais – traduction d'une vision, d'une image, d'une pensée.*
      C'est le dernier livre **vu** par Jean-Paul Delamotte.
*Bookwarm*, poème de Jean-Paul Delamotte, 2019, technique mixte sur tissu, VI exemplaires reliés; élastique, papier de verre, Paris 2019.

« Bookwarm »*

*Qui nescit userus tamen audet fingere; quidni? / Il n'y connaît rien … pourtant il fait des pas* ? (Horace, *Art poétique*, 382)

La nuit tombe et je pense aux livres que j'ai lus
Il me semble ce soir avoir lu tant de livres !
Le détail de chacun, je ne m'en souviens plus
Mais je leur dois à tous le soin que j'ai de vivre !

\* *Jeu de mot*: bookworm = *rat de bibliothèque*; bookwarm = *passionné des livres*.

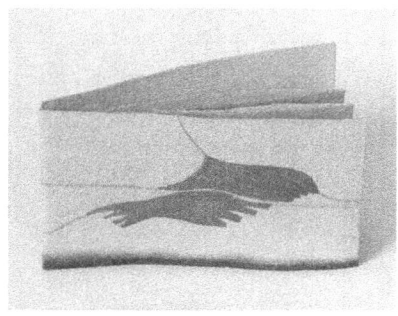

'Plutôt deux fois qu'une' (2014)

'Message de Sydney' (2016)

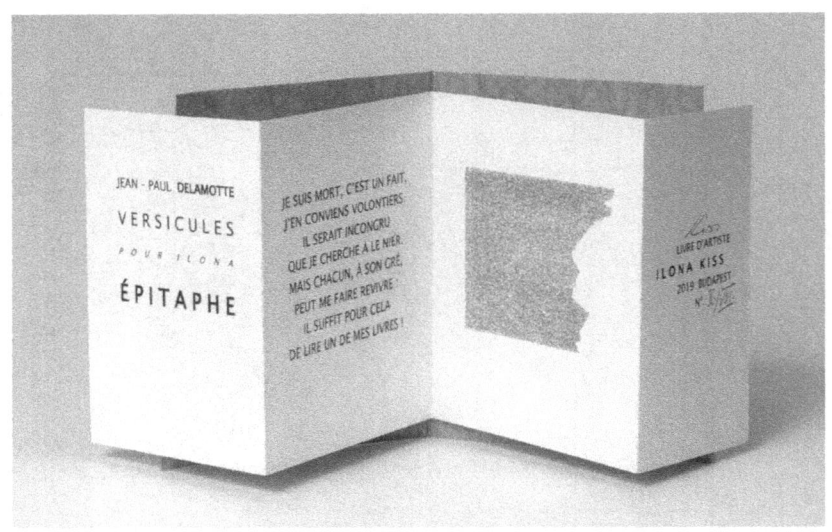

*Atelier Ilona Kiss rend hommage par ses livres à Jean-Paul Delamotte qui nous a quitté en 2019. Il était écrivain, traducteur, cinéaste, éditeur. Le couple Delamotte a fondé « La Petite Maison – ALFA (Atelier Littéraire Franco-Australien) » pour leurs publications. Jean-Paul Delamotte, le Littérateur, grand ami de la bibliophilie et des livres d'artiste a laissé ses traces … Mes livres répondent : merci !*

**IN ESSENCE** (G Collins) :  Swiss-born contemporary artist Ilona Kiss, uses her artistic flair to produce books, including some of Jean-Paul's poetry in an artistic form. It is her way of paying homage to him. The result is artistic beauty that is a wonderful tribute to a man who did so much for the French and Australian literary worlds.

# DO YOU REMEMBER

## By Monique

Do you remember? It always began, do you
Remember? How it was …

Excerpt from VERANDAHS for Monique Delamotte, by Robert Brissenden, in the *Bulletin, Centenary Issue,* January 29, 1980, 159.

I had mentioned to Robert how impressed I had been after the discovery of 'Rosemount', a beautiful homestead and he offered me this beautiful poem as a gift. Thank you, dear Robert.

Et MERCI MERCI MERCI MERCI MERCI MERCI MERCI MERCI MERCI, **CHERS AMIS NOVOCASTRIANS :**
Professor Ken Dutton (Guibourg's godfather) who welcomed us at the **University of Newcastle**; the French Department : Jan Rubenach, Colyn Whitehead who welcomed us at the station and loved Baudelaire; Norman Million (Medievalist who taught us where to find the story of 'Guibourg'); Kath Dockrill; Gay Reeves … and Mrs Regan …

**Perkins Street :** Mr GRUG (Ted Prior), Nan & Chesney Gardner, Helen Mansfield (our babysitter), Jill Johnston who organised our moving into N° 35 and mentioned the name of 'this French writer Paul Wenz' on the Saturday of our arrival! The Fenton-Smiths, famed artist Aldona Zakarauskas … They all made our life enchanting and easy. Opposite side at N° 33 lived Jan whose house welcomed us on our arrival day and later in December 1978.

On The Hill, **Wolfe St**, our dear friends Kay and Brian always welcoming us at (or driving ) us to the airport. Over the years, we became one – the same family. They visited La Milesse in 1977[1] where they stayed in the 'Grand Hotel' ! and Andelu … We holidayed at

Boomerang and created the 'Society of Defense of the Bidet' and drove together for our first visit – how memorable – to NANIMA ... and all the way to Uluru through Kakadu National Park and Darwin. Fond memories.

Kim and Margie Ostinga whose lovely home welcomed us; Carol Carter and Allan Chawner whose beautiful book ***Chartres*** is dedicated to Jean-Paul; Julian Ward, who gave birth to our lovely daughter, Guibourg, at the Royal Newcastle Hospital with a view on the Ocean, on Victory Day!

**And do you remember ...?**

I remember Philip Short who helped JP collect our trunks at the station – it was on the Monday, the very day we moved into N° 35, sitting on the trunks and Philip opened a bottle and we toasted with a good Hunter Valley bottle, our first taste of Australian wine.

**I remember ...**

Charlie Goffett and Joy, Michael Taper and Mr Lynch (his famous Hunter River prawns), Mr & Mrs Doyle (their horse was called "Chirac"!) and Mr & Mrs Knight (our good butchers).

This was the life **in Newcastle**: Hunter street and, of course, there was David Jones! And Mr BRUCE's shop on the other side ...

And in these days, we never locked the front door. It remained open to welcome a friend walking up the steep street or a student for a cuppa tea.

Further away at **Toronto,** by the Lake, there was a talented artist who taught me engraving techniques: Patricia Wilson who lives with Phil Adams in a beautiful home where orchids have found an Eden.

**Do you remember?**

Yes, I remember Paul Kavanagh's visit in Paris particularly. Paul was working on his project 'Heloise & Abelard'. Early that Saturday morning, we set off and while walking around Notre-Dame, in a very tiny street, a gate opens just when we are passing. JP speaks solemnly to the priest who closes the gate silently behind us and, across a small garden, leads us to the secret chapel where Heloise and

Abelard were secretly married. So emotional was this sacred moment forever engraved in my soul. Back on the street, we remained speechless for quite a while A high spiritual experience it was. We were just so lucky ...

**Do you remember?**

Yes, I remember the warm hospitality of the BRUCE family at NANIMA,[2] the delicately set tables with candelabras. John and Barbara were so happy to show us the homestead built by Paul WENZ, his irrigation system still working, walk us to Madame's woods and every room inside beautifully furnished. Jean-Paul was taking notes – this was Paul's *bibliothèque*, etc – the wine cellars (unique). Guibourg learned to drive on the property when she was 14!

Such fond memories. Thank you dear John and Barbara for welcoming us many times.

Cf *LA ROUTE DE NANIMA*. A la découverte de Paul Wenz – 4 Feb 2008 : *Inauguration de la rue Paul Wenz à Reims*.

**Do you remember?**

Yes, I remember SYDNEY and our gentle hosts Gough and Margaret,[3] who invited us so often to share a fine lunch and literary conversations together with Ross [Steele] and Frank [Moorhouse].

They loved French culture, Aix en Provence, Latin and Greek. So did Jean-Paul.

Gough called himself "Edouard" and "Marguerite"! to sound more French.

I have a red little tin box here which once contained meringues from Dalloyau, a gift from Margaret who, on her visit to Boulogne, said to me: 'It's like bringing coal to Newcastle'! In confidence, I treasure that little tin box like an ingot.

When *POETRY AUSTRALIA*[4] was launched at the Embassy in 1984 under the auspices of Gough, then Ambassador to UNESCO, I presented to Gough his Latin dictionaries repaired and dressed with a new binding. He was so grateful and pleased. (lovely photo here in J-P's Studiolo with Ken and Guibourg) ...

I remember Margaret's contribution in the DOUBLE BUSH BINDING exhibition.[5] She translated one of the Paul Wenz' stories

'Charley' from French into English. Our artist-painter friend, Daniel Pata, made the lovely engravings that enhance the exceptional quality of this limited edition book.

Yes, I remember our Kirribilli friends, **Margaret and Michael Costigan**, unfailing friends over the years. We shared happy times and sobbed together shattered by a dreadful tragedy.

I am forever grateful to Michael for the Obituary he wrote in the *Sydney Morning Herald*. *Merci cher* Michael.

**Anne et Daniel Pata** often travelled to Europe and never failed to visit us. Artist painters, art lovers, they always enriched the conversations with their discoveries. Daniel was very involved in the PENS & PENCILS Society and some of those artists visited in Boulogne.

Anne studied Delacroix in Paris (Place Furstenberg) and Iso Rae. We visited Etaples together to meet Jean-Claude Lesage, the author of this beautiful book *Peintres australiens à Etaples*.[6]

On her last visit, Anne was in a wheelchair pushed by Daniel. She never complained and still enjoyed the Paula Modersohn exhibition at the Musée d'Art Moderne we discovered together. She died soon after in Sydney and I remember Daniel's fatal call on 7 February 2017. She was a fair lady. God bless her soul.

**Tom Thompson and Elizabeth Butel** are long-time friends. Angelica was a baby when they first came to Boulogne. She is now the mother of two little ones and Tom and Liz have naturally turned grandparents!

I remember Jean-Paul and Tom discussing a Paris-Sydney Link or Sydney-Paris Link and Tom materialised the idea with the publication of *The Thorn in the Flesh*,[7] the launching of which took place on 18 January 2005 in the presence of Margaret Whitlam.

Tom's decision to create ETT IMPRINT was a major step forward. He has since published, dedicated to Jean-Paul's memory, *THEIR FATHERS' LAND* (translated from the French by Marie Ramsland) – *Le Pays de leurs pères*; *DIARY OF A NEW CHUM* (translated by Maurice Blackman, Patricia Brulant and Margaret Whitlam; notes by Jean-Paul); *A CORAL EDEN* (translated by Maurice Blackman), *Le Jardin des Coraux*.

Thank You, dear Tom, for remaining faithful to Jean-Paul's memory.

**Sydney** was also Patron of the Arts **Susie Carleton** who welcomed us first at Riverview and later at the Belleview. Around large tables *l'intelligentia* were sitting and expressing new ideas, the food and the good wine were contributing to joyous exchanges and great spurs of laughter to which Frank Moorhouse never failed. Susie made the place magic and a famous intellectual meeting place.

**Do you remember?**

Yes I remember Nance Irvine, Nancy Cato, Nancy Keesing and Mark Hertzberg and Lloyd Rees and his family who visited us and whom we visited in **Hobart** on the way to **Port Arthur** (JP was translating Marcus Clarke's *For the Term of His Natural Life*. Port Arthur – unlike the Belleview! – is the resting place of so many condemned souls, it requires silence. When we were visiting the Museum and watching what remains of the original film, Jean-Paul engaged a quiet conversation with the gentleman by his side: 'I am the French translator of Marcus' book' and this gentleman, unable to keep the secret, revealed it to the audience and approximately 20 people applauded!

**Do you remember?**

Yes, I remember ... on the way south, I remember **Braidwood,** the home of **Robin and Virginia Wallace-Crabbe**, their horses and the wombat and the dog. The lit fire place and Robin's laughs and good jokes. His atelier and painted artworks. Virginia was a professional photographer and she took this series of 6 photos. Memorable clichés we owe Virginia. Part of History now. Thank you Virginia – when Gough and Margaret had lunched in Boulogne and were in front of the house waiting for the No 72 bus to take them back to the Embassy. It was on a Sunday, the bus was long to arrive, after 20 minutes of chatting on the sidewalk, we see Gough and Margaret waving back at us and walking to the Metro !

**Do you remember?**

Yes, I remember Melbourne and the Windsor Hotel where we would meet friends, writers and academics Patricia Clancy, Colin Nettlebeck and Colin Thornton-Smith, all devoted to the Study of Franco-Australian Links.

"Reciprocity"[10] by Jean-Paul Delamotte
'Book Review' by Patricia Clancy

Melbourne, city of famed *Chloé* by Jules Lefebvre proudly exposed in the Jack & Jackson pub where we discovered her. Jean-Paul made it the setting of his novel *Un Dimanche à Melbourne*.

I remember the kindness of Joanna Murray-Smith and Ray Gill inviting us to visit Nita's home, and how Jean-Paul was moved discovering Stephen's beautiful library and writing environment.

I realise it is time for me to close and read again 'RECIPROCITY'. *Vive la Réciprocité culturelle !*

Thank you Dr Marie Ramsland who initiated this project as a tribute to Jean-Paul 's work.

(in **Reciprocity**, 32-3: 'Thanks to our visitors, Paris (or rather Boulogne ...) has provided us ... with both a foretaste and an aftertaste of Australia, culturally speaking Monique and I would probably never have met on friendly terms so many talented Australians if we had remained in our little niche in Australia ... At home, we have had a great (Aussie) life. Limiting myself to one memory ... I treasure the evening when Bob Brissenden came to dinner, bringing instead of flowers or wine his poem "Verandahs", dedicated to Monique ...'

> They don't build houses like that anymore – not
> With verandahs the way they used to : wide verandahs
> Running round three sides of the place, with vines
> Growing up the posts and along the eaves – ...
> ....
> That's where the talking happened – over a cup
> Of tea with fresh sponge cake and scones, or a drink
> ....
> On Sunday afternoons or warm dry evenings:
> Do you remember, it always began, do you
> Remember? ...

Shall we gather under the shade of Nanima's verandah in memory of Paul Wenz, Jean-Paul and Bob Brissenden, writers and poets who above all loved beauty and reciprocity.

\*\*\*

Our motto was *AMOUR et LABEUR*. Both fulfilled our lives.

Jean-Paul's last words to me: 'JE SUIS HEUREUX, JE SUIS COMBLE'.

He accomplished so much.

In memory of Jean-Paul: Long Live French-Australian Cultural Reciprocity!

I am grateful to Ross who spent an afternoon with me in November and, of course, thank you on behalf of Jean-Paul to Marie Ramsland and John, her husband, to the friendly contributors who remember Jean-Paul's generosity to the cause of French-Australian Cultural Reciprocity which was a lot of work and sometimes led to some frustration when doors remained closed despite his efforts.

**Notes**:
1. La Milesse (Sarthe) is my grandparents' village. Our then apartment, rue Vital, was occupied by Serge Doubrovsky. Kay & Brian visited us with Richard & Stephen. At the time, it was a rather sad looking village. It is not the case today!
2. NANIMA is now a National Trust Home.
3. Jean-Paul Delamotte, *GOUGH et MARGARET, Hommage d'un ami français à Gough et Margaret, Australiens par excellence,* La Petite Maison, 2010.
4. *Poetry Australia*, no 94/95, 1984, *French Poetry Now*, collected and translated by Kenneth Dutton.
5. Initiated by Sabine Pierard (Bookbinding Exhibitions Australia), rallied in Paris by M, the exhibition visited Tokyo (through the Bookbinding Tokyo Club whom I knew), went to Reims (Paul Wenz' native city) and to Forbes where Frank joined us and made a speech. It was a major success. I made a special binding for Margaret's copy; A grateful gesture towards a dear lady.
6. *Australian Painters in Etaples* is the translated version from French by Pauline Le Borgne. Published by ETT IMPRINT A Sydney-Paris Link Publication in memory of Jean-Paul D.   Thank you dear Tom. I know how much you loved Jean-Paul.
7. *L'Echarde*, Paul Wenz, translated in English by Maurice Blackman.
8. In *LA ROUTE DE NANIMA*, 328 : '*L'écrivain australien que j'aime et j'admire entre tous ; l'ami qui m'a permis de découvrir la qualité de la vie "en littérature" à Sydney*'. Frank could not have hoped for a finer pen. (M note)
9. CB Thornton-Smith, 'The Delamotte Phenomenon – Cultural Reciprocity', *Explorations,* no 24, April 1999, 6-16.
10. RECIPROCITY for John Rowland in The Kelver Hartley Fellowship Address, 1997.

# Contributors:

**Solène Anglaret** is a speaker, author and entrepreneur. Founder of Be Beyond Borders, she has published four books, including travel memoir *Where to Next?* Her books are inspired by her extensive travels and insatiable quest for home and belonging.

**Linda Barcan**, BA (French & English, Hons), with spoken and singing voice performance and pedagogy at the NIDA and the Sydney Conservatorium. She has performed in art song recitals Australia-wide, in France, Germany and South-East Asia, including frequent concerts in French cultural and diplomatic circles. For nine years, she lectured at the Western Australian Academy of Performing Arts. She is a lecturer (Voice) at Melbourne Conservatorium of Music.

**Virginie Bauer** is a French translator, an English teacher and an equestrian journalist. She co-founded and co-directed FROGZ, a Franco-Australian film production service (1989-1996) and has been writing articles and books about horses in France and abroad.

**John Beach** is a retired primary school principal with a lifelong love of French language and culture, inspired by watershed moments with his charismatic high school French teacher. He was Chief Editor of *To Climb the Hill*, Newcastle East Public School, 2016, launched by former prime minister Julia Gillard.

**Maurice Blackman**, PhD, was Head of the Department of French at the University of New South Wales and Director of the French-Australian Research Centre of the university. His principal translations of Paul Wenz, all published by ETT Imprint, are *Diary of a New Chum* and other lost stories (1990 and 2018); *The Thorn in the Flesh* (2004 and 2018); and *A Coral Eden* (2021).

**Gay Bookallil** is a retired Pharmacist who, as a mature-age student, was able to follow her special interests in History and Languages, graduating with a BA Hons (French) at the University of Newcastle.

**Margie Bryant** is a documentary film maker in Sydney, owner and Managing Director of Serendipity Productions, a boutique company making factual stories for TV and occasionally cinema.

**Alex Byrne**, PhD, AM, FALIA, *Chevalier de l'Ordre des Arts et des Lettres*, a retired librarian, university vice-president, researcher and writer, now focusing on printmaking. His career took him to leadership roles at universities across Australia and culminated as the CEO of the State Library of New South Wales, Sydney. Internationally, he contributed to the establishment of FAIFE, through

IFLA's advocacy at the World Summit on the Information Society, as president of IFLA and in facilitating the consideration of Indigenous matters, a lifelong concern.

**Allan Chawner**, PhD (Fine Arts), retired as Associate Professor from the University of Newcastle in 2011. Allan produced photographic exhibitions which have been shown in galleries in Australia and internationally. He and his wife Carol Carter published a book in 2022, *Spirit of Place – Aboriginal Sites of the Hunter Region*, with Aboriginal elder Warren Taggart. The book will be featured in a major exhibition in the new Singleton Art Gallery, NSW.

**Gerry Collins** is a former ABC sports broadcaster, whose recent memoir, *A Fortuitous Foray into France*, tells of his experiences as an exchange student at the University of La Rochelle. He had earlier written the memoir of Australian Test cricketer Andy Bichel. In 2012 he interviewed Jean-Paul Delamotte on ABC Radio Newcastle and visited him later that year at his Parisian home.

**Peter Collins**, AM, KC, was NSW Minister for the Arts 1988-95. Since leaving parliament in 2003, he has served on several public boards; established Barton Deakin Government relations; chaired Industry Super Australia and currently President of the Powerhouse Museum – the largest NSW cultural project since the Sydney Opera House.

**Hélène Savoie Colombani,** PhD en Lettres et Sciences Humaines, poète, écrivain, essayiste et conférencière, est Conservateur en chef des Bibliothèques (ENSB Paris) et Chargée de Mission (retraitée) pour le Livre et la Lecture auprès du Haut-Commissaire de la République. Elle créa *Flamboyant Imaginaire, ainsi que deux collections qu'elle dirige chez* l'Harmattan (Paris), '*Lettres du Pacifique*' et la collection de recherche universitaire '*CIRMAIOS, les Champs de l'Imaginaire*'.

**Michael Costigan**, PhD (Civil and Canon Law), writer, editor, former Roman Catholic priest, senior public servant and social justice advocate, was the first Director of the Literature Board of the Australia Council for the Arts (1973-1983), promoting Australian literature in France, Denmark, Barcelona, Germany. He retired in 2005.

**Guibourg Delamotte**, is Professor, Japanese Studies at the French Institute of Oriental Studies (Inalco), Research Fellow with the French Research Institute on East Asia; also with the Japan Forum on International Relations (JFIR) and Adjunct Fellow at the Temple University, Japan. She is widely published in Japanese foreign and defense policies, domestic politics and Japanese political system.

**Gionni Di Gravio** OAM, ASAAP, BA (Classics), University of Newcastle Archivist, Special Collections (Archives); Chair, Hunter Living Histories Initiative.

**Ken Dutton**, Emeritus Professor AM FRSN FACE *Officier des Palmes Académiques*, occupied the Chair of French at the University of Newcastle from 1969-98. He is the author or co-author of 26 books and the author of over 60 articles and monographs in various fields including French Language and Literature, biography and French-Australian relations.

**John Emerson** has a *Diplôme d'Études Approfondies* from the University of Paris III and a PhD from the University of Adelaide : 'The representation of the colonial past in French and Australian cinema, from 1970 to 2000'. He was director of the University of Adelaide Press and is currently an independent writer and publishing consultant.

**Suzanne Evans** BA, Dip Ed (Newcastle University) Secondary school teacher-French, Japanese, EAL/D (English as an Additional Language/Dialect). NSW Department of Education 1976-90, 1992-2003, 2013-18; Ministry of Education, Japan 1990-91; Education Bureau, Hong Kong 2003-12.

**Merrill Findlay**, PhD, MSS, author, a librettist, independent scholar, storyteller and community cultural development practitioner, believes in the power of narratives to effect change. She has published widely in magazines and journals. Her *Kate Kelly* Chamber Opera (co-created with Ross James Carey) was produced online for a global audience in 2020.

**Marion Halligan**, AM, born and educated in Newcastle, was a teacher and journalist before becoming an award-winning full-time writer of novels, short stories, reviews and essays. Her most recent book *Words for Lucy: A story of love, loss and the celebration of life* was published in 2022.

**Israel Horovitz** (1939-2020) was an American playwright, director, actor and co-founder of The Gloucester Stage Company. Well known in French theatre and cinema, he became *Commandeur de l'Ordre des Arts et des Lettres* in 2012.

**Hélène Jaccomard**, BA, PhD (UWA), *Chevalier des Palmes Académiques*, Professor School of Humanities, Discipline of European Languages and Cultures, is an certified translator in English, French and Italian. Her recent publication is *Yasmina Reza et le Bonheur: Théâtre et romans*, L'Harmattan, 2022.

**Barbara Kelly,** BA, Dip Ed (Newcastle), is a retired secondary teacher with a special interest in literacy and numeracy. She enjoys writing and is active in animal rights.

**Ilona Kiss**, diplômée de l'Académie des arts décoratifs de Budapest à la faculté du Livre (1979), est peintre et graphiste au style très original de notoriété internationale. Elle expose régulièrement depuis 1993 ses œuvres et ses livres en France, dont *Les Versicules* de Jean-Paul Delamotte. De nombreux ouvrages qu'elle a réalisés figurent d'ailleurs dans les institutions nationales de son pays ainsi qu'en France, en Suisse ou en Allemagne.

**Jean-Pierre Langellier** is a French journalist. He worked for 35 years for *Le Monde*, including 20 years as a foreign correspondent based in Nairobi, Jerusalem, London and Rio de Janeiro. His last of several books is a biography of Léopold Sédar Senghor, French and Senegalese statesman and poet (Perrin), which won the 2022 Goncourt prize for biography and the Guizot prize of the *Académie Française*.

**Helen Ledwidge,** PhD, taught as a language teacher at numerous schools in Australia, at French Government schools in Warsaw and Manila, and at UNESCO in Paris. In retirement she teaches Latin at U3A (University of the Third Age) in Sydney.

**Tony Maniaty** is an award-winning Australian journalist, author and photographer based in Paris and Sydney. His published works include *The Children Must Dance* and *Smyrna* (shortlisted for the Miles Franklin Award) and his memoir *Shooting Balibo*. His photobook of Paris during the Covid crisis, *Our Hearts Are Still Open* (*Nos cœurs sont toujours ouverts*) – text by Raimond Gaita, was published in 2022.

**Joanna Murray-Smith** is an Australian playwright, screenwriter and novelist.

**Will Noonan** was resident at La Petite Maison from 2009 - 2018. He completed a PhD (USyd) project on the history and theory of humour. He taught at the Sorbonne Nouvelle Université from 2009-2012 and has been lecturing in English and translation studies at the Université de Bourgogne, Dijon, since 2012 where he is a member of the Texte-Image-Langage (TIL) research centre.

**Daniel Pata**, MA (Fine Arts, UNSW), is a Sydney-based *plein-air* landscape artist, who studied at the Julian Ashton Art School and the College of Fine Arts. In 1987 he was awarded an Artist-in-Residency at the Cite International des Arts, Paris, and has since maintained strong links with France. He has exhibited widely in Australia, Asia, France and the UK. He currently lectures at the National Art School, Sydney.

**Xavier Pons,** Emeritus Professor of English at the University of Toulouse-Jean Jaurès, has lectured and researched at various Australian universities, including Newcastle University and the University of New South Wales. Hehas published widely on various aspects of Australia's culture; his books include *Out of Eden* (1984), *A Sheltered Land* (1994) and *Messengers of Eros* (2009). He remains as fascinated as ever by the country.

**John Ramsland**, OAM, FACE, F CollP, Emeritus Professor of History at the University of Newcastle, is an award-winning author of 30 non-fiction books and many articles. He has made contributions to education and social history, particularly in child welfare, biography, the impact of war, film history and the Aboriginal presence.

**Marie Ramsland,** BA, MLitt (French), PhD, *Chevalier des Palmes Académiques*, is an Honorary Lecturer of the University of Newcastle. Her interests are in French language, literature and culture, especially French-Australian contacts. Her work on Paul Wenz' writing, *Their Fathers' Land: For King and Empire*, was published by ETT Imprint (2018).

**Dianne Reilly**, AM, FRHSV, PhD (Melbourne), Fellow (Monash University), *Chevalier des Palmes Académiques*, was La Trobe Librarian at the State Library, Victoria, from 1982-2008. In 1977/78, she was a stagiaire in Paris working at the Bibliothèque Nationale de France (Richelieu) and at the Bibliothèque Publique d'Information (Centre Pompidou). She was a co-founder of the La Trobe Society in 2001 and is currently its Secretary. **Kevin Tang** is a Barrister in Sydney. After receiving the Kelver Hartley Scholarship and completing an Honours Degree, he taught French for a short time. He read Law at the University of Sydney and practised for some years as a Solicitor. Before being admitted to the Bar, he lived and studied in the UK at the London School of Economics. He remains a fluent French speaker and an enthusiast of French literature.

**Emmanuelle Souillac,** née le 29 décembre 1948 en Allemagne. Vécu en Australie de 1958 à 1969 puis de 1972 à 1977. Titulaire d'une maîtrise et d'un DEA sur l'éducation auprès des Aborigènes dans les années soixante-dix. Professeure d'anglais de spécialité à l'université de Cergy-Pontoise.

**Ross Steele** is Honorary Associate Professor of French Studies at the University of Sydney. He has authored 33 books published in France and the USA, teaching French to foreigners, integrating language and contemporary culture in a sociolinguistic and communicative context. He has received French Awards: *Officier de la Légion d'Honneur, Officier de l'Ordre National* *du Mérite and Officier des Palmes Académiques.*

**Brian Suters** AM, LFAIA, Hon PhD (University of Newcastle), Freeman of the City of Newcastle (2022), is a multi-award-winning architect and lifetime community activist. His projects have shaped the city's landscape over decades. At the time of his retirement, his Newcastle firm had become part of an international practice. He was, and still is, a lifelong friend of the Delamotte family.

**Tom Thompson** continues to publish Australian literature through his company ETT Imprint, including a Sydney-Paris Link series. Correspondence for ACFA between the Delamottes and Moorhouse are in the State Library of NSW.

**Alan Ventress**, Mitchell librarian (1993-2001; 2001-2012), worked at the NSW State Archives and ended up as Director before retiring. He continues to work for Sydney Diocesan Archives in a voluntary capacity.

**Marie-Laure Vuaille-Barcan**, PhD (Newcastle), Maitrise, BA Litt, DESS (Université Lumière, Lyon II, France), is a senior lecturer in French Studies at the University of Newcastle and Group Leader for Screens, Languages, English and Writing. She has a keen interest in translation theories and practices and has collaborated in the translation of novels by Māori author Patricia Grace.

**Virginia Wallace-Crabbe**, BA, Dip Ed, married Robin (artist and writer) in1961. They began raising cattle in Gippsland in 1970 and Robin taught at the Institute of Advanced Education. They moved to Braidwood NSW in 1979. Virginia taught herself photography and Robin continued with his art. In the '80s and '90s, Virginia's work is held in the National Library

**Sandra ("Sandi") Warren**, BA, (Hons I, Classics), PhD. Completing an Open Foundation Course at the University of Newcastle in 1997 allowed Sandi, who had worked in Banking and later in her own retail business, to commence tertiary studies. She spent six months studying in France as a Hartley Bequest recipient. Her second Hartley scholarship assisted her doctoral research.

**Travis Watters** undertook a BA (Hons) in French at the University of Newcastle, before studying Translation and Interpreting at Macquarie University and Romance Linguistics at the Sorbonne. Based in London, he is a certified translator and student of Classics.

**Peter Weir**, AM, retired award-winning film director, wrote and directed his last film (2010). 'For film directors, like volcanoes, there are three major stages: active, dormant and extinct. I think I've reached the latter! Another generation is out there calling "action" and "cut" and good luck to them.'

**John West-Sooby**, BMath, BA(Hons), DipEd (Newcastle) DEA, PhD (Stendhal University, Grenoble), *Officier des Palmes Académiques,* is Emeritus Professor of French Studies at the University of Adelaide. Previously, he taught French language and culture at the University of New England and La Trobe University. His work includes studies of the French nineteenth-century novel and of French and Australian crime fiction. He has also co-published several books on Nicolas Baudin's scientific voyage to Australia (1800-1804).

**Colyn Whitehead**, BA (Hons, New England), MA (Hons, Sydney); tutor and lecturer in French Language and Literature at Newcastle from 1968 to 1992. His thesis was '*L'Idée du moderne chez Baudelaire* (1964).

**Denise Yim**, PhD is an Honorary Associate, Department of French and Francophone Studies, the University of Sydney. Her research focuses on the eighteenth-century English Chinnery family, their relationship with violinist GB Viotti and with author Madame de Genlis. Her latest publication is *A Genlis Education and Enlightenment Values: Mrs Chinnery (1766–1840) and her Children* (Routledge, 2022).

# Table des matières

in

***Amours de Rencontre (Papiers australiens) (1) & (2)***

La Petite Maison, Boulogne, 1993

1. Le temps long (*Le Monde*)
2. Le Festival de Sydney (*Signe de Vie*)
3. La Jeune Fille borgne (*Signe de Vie*)
4. Newcastle gets a Film Festival (*Newcastle Herald*)
5. De Signe de Vie 2
6. Lettre de Melbourne
7. Signaux des Antipodes (*Le Monde*) Patrick White ou l'Œil du Maître (*Le Monde*)
8. Ecrivains d'Australie (*Magazine littéraire*)
9. Correspondance
10. Semaine du Cinéma australien
11. Patrick White ou le Vif du Sujet (*Le Monde*)
12. La Colleen inspirée (*Magazine littéraire*)
13. Gallipoli, Victoire du cinéma australien
14. Charme de la culture australienne (*Le Monde*)
15. La littérature incarnée (*Le Monde*)
16. Métamorphoses australiennes (*Magazine littéraire*)
17. Australophilie (*Magazine littéraire*)
18. Les Ecrivains d'Australie (*Magazine littéraire*)
19. Fiction et réalités australiennes (*Le Monde*)
20. Australire (*Magazine littéraire*)
21. Australire (*Magazine littéraire*)
22. Une révolution à Djakarta (*Magazine littéraire*)
23. L'enthousiasme d'un « Aussiephile » (*Le Monde*)
24. A la recherche d'un écrivain perdu (*La Petite Maison*)
25. Une destinée de peintre (*Magazine littéraire*)
26. La Justice des Hommes (*Presses de la Renaissance*)
27. FM (*La Petite Maison*)
28. Nevil Shute en poche (*Magazine littéraire*)

29. Austra-lire (*VSD*)
30. Lettre à M Bernard Pivot (*Terre de l'Homme*)
31. Etat de l'enquête (*Le Lérot*)
32. La littérature australienne (*L'Express*)
33. Whitlam et la vérité
34. Visite à l'Australie des Ecrivains » (*Le Monde*)
35. A la rencontre des Ecrivains (*Le Lérot*)
36. Lointaine et proche Australie
37. Addendum
38. Rod Jones ou Les mots à dire (*Le Monde*)
39. Brian Castro (*Le Monde*)
40. A la passée (*Magazine littéraire*)
41. Un cinéphile « aussiephile » (*Le Monde*)
42. Un coup de théâtre (*Le Monde*)
43. Australiennes (*Magazine littéraire*)
44. D'un extrême à l'autre
45. A note from Paris (*ABR*)

*Triste FIN en forme d'Hommage à Nancy Keesing*

*La littérature australienne à vol d'oiseau*

*Heureuses rencontres*

*Propos déplacés*

Paris, le 9 mars 1974

Professeur K.R. Dutton
Head, Department of French
The University of Newcastle
New South Wales 2308
AUSTRALIE

Monsieur,

Je connais Jean-Paul Delamotte depuis quelques années. Il me semble être très indiqué pour faire connaître et aimer la littérature et la langue françaises en Australie où son excellente connaissance de l'anglais le rendra plus proche encore de ses étudiants.

Il a fait des études à Harvard où il a également enseigné.

D'autre part, ses romans et ses contes font de lui un espoir de la nouvelle littérature française.

Je me permets donc de vous le recommander très chaleureusement.

Agréez, Monsieur, je vous prie, l'expression de ma profonde considération.

Eugène Ionesco
de l'Académie Française.

# NEWCASTLE GETS A FILM FESTIVAL
## French writer says 'go'*

'Look', said Monique, 'are you really going to write that in English?'

She spoke in French. We arrived in France a year ago and speak French from time to time together lest we forget the language and, since we teach it here, lose out jobs.

'This is a very important matter,' she added. 'A film festival coming to Newcastle …'

She sounded so professional I felt nostalgic. I have spent a dozen pleasant years moonlighting in feature film production since literature (mine at least) does not pay, and she has worked in the past seven of them with the European Publicity Department of MGM in Paris.

… These were memorable days, happy days.

I venture, to say that next weekend will be happy and memorable in Newcastle, thanks to the Travelling Film Festival.

Now I had to answer Monique's objection about my writing in English.

'My cabbage,' I retorted [endearingly]. 'The minor mistakes which I could inadvertently make in the tongue of Joseph and Vladimir Nabokov would not matter. […]

'The real problem is to catch the attention of readers. They may have planned family reunions, school gatherings, fishing expeditions … and it is most essential and most urgent that they care to modify slightly their intentions, and rush, that's the word, rush to book tickets, at David Jones [in Newcastle Mall], the CAE [College of Advanced Education], the University Shop or the Civic Theatre for August 15, 16 and 17.'

'You are a dreamer,' said Monique. 'Let's be realistic. What's the festival's publicity budget?'

'They don't have a publicity budget to speak of,' I replied. 'But they have good films. Good films have an enormous appeal.' …

'How much are the seats?' Monique asked.

'A trifle! Eight dollars for a subscription for seven films'

'In this day and age,' Monique commented (just to see how I would translate the French idiom, which is quite different), '... shouldn't the festival charge more?'

[...]

'As a special gesture for Newcastle, "The cars that ate Paris" [Peter Weir] will open the festival,' I replied.

'Is it some sort of Franco-Australian co-production?' asked Monique as a joke because she could tell that through sheer enthusiasm I was getting as tense as Norman Gunston'.

'No,' I told her. Unhappily, we have not reached that stage yet. [It] has nothing to do with Paris. It deals with an imaginary Australian town whose inhabitants live by causing car accidents. Curiously, however, it has been released in Paris before reaching Newcastle. The director, Peter Weir, outstanding among the younger generation, attracted a lot of attention at Cannes last year. The actors ... are good: John Meillon, Terry Camilleri, Max Gillies, Kevin Miles and Bruce Spence.' ...

'And what else shall we see?'

[... "*The Pedestrian*", Maximillian Schell; "*Help, the Doctor is Drowning!*, Nicolai Van Der Heyde; "*The Phantom of Liberty*", Bunuel].

I got distracted. I remembered that last year, when we arrived, Mr Theo Goumas had "*Discreet Charm of the Bourgeoisie*" on at the Roma. Thanks to people like him and the "*Herald*" film critic Allan Watkins, I thought, the name of Bunuel, one of the greatest names in the history of cinema, must be appreciated around here. Now, if the Film Festival succeeds, it will be beneficial for the whole community locally. Even bigger audiences will go to the Roma, the Lyric, the Strand, the Royal, Kings, the Regal ...

'What about Sunday?' asked Monique.

["*Belle*", Andre Delvaux; "*Brother, can you spare a Dime*", Philippe Mora [An Australian of French ancestry]; "*The Passenger*", Michelangelo Antonioni]

'... pour finir en beauté!'

'I hope you won't leave that in French,' said Monique.

'Why not? It means last but not least.'

[…]

How I wish that influential persons, long-time members of the community (not newcomers like us), […] and why not the [newly-elected] Lord Mayor herself [Joyce Cummings] …

[…]

Let film lovers speak, now.

* *Newcastle Morning Herald and Miners Advocate*, 12 August 1975; see also *Amours de rencontre (1)*, 23-29.

# *Livres d'Or*

## Ken Dutton

*Impressions d'un Aussie de passage*

Le parapluie ?
M'a à l'abri
Celle (ou celui)
Qui, par oubli,
Laisse le sien en Australie.
Le joli lit ?
Si bien décrit
Où Nancy Keesing a dormi
M'a accueilli.
Ici Aussi.
Et, moi aussi,
Je m'suis assis
Où Frank Moorhouse a fait pipi.

Le paradis
Si bien garni
De végémi-
-(te) et d'choses qu'on lit
À rafraîchir
Corps et esprit !
Si je publie
(comme j'ai envie)
Certaine autobiographie,
Faudra que j'y
Evoqu' pour qui
La lira, cette nostalgie
Que je ressens, une fois parti.

Bien chers amis,
Jean-Paul, Moni-
-(que) et Guibourg, mille fois merci.
C'est grâce à votre courtoisie
Que, moi Aussi [E],
Je suis Ici !

12–27 janvier 1998

Renvois: (1) Voir message du 12/12/97 (2) Message du 7/11/95
(3) Message du 7/9/93

---

LE POÈME DU TRANSPARISIEN

(Apologies to Valery Larbaud)

Et si nous partions d'Austerlitz ?
Quelle ligne choisir, d'abord ? La Dix.

Partir oui, mais pour aller où ?
Vers la Porte de Saint-Cloud !

À Jussieu, rien ne nous tente
(Mais, attention à l'amiante !).

Lemaine (Cardinal) monte au ciel :
Pour Maubert est-ce mutuel ?

De Cluny la cloche qui sonne
Me rappelle ma « vieille » Sorbonne.

(Renaud-Barrault à l'Odéon,
Restaurant V « le Mabillon »).

Continuons. La voie est bonne
Qui mène à Sèvres-Babylone.

Vaneau, Duroc et Ségur :
6e ou 7e ? Pas sûr.

# Aprononcer dit z : Lat. decius.
Cf. Roland. [n.d.l.r.]

(Delamotte piquait Grenelle ?
Malheur à moi si je m'en mêle.)

Soudain, je me réveille : holà !
Déjà l'avenue Émile Zola

Dont les œuvres sont si belles.
Mais qui donc était Charles Michels ?

(Conduisait-il peut-être une benne
Marquée : « André Citroën » ?)

Les Auteuil passent en cohorte :
Église — Michel-Ange — et Porte.

Patientez, car rien ne presse :
Deux minutes à Jean Jaurès.

De la Sortie n'y a qu'un saut :
On retrouve le studio

66, rue d'Aguesseau.
Y habiter, que c'est beau !

Ken Dutton

septembre '02

Letter from Margaret Whitlam          At Sydney airport -keen on travelling

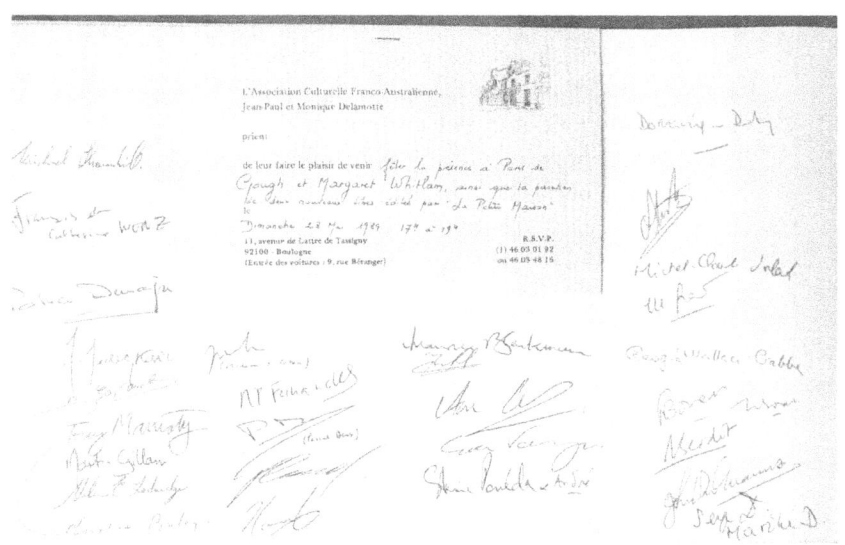

*Fêter la presence à Paris de Gough et Margaret Whitlam*

# Poetry by Jean-Paul

*Versicules 1*

*Pas de nouvelles, bonne nouvelle*

Ce matin, du balcon, un peu avant dix heures,
[...]
Baissant les yeux, je vis, qui grimpait notre rue
(En pente raide et qui vous mène au pied du mur
Où s'accroche un escalier, dans la verdure),
Je vis notre facteur, léger et court-vêtu.
Tati, ce facteur-là n'a pas de bicyclette.
Sa chemisette est bleue et son short bleu foncé.
Jamais il n'a porté de képi ni casquette.
On ne l'invite pas à boire un coup de vin.
Il passe ... il est passé avec indifférence
Devant notre maison, qui ne l'arrête pas.
La boîte à lettres vide a l'air d'un trou stupide
Et mon cœur est chagrin d'avoir battu en vain.
Pas même un petit mot, une carte postale ...
Pour combler ce grand vide, il suffit d'un poème
Un poème de pluie ou de brume et de vent.
Un poème est toujours une lettre à soi-même
Et le destinataire en est un peu moins seul.

*Versicules 2, (4)*

Paris me manque à la folie,
Que faites-vous, ô mesa mis ?
Ecrivez-moi, je vous en prie,
Sinon je m'enfuirai d'ici :
Paris me manque à la folie !

*Le toboggan de King Edward Park*

Dans ce parc aux grands pins, qui longe l'océan
    Un toboggan se dresse où il paraît séant
    A Guibourg, aussitôt qu'elle arrive céans
    De se précipiter pour poser son séant.
    Il semble que ce jeu infiniment lui plaise …
    Elle n'a que vingt mois mais se sent très à l'aise :
    On dirait un oiseau, perché sur un mélèze
    Qui va prendre son vol plus haut que la falaise.
    Elle glisse et regrimpe et glisse et grimpe encor.
    Puis, sur l'herbe et les fleurs qui caressent son corps,
    Elle s'endort enfin et doucement respire,
Plus heureuse à présent qu'un conquérant d'empire.
    La vie est glissement (vif ou lent peu importe !)
    Vers le but trop connu où le destin nous porte …
    On ne remonte point le toboggan de fer.
    Alors, je lis Plutarque – ou regarde la mer …

*Le toboggan (variante)*

    Dans ce parc, au bord de la mer,
    Un toboggan luisant se dresse
    Et mon enfant avec adresse
    Y grimpe quand je fais des vers.
    D'en haut, elle a un regard fier
    Avant de glisser sur ses fesses.
    Elle éprouve une douce ivresse.
    J'ai eu son âge … avant-hier.
    Ce toboggan, j'ai glissé,
    Ici ou ailleurs, peu importe !
    La vie, on l'a et elle est morte …
    L'avenir est déjà Passé !

*En Vol !*

Quand on voit la terre ainsi
　　Brulée, ingrate et stérile,
On se dit que l'homme aussi
　　A un destin difficile,
　　Puisqu'il doit finir ici …
　　Ici-bas, comme un fossile !
*28 oct 2000 dans l'avion survolant* Nullabor


*L'autobus 460*

J'ai une passion dans ma vie
　　Et j'en ai même plusieurs,
Mais celle à quoi je vous convie
　　Est d'un ordre supérieur.
Sachez donc, je vous le confie,
　　Que je ressens une ferveur
　　　Empreinte de jalousie
Pour un simple transporteur
　　Il faut que je vous l'avoue
　　　Celui que j'aime le plus,
Et qu'à tue-tête, moi, je loue,
C'est simplement le bus.
L'autobus qui nous emmène
　　Ici ou là, sans façons
Et qui bien sûr nous ramène
　　Aisément à la maison.
*Hommage au Quatre-cent-soixante,*
　　*A la montée, à la descente !*

# Jean-Paul Delamotte, le cosmopolite
## Alfred Eibel, *Express*, no 68, février 1996

> Auteur de romans, de livres de voyage et d'un 'gros' journal intime, **Jean-Paul Delamotte s'inscrit dans la vieille tradition de Voltaire et de Swift.** Mais ce gentleman boulonnais est aussi serviteur d'une autre culture, celle de l'Australie.

Cosmopolite, Jean-Paul Delamotte l'est authentiquement. Après ses études en France et aux Etats-Unis, il est revenu aux studios de Boulogne dans le cadre d'une société franco-américaine. Il a été le principal représentant des équipes de production française dans le contexte américain et a participé, par exemple, au tournage du *Jour le plus long* ou du *Compartiment tueurs* de Costa Gravas. Par ailleurs, il voue une grande admiration a1 Jacques Deray, autre Boulonnais, remarquable réalisateur de *Symphonie pour un massacre*.

Mais en 1974, Jean-Paul Delamotte se marie, prend le bateau pour l'Australie et va enseigner le français dans les universités de Newcastle, Sydney et Melbourne. Il entretient ses élèves à l'œuvre de Paulhan, Beckett, Ionesco. Mais il découvre surtout avec éblouissement la littérature australienne. Ainsi Frank Moorhouse dont il traduira *Un Australien garanti d'époque, Quarante/Dix-sept* et le célèbre *Coca-Cola Kid*. Ce qui ne l'empêche pas de dénicher aussi dans un bibliothèque un écrivain français, Paul Wenz (1869-1937) ami d'André Gide, établi en Australie en 1897 où il exerça la profession d'éleveur de moutons. Delamotte crée donc tout naturellement en 1980 l'association culturelle franc-australienne qu'il anime avec une rare constance et un désintéressement total. Il fond également sa propre maison d'édition en 1986 qu'il appelle *La Petite maison* [sic] et il réédite trois œuvres de Paul Wenz. De 1984 à 1994, Jean-Paul et Monique Delamotte reçoivent à Boulogne une foule d'hôte de passage, comme ces écrivains australiens venus à Paris, dans le cadre de la manifestation 'Les belles étrangères'. Il multiplie les rencontres entre enseignants, soutient les professeurs de français bilingues en partance, noue des contacts avec les services culturels des différents municipalités. A ses invités, il fait découvrir Boulogne. Jean-Paul Delamotte y est né en 1931, y a vécu jusqu'en 1960 puis, après une absence de vingt ans, s'y réinstalle en 1981 parce qu'il ne peut plus s'en passer et que Boulogne est pour lui la base essentielle de ses activités.

Lorsque l'enthousiasme d'une lecture suscite en Jean-Paul Delamotte le besoin de propagande, il entreprend l'exemple de son maître Labaud, '*une politique intellectuelle interlinguistique* et traduit non seulement Moorhouse mais d'autres livres dont *La justice des hommes* de Marcus Clark, cet écrivain australien mort à 35 ans qui aimait la littérature française, Balzac et Dumas.

Lorsqu'on demande à Delamotte s'il ne se sent pas décalé au sein de ce siècle, il sourit. Il répond simplement qu'il y a des survivances partout. Alors, pourquoi pas lui, la qualité française pourquoi pas après tout ? son journal intime, qu'il a intitulé *Vivre et revivre,* est toujours à la recherche d'un éditeur de goût. Et pourtant, quelle richesse ! Ce sont les rencontres avec une foule de personnages : Louis Guilloux, Maurice-Edgar Coindreau, le grand traducteur de Faulkner, de nombreux écrivains français ... Ceux qui ont eu la chance de lire ce journal nostalgique ont découvert chez Jean-Paul Delamotte un styliste comme on n'en fait plus, sans faux-semblants, doué d'une écriture incisive. Si l'Australie peut s'enorgueillir de connaître François Mauriac, Michel Foucault, Jean Baudrillard, Michel Serres, il est dommage, en revanche, constate Delamotte que la France ne connaisse pas encore Henry Lawson (1867-1922), le père de la littérature australienne. Qui prendra un jour le risque d'éditer ce Mark Twain des terres reculées, ce Jack London de la brousse ? voilà une question qui mérite d'être posée.

Aussi à l'aise dans l'œuvre de Rousseau que dans celle de Thomas Wolfe, auteur américain de premier ordre, Delamotte possède un caractère cosmopolite. Il rêve d'une Australie aux couleurs de la France, d'heureux amants français de la littérature australienne et le plus secret conseil qu'il dépense est celui-ci : « *Il faut sortir de l'isolement. L'Australie compte un nombre incroyable de revues littéraires. Elles rendent comptent chaque fois qu'il est possible des écrivains français traduits là-bas. Il faudrait qu'ici, dans mon pays, l'accueil des écrivains australiens trouve une résonance égale.* »

Jean-Paul Delamotte veut maintenant se consacrer exclusivement à l'écriture. Il note dans le tome I de ses *Amours de rencontre* [...] « *Sans vouloir en remontrer à quiconque, j'ai une conception assez tonifiante du rôle d'un écrivain, même obscur. J'aime qu'il s'efforce d'être un peu utile à l'occasion, dans la tradition voltairienne, à l'inverse des joyeux drilles dont Voltaire disait justement : chacun d'eux brigue une place de valet et une réputation de grand homme.* »

On ne saurait mieux dire.

# PUBLICATIONS – Jean-Paul Delamotte: author, translator, subtitler

**Author/Editor - with La Petite Maison**

Jean-Paul Delamotte

*Amours de rencontre (papiers australien) : à la rencontre de la culture australienne,* vols 1 & 2, 1993

Frédéric Moreau (alias), *Un Bienfait des Dieux (facétie)*, 1997

*Paul Wenz (1869-1939), sa vie son œuvre,* 1998

*La Place de la Concorde (conte parisien),* 1998

*Allumettes et brouteilles : dix nouvelles,* 1998

*Un Dimanche à Melbourne,* 1998

*L'Instinct de reproduction : dix nouvelles quadragénaires,* 1999

*Douce illusion : factum,* 1999

*Vivre et revivre. Journal littéraire (Australie, 29 janvier - 20 février 1977),* 2000

*L'Indien-Pacifique, conte franco-australien,* 2000

*Innocentes plaisanteries : dossier de Rien de Presse,* 2002

*Le Vain labeur ? : Conte cantabrigien écrit à Harvard en 1957,* 2008

*Gough et Margaret. Hommage d'un ami français,* 2010

*La Route de Nanima. A la découverte de Paul Wenz 'the Master of Nanima' et de la richesse Culturelle australienne (Vivre et revivre),* 2011

*Carpe diem, dix nouvelles quadragénaires,* 2014 (Gallimard, 1968)

**Author/Editor - with other publishers**

[under the name Jean-Paul Dominque], 'American College', *Hommes et mondes* [Gallimard], no 61 juillet, 1951, 246-53

'French Line', no 103, juillet 1961, 41-50

*La Communauté,* Collection jeune, Gallimard, Paris, 1962

*Sans hâte : cette nuit. Roman,* Plon, Paris, 1967

'Appartenances', *La Nouvelle Revue Française,* Gallimard, no 173, mai 1967, 997-1007

*Signe de Vie 1 & 2, Le bout du monde,* Newey & Beath, Newcastle, 1975

'L'Imagerie', in Jean-Paul Aron (ed), *Qu'est-ce que la culture française ?,* 1975, 73-79

*La Bourelle : Gentillesses, trois récits,* Plon, 1978

(ed), *A La recherche d'un écrivain perdu : Paul Wenz, Français et Australien,* in *Le Lérot rêveur,* no 46 Aigre : Lérot , 1987

'A Note from Paris', in *Australian Book Review*, no 130, 1991, 33

*Amours de rencontre*, in *Antipodes* (Brooklyn) vol 9, issue 2, 1995, 152

 (ed), 'Ecrivains d'Australie I', *La Nouvelle Revue Française*, no 566 2003, 109-230

 & Xavier Pons (eds), 'Ecrivains d'Australie II', *La Nouvelle Revue Française*, no 567, 2003, 111-232

'Du côté de chez Frank [Moorhouse], *L'Atelier du Roman* [Flammarion], décembre 2003, 189-99

'La Manifestation', *L'Atelier du Roman*, décembre 2003, 208-14

**Translator**

Frank Moorhouse, *Coca-Cola Kid : et autres recits,* Presses de la Renaissance, Paris, 1985

 & presenter, *Un Australien garanti d'époque* (*Le Fibre Paternelle et Les Lettres à Twiggy*), Petite Maison, 1987

 *Quarante/dix-sept,* Quai Voltaire, Paris, 1992

 *Tout un monde d'espoir,* Belfond, Paris, 1996

Marcus Clarke, *La Justice des hommes,* Presses de la Renaissance, 1987

 *L'Histoire d'un communard,* Petite Maison, 2006

JR Rowland, *Paris-Canberra, 1982,* Paris : Petite Maison, 1989 Katharine Susannah Prichard, *Coonardoo* (with Hélène Jaccomard), Petite Maison, 1991

Maurilia Meehan, *Ah, Simone ...* , Petite Maison, 1995; includes '*Rêves au porteur* (extrait de *Fury*), 19-25

Geoffrey Dutton, *Et Voilà !,* Petite Maison, 1998

David Malouf, *En fin de contes: Nouvelles*, Petite Maison, 1999

Chris Andrews, *Septuor : poèmes,* Petite Maison, 2001

William La Ganza, *Meeting her in Paris/Rendez-vous à Paris* (alias Frédéric Moreau), Petite Maison, 1998

**Subtitler** – as revealed by Tom Thompson (Sydney, 2019)

In a long visit to France in 1994, [Tom's] family lived with Australian writer and radio broadcaster Alister Kershaw near Sancerre and with the Delamottes in Paris, where Jean-Paul arranged meetings for me with the publisher Robert Laffont. At this time I became aware of Jean-Paul's 'other' role as a subtitler for Hollywood classic films to be shown on French TV. His understanding of American idiom enabled forty classics to appear and these continue to bring French audiences to classic cinema.

In order of work – and year of release – they are: *Yankee Doodle Dandy* (1942); *The World, the Flesh and the Devil* ('59); *Red Headed Woman* ('32); *Little Women* ('49); *Dance Fools, Dance* ('31); *The Unholy Three* ('30); *Mrs Skeffington* ('44); *The Group* ('66); *Kiss Me Deadly* ('55); *Red River* ('48); *The Earl of Chicago* ('40); *The Last Run* ('71); *Moonfleet* ('55); *Silver River* ('48); *Man With the Gun* ('55); *Satan Met a Lady* ('36); *Mad Love* ('35); *Alexander The Great* ('56); *Painted Veil* ('34); *Ambush* ('50); Abbot & Costello – several movies; *Gaslight* ('44); *San Francisco* ('36); *Woman of the Year* ('42); *Three Little Words* ('50); *Mutiny on the Bounty* ('35); *The Last Mile* ('32); *Hallelujah* ('29); *Viva Villa* ('34); *The Thin Man* ('34); *Adam's Rib* ('49); *Waterloo Bridge* ('40); *Toy Wife* ('38); *Soldiers Three* ('51); *Many Rivers to Cross* ('55); *A Lady Without a Passport* ('50); *The Adventures of Robin Hood* ('38); *Casablanca* ('42) and *Downstairs* ('32).

Jean-Paul published a French version of my own memoir of Australian writers, *Coming out from behind: the unprinted stories behind the published books*, as *Hors-texte : confidences d'un éditeur* (trans by Anne Sauvêtre, La Petite Maison, Boulogne, 1996). This served as a 'calling card' for French publishers. It coincided with the creation by the Delamottes of the Atelier Littéraire Franco-Australien, which welcomed many Australian artists and writers to France, and with Jean-Paul's translation of Moorhouse's *Grand Days* (*Tout un monde d'espoir*, Belfond, Paris).

Robert Laffont and his wife then visited us in Sydney. He was critical to my decision to name my publishing company Editions Tom Thompson (ETT) in my management buyout of 250 Angus & Robertson and Imprint titles, which formalised in 1996.

In 1997 the University of Newcastle made Jean-Paul an Honorary Fellow and, as the inaugural Kelver Hartley Foundation Fellow, he delivered a speech on 'Reciprocity' which was published the following year along with Colin Thornton-Smith's essay 'The Delamotte Phenomenon—Cultural Reciprocity' (*Explorations*, 24, June 1998). This seemed to give Jean-Paul renewed energy and that year he co-wrote *Aimer l'Australie* (for Larousse's 'Monde et voyages' collection) and then in 1998 published his own translation of the first three chapters of Geoffrey Dutton's memoir *Out in the Open* (*Et voilà ! : souvenirs d'enfance*) as well as *Récits du bush* by Paul Wenz.

Two short stories by Paul Wenz – 'Charley' (trans by Margaret Whitlam) and 'Jim et Jack' (trans by Maurice Blackman) were published in a bilingual edition for Double Bush Binding (2005) – within an exhibition of individual binders shown in Sydney, Tokyo and Rennes.

Jean-Paul also translated the play *Acrobates* by his close friend Israël Horovitz for the collection *Dix pièces courtes* (Éditions Théâtrales, 2007).

A long-term ambition was finally realised when Jean-Paul's translation of Marcus Clark's classic novel *For the Term of His Natural Life* appeared in France as *La Justice des hommes* (Houdiard, Paris, 2009). As Jean-Paul noted in his journal: '*Je suis l'esclave de Marcus*'.

**Note**: extract from *Le Courrier Australien*, 10 March 1989, 12 :

**Pour faire connaître la littérature australienne aux Français**

Passionné de littérature australienne qu'il a découvert en enseignant le français à l'Université de Newcastle en 1974, Jean-Paul Delamotte était de retour à Sydney le mois passé. Auteur et traducteur, il a récemment été distingué par l'ambassade d'Australie à Paris qui lui a décerné son premier Prix de traduction pour For *The Term of His Natural Life* (*La Justice des hommes*) de Marcus Clarke. Ce prix a été fondé par le Literature Board of the Australia Council.

Also in 2009 he published *En époussetant la mappemonde* by Paul Wenz.

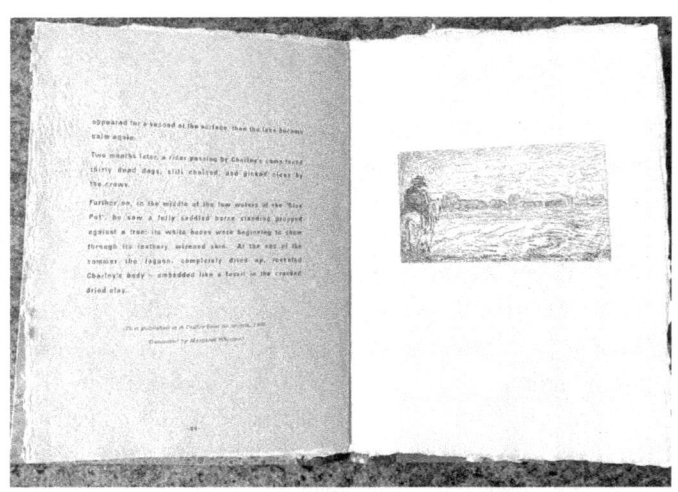

"Charley" trans by Margaret Whitlam; artwork by Daniel Pata on handmade paper by the Euraba Paper Company of Boggabilla. From volume bound by Greg Atcheson, Australia:

*plats en patchwork de crapaud et dos en peau de serpent*

# ASSOCIATION CULTURELLE FRANCO-AUSTRALIENNE (A.C.F.A)

### Note d'information sur l'ACFA

L'ACFA a été fondée en 1980 par Jean-Paul et Monique Delamotte. Sa Présidente d'Honneur est Madame Margaret Whitlam. Sa liste de members est remarquable, en particulier du côté australien. Le recrutement en a été délibérément ralenti pour ne pas accroître les tâches administratives et permettre de concentrer l'effort entrepris sur les points suivants :

1. Démarches du haut niveau. La machine administrative français prend fort peu en compte l'Australie. Le fait qu'il s'agisse d'un Etat fédéral n'arrange pas les choses on ne connaît a Paris, le plus souvent, que Canberra. Nous nous attachons actuellement à faire sentir le besoin de relations plus étroites entre la Ville de Paris et Sydney. Une lettre du Président de la République nous a ouvert diverses portes et constitue un précieux encouragement.

2. Sociabilité. Dans le petit hôtel particulier où elle est hébergé à Boulogne, l'ALFA a reçu au fil des années des centaines d'Australiens, écrivains, journalistes, universitaires, étudiants, artistes, cinéastes, éditeurs, etc en leur faisant rencontrer des Français proches de leurs activités. Sous le signe de la réciprocité culturelle et dans l'intérêt bien compris de la culture française (que les collèges et Universités d'Australie ont si bien servie) nous avons tenté de montrer à ces visiteurs qu'à Paris aussi l'on peut être sensible à leur propre culture.

3. Deux studios situés à Boulogne favorisent les courts séjours d'Australiens à Paris.

4. Edition. Sous le label de la Petite Maison, douze titres ont été publiés. L'œuvre de Paul Wenz (1869-1939), d'une importance capitale parce que c'est le seul français de l'Australie (où il a vécu la vie du Bush et est enterré auprès de son épouse australienne) est ressuscitée et la Télévision s'y intéresse. Un chef d'œuvre de la littérature australienne, Coonardoo ou le Puit dans l'Ombre de Katharine S Prichard a été traduit pour la première fois en français. Un reportage sur la Nouvelle-Calédonie en 1878 mérite aussi d'être mentionné pour son exceptionnel intérêt. Les Belles Etrangères/ Australie de 1990 ont été initiées par l'ALFA. Dans les années 80, son fondateur a donné bon nombre d'articles au Monde et au magazine littéraire. Un travail de traduction a également été effectué, attirant l'attention d'éditeurs importants sur des auteurs australiens.

5. Honneurs. L'ALFA a effectué les démarches nécessaires pour que le grand peintre Lloyd Rees reçoive une Médaille de Vermeil de la Ville de Paris ainsi que le Professeur KR Dutton ; pour Joan Sutherland et son mari Richard Bonynge soient faits Officiers des Arts et des Lettres.

6. Précisions concernant le fondateur (et principal mécène) de l'ACFA : né en 1931, ancien élève de Sciences Po, Master in Public Administration de Harvard, Docteur du 3ème Cycle en Etudes Politiques (Sorbonne). Cinéaste dans le secteur franco-américain de la production (en dernier lieu Directeur général des Productions Artistes Associés, 1979-1981). Ecrivain avant tout (romancier publié à ses débuts par Gallimard, Plon, etc). Chargé de cours dans trois Universités australiennes de 1974 à 1977. AM (Order of Australia – remis en 1992 par le Gouverneur général, en sa résidence de Canberra. Honorary Fellow de l'Université Macquarie (Sydney).

Il est difficile de résumer un effort de cette ampleur ...
Au moins a-t-il le mérite de la ténacité, au service de l'intérêt général.

Amours de rencontre/ Papiers australiens, recueil d'articles publiés dans le Monde, le Magazine littéraire et diverses revues par J-P Delamotte rend compte de son activité, sous le signe de la réciprocité culturelle.

**Note** — David McNicholl announced in the *Bulletin* (10 June 1997, 25) :
'the inaugural Kelver Hartley Fellow, Dr Jean-Paul Delamotte, will speak on 'French-Australian cultural relations, past and present'.

*Livres d'Or* – Bon Voyage Lloyd Rees ...

# Promotion of Australian Culture in France

## ARTICLES:

| | | |
|---|---|---|
| *Le Monde* | 1 Sept 1978 | Australian Literature |
| | 15 June 1979 | Patrick White |
| *Le Quotidien* | 15 March 1982 | Gallipoli (Peter Weir) |
| *Le Monde* | 5/6 Dec 1982 | Australian cultural life |
| | 6 May 1983 | Patrick White, David Malouf |
| | 1 June 1984 | Nancy Cato & others |
| | 14 June 1985 | Australian cultural life |
| | 27 Feb 1988 | Australian literature |
| | 15 July 1988 | Rod Jones |
| | 23 Dec 1988 | Brian Castro |
| | 27 April 1989 | Australia Cinema |
| | 2 June 1989 | Thomas Keneally |
| *Magazine littéraire* | Jan 1982 | Colleen McCullough |
| | April 1984 | Australian Writers |
| | Oct 1987 | Nevil Shute |
| | Feb 1989 | Brian Castro |
| *VSD* | January 1988 | Australian literature |
| *L'Express* | 22 Jan 1988 | Australian culture |
| *Terre de l'Homme* | Jan 1988 | Lettre à Bernard Pivot [...] Australian writers |
| *Distance* | May/June 1988 | Paul Wenz |
| *Le Lérot* | June 1988 | Cultural life in Australia |

## TRANSLATIONS:

Marcus Clarke    *For the Term of his Natural Life*
Frank Moorhouse  *Coca Cola Kid; Filming the Hatted Australian & other short stories; 40-17*
John Rowland     *Paris-Canberra,* 1982

**Awarded** the first Translation Prize from the Literature Board of the Australia Council, presented by HE Ambassador ER Pocock, 23 November 1988

## FILMS:

- Tribute to the Australian cinema at the French Cinémathèque, 1979 (presentation n in catalogue
- French sub-titles    *The FJ Holden; The Last Wave; Long Weekend; Young Einstein*

## PUBLISHING:

(Through the publishing venture I initiated called "La Petite Maison")
Paul Wenz   L'Echarde (A Thorn in the flesh)
Diary of a New Chum (first published in 1908) French translation
Frank Moorhouse   (three stories)
John Rowland   Paris-Canberra, 1982
The Vagabond   The War in New Caledonia, 1878
KS Prichard   Coonardoo (due next)

## THE CULTURAL ASSOCIATION:

In 1980 I founded the Association Culturelle Franco-Australienne, ACFA [members, yearly reports 1983-1988]

Under the auspices of this Association my wife and I have started a free 'stop over' programme intended to allow writer and other cultural people from Australia to spend a week in Paris. The list of these guests will be found in the yearly reports. A small contribution to costs is now requested due to budgetary problems.

The ACFA has been morally and financially supported by the Literature Board of the Australia Council.

My wife and I have always financed the ACFA with our own funds to a large extend [...] We are very happy and indeed somewhat proud of this situation.

We have naturally established a good relationship also with French authorities in Paris. This enabled us for instance to have Lloyd Rees, when he came and, more recently, Joan Sutherland honoured in the proper official way with French 'decorations'.

(Addendum) ARTICLES from the AUSTRALIAN PRESS:

| | | |
|---|---|---|
| *Bulletin* | 5 Jan 1988 | Patricia Rolfe |
| *Australian* | 30 Jan 1988 | Elizabeth Swanson |
| *Bulletin* | 17 Jan 1989 | Patricia Rolfe |
| *Artforce* | No 64 1989 | Tom Shapcott |
| *Australian* | 11/12 Feb 1989 | Barry Oakley |
| *Australian* | 14 May 1989 | Tony Maniaty |
| *Bulletin* | 4 July 1989 | Patricia Rolfe |
| *Australian* | 11 Aug 1989 | Paul Wenz |

# Australian Honours

Receiving the Order of Australia AM with Governor-General Bill Hayden, 6 February 1992: 'For service to Australian/French relations'.

In the courtyard of Macquarie University with Margaret Whitlam after the Ceremony for the Conferring of an Honorary Fellowship, 21 April 1994.

## *Livres d'Or* – Keryl & Paul Kavanagh

> 10/4/97 "April in Paris ..."
>
> Someone should write a song about it! They'd have to include a verse on the wonderful hospitality of Monique + Jean-Paul. I look forward to seeing them both again soon in Newcastle. Thanks also to the Noëls for the use of the studio. One can pretend to be a real Parisian.
>
> love Keryl Kavanagh
>
> All we have to thank Pa Monique for... the studio, the hospitality, the yabbies, St. Cloud gardens, cous cous, the Musée Albert-Khan... and La Tourelle's beef, and, perhaps best of all, Chapelle Saint-Aignan!
>
> Let me give a little back in the form of a charming restaurant in Rue des Barres (4th Arr.) near the Quai de l'Hôtel Ville, called (I think) L'Ébouillant...!? Look for the waitress with blue-electric hair, called Fa:tif. Love, Paul

Tom Thompson in Boulogne, 1994

# *Livres d'Or* – Tom, Elizabeth & Frank

> September 5–12 1986
>
> Thank you for such a haven wherein to dwell upon the good things of life – french food, art – and Australian literature! Amongst the ivy in St. Cloud we have both written articles on Tokyo, interacted with Government (met Mitterand on the street!), and slaved over a film script on English social history. All this to the bush sands of Monique's "Coo-ee" —
>
> Viva the Delamottes!!
> Monique, Jean-Paul
> & Guibourg
>
> Tom Thompson • Elizabeth Butel

> After ten years
> 2nd September 1990
>
> I have just read the report of the first ten years of the Association Culturelle Franco-Australien compiled and written by J-P.D.
> I said to him that he has created, from thin air, a living work of human art. Unlike the sculpture or the building, the "Association" is intangible. It is the sum of human contacts and encounters which occur and pass. There are the books published, translated, and the articles in journals, but the essential work of the "Association" remains invisible, ever-changing, seemingly only of the moment yet it lives in many memories and in the life histories of many of us.

> It has taken, though, as a significant life work of J-P & M's. It may not be an institution but it is a life work.
> It may be fragile but Briande Clemenceau? said that creativity in human endeavour comes from the impermanent and fragile and threatened circumstance, the institutionalising in palaces and monuments represents the exhaustion of the creativity.
> J-P D & M's creativity in their life work is far from exhausted.
>
> Frank Moorhouse
> 2-9-90
>
> Frank returned on October 13 and left on the 21st (which happens to be my birthday – J-P.)
>
> (at 6
> 11–13 may 91)
>
> By hook or by crook I'll be back in this book.
> F.

351

# Enduring friendships – from 1974

Monique and Jean-Paul, with Kay and Brian Suters.

# Ici Aussie (for Jean-Paul and Monique Delamotte)

Lynn Hard*

In June in Boulogne by the Bois
the nights are short
and astronomers, nightingales and vampires
must take either their rest
or chances.

Lots of daylight
to watch
from the window
the workings of the courtyard:
the tenants
mostly foreign, still in the migratory process,
following the paths
past the roses
and half trees
like shabby jewels
in a Swiss movement.

Outgoing
with their string bags of intent;
and last words;
incoming
with biplane struts of baguette
a bulge of what's on special today something
in their eyes
about what was out of stock
and their next words.

The Conversations
are caught
in the seamless, right-angled
yard
drifting in the air
shifting like old newspapers
in the corners.

The gardienne and her assistant
have grown old in their jobs
tending the paths
heaping stuff at the feet of trees
moving the trash out each day
with the sound of tumbrils.

It's 10
and the night comes again:
time for a last look at the courtyard
and the plants in their places.

That they don't move
is their solution
to the maze.

June 1991

* Lynn Hard was librarian at the Australian Defence Force Academy (ADFA). This poem was first published in *Dancing on the Drainboard* (A&R, 1992) and in *Poems, New & Neglected* (ETT Imprint, 2016).

# Monique append ses ancêtres

Eva & "Papolo" (2016) : "Les livres, c'est ma vie",
Eva aged 11, at Berkelouw's, Sydney May 4th 2023.

Jean-Paul m'a épousée contre sa famille (bourgeoisie Parisienne – issue de la noblesse du côté de sa mère). Pour m'impressionner, la première fois que je rencontrai la maman de JP, elle me dit : 'Vous savez mon père (Paul Guibourg) était comte'.

Ma famille était originaire du Mairie (fief des Plantagenêt) et terrine. J'ai appris depuis le décès de JP que nous sommes rattachés au papa d'Aliénor d'Aquitaine d'un côté et descendants de Charlemagne ! – preuves à l'appui de longues recherches d'historiens.

Jean-Paul ne l'a pas su, c'est dommage. Il m'aurait sans [doute] dit : 'Cela ne m'étonne pas de toi !'

Guibourg a une double ascendance car son prénom (devenu le nom de famille des grands-parents de JP) et Carolingien comme nous l'avait appris le cher Norman Million, Médiévaliste au département de français à Newcastle : 'Mais oui, Jean-Paul, c'est un prénom de fille bien connu dans la Geste de Guillaume d'Orange'! Bonheur de Jean-Paul, je me souviens, qui voulait faire revivre le nom de famille de ses grands-parents chéris (Paul et Marie Guibourg).

**Note** from Monique : Standing on my left is my witness Richard Klehe whose father created Art Cinema Television. Richard was young and asked Jean-Paul … to join the company and he did. On JP's right is an old friend, Christian Gaudin, famous chief film editor. Right of Christian is Anne Klehe, la marraine de Guibourg, que Ken a rencontrée (étant le parrain) pour la première fois le 26 septembre 1984 !

15 January 1974, Hôtel de Ville, 16e arrondissement.

In *L'Indien-Pacifique* (219) : **Journal de bord** – (*Parcours migratoire, de Paris à Perth (Australie Occidentale)*), Samedi 4 mai 1974 : Dans le train, départ. Après avoir déjeuné avec Christian à la gare de Lyon. Il pleuvait un peu. Nous étions un peu mélancoliques. Christian a dit : "C'est une assise qui va manquer."

**Websites:**

https://www.isfar.org.au/wp-content/uploads/2020/02/67_JEAN-PAUL-DELAMOTTE-OBITUARY.pdf
https://dailyreview.com.au/jean-paul-delamotte-champion-of-australian-culture-in-france-dies-at-87/    Obituary
https://www.isfar.org.au/fadb/    French-Australian Dictionary of Biography
https://www.isfar.org.au/wp-content/uploads/2016/10/24_C.B.-THORNTON-SMITH-The-Delamotte-Phenomenon-—-Cultural-Reciprocity.pdf
https://www.isfar.org.au/wp-content/uploads/2016/10/24_JEAN-PAUL-DELAMOTTE-Reciprocity.pdf
https://www.isfar.org.au/resources/delamotte_alfa_archive_index/
https://www-australianliterarystudies-com-au.eu1.proxy.openathens.net/articles/wenz-reinvented-the-making-and-remaking-of-a-french-australian-transnational-writer

# In the 'Studiolo'

"Finish it? Why would I want to finish it?"

www.ingramcontent.com/pod-product-compliance
Lightning Source LLC
Chambersburg PA
CBHW032031150426
43194CB00006B/237